THE TAMIL GENOCIDE BY SRI LANKA
SECOND EDITION

SECOND EDITION

THE TAMIL GENOCIDE BY SRI LANKA

THE GLOBAL FAILURE TO PROTECT TAMIL RIGHTS UNDER INTERNATIONAL LAW

BY

FRANCIS A. BOYLE

TAMILS AGAINST GENOCIDE   CLARITY PRESS, INC.

In-house editor: Diana G. Collier

Tamils Against Genocide
P.O. Box 529, Glen Echo
Maryland 20812
http://www.TamilsAgainstGenocide.org
tagdesk@gmail.com

Clarity Press, Inc.
2625 Piedmont Rd. NE, Ste. 56
Atlanta, GA. 30324, USA
http://www.claritypress.com

**THIS BOOK IS DEDICATED TO
S. A. GANDHIYAM DAVID**

DAVID AT THE AGE OF 60

"The late Gandhiyam David was an example of a very cultured Tamil, soft-spoken, strong in his views, dedicated to his land and rooted to the soil – he was definitely a person who represented Tamil Eelam. Very few people in history make such determined effort to save their community and hold on to their principles. Even today, many of us hold on to very strong views about our future. We may not be there. But the dream will be there. David's dream will be there. His dream was human emancipation through Tamil emancipation. He was dreaming for the community, not because he loved those around him, but because he loved the humanity."
Ma'ravanpulavu K. Sachithananthan,
a senior activist and former UN consultant,
remembering the contributions of the
veteran Gandhiyam leader of early 1970s

Even at the age of 92, Mr David was talking about continuing what he did in early 70s. He was talking about possibilities of developing cashew plantations in the East.

Gandhiyam David was always interested in farms and making Tamils self-sufficient.

He was a historical variant with vision. He never wanted anything to him personally. To be very frank, he was a detached person. Detached to the core. To the last, he held one view: Tamils should rule themselves.

David would talk continuously of achieving self-rule or a separate State for the Tamils. He would never bargain on that. He would never give up his ideas because of "changing situations". He was very clear.

David was not a very strong believer in violence. But, he said there was no other way at the time when the young men took to violence. Even though he was a Gandhiyan, he felt he was not there to block them.

Sachithananthan remembered how hopeful David Aiyaa was in January 2009 when Barack Obama was elected US President. "He had high hopes. Obama has come. We are definitely going to have some change in the American policy, Mr David was saying. But, when Mr Obama failed, when he did not grow up to the expectations of David Aiyaa, he fumbled."

"Satchi, this American Establishment is against us, David Aiyaa would say."

David Aiyaa's dream is not limited to his life. It is a continuous process, because subjugation is also a continuous process. "We think subjugation is time-bound process and that somebody would conquer it. No. History repeats continuous situations."

"The history also repeats David Aiyaas."

TABLE OF CONTENTS

FOREWORD*

From: S.A.David Gandhiyam [mailto:soloman_david88@yahoo.in]
Sent: Monday, April 15, 2013 10:52 AM
To: Boyle, Francis A <fboyle@illinois.edu>

The Eelam Tamils in Singhala Sri Lanka are living in mortal Fear and horror.

No Country in the world came to their help.

On 17th and 18th May 2009 at Mullivaikkal in Vanni, 200,000 Singala soldiers armed to the teeth supported by Indian Commanders attacked the Eelam Tamils by land, sea, and air. They used poison gas, cluster bombs, multibarrel cannons. They used most modern arms from Moscow, China, Korea, Pakistan and Israel. They attacked by day and night.

In two days one Lakh and thirty thousands men, woman, and children lay dead. There was no medical aid. The wounded were left to die and rot.

No visitors were authorized inside, not even U.N. officers or Red Cross Personnel.

Six hundred persons who came behind LTTE Leader Nadesan with White Flags were shot to death at short range.

Nearly six thousand women, young and old, were raped by Singala Army and Indian soldiers.

In 2010 the Book *Tamil Genocide by Sri Lanka* was published by Prof. Francis A. Boyle. He is Head of the International Law Faculty at Illinois University, U.S.A.

He has studied the problems of the Eelam Tamils minutely, written his book with deep feeling and sympathy. He wants to present his case at the International Court of Justice at The Hague in Holland.

There is no doubt he will win the case and bring freedom to Eelam Tamils, He has already won Freedom for Bosnians in 1993. He also sent the murderer of Bosnians to jail.

The book written by Prof. Francis A. Boyle to bring freedom to Eelam Tamils is a treasure. The book must be kept in every Eelam Tamil home and passed on to every Generation.

When I.C.J. declares the Eelam Tamils a free nation, they must be ready to take over Tamil Eelam and manage it as a Peaceful and

---

*This *Foreword* by Gandhiyam David was originally written for an uncompleted Tamil translation of this book that he commissioned at his suggestion and with my permission.

Prosperous Nation. If there are several groups fighting with each other for power and position, there can be chaos and commotion.

Therefore it is advisable to create solid unity among Eelam Tamils at the start itself.

To achieve this each person must have 1)Truthfulness 2) Simple Lifestyle 3)Hard work. These were the qualities of Mahathma Gandhi and Our own Leader Thanthai Chelva.

In Conclusion

"United we stand,

Divided we Fall"

Wish all the Eelam Tamils a Glorious Future.

15.4.2013

S.A.David

Talking to *TamilNet* from his Anna Nagar Residence, Mr. David said, "I appeal to the expatriate Tamils to continue the struggle in the Gandhian way to impose the moral responsibility on the leading Governments of the West to facilitate the birth of Tamil Eelam. There is no question in my mind that Tamils have the right to live freely in their own homeland. Mr. David added, "I salute Professor Francis Boyle's contributions to our struggle, and when the time is appropriate I am certain that he will help our people to fight the legal battle in the International Court of Justice (ICJ), and in the International Criminal Court (ICC), if the Security Council accepts to take our case."

To which this author responded:

Dear Friend:

Thank you very much for your kind and gracious tribute to me. It is mostly greatly appreciated coming from someone who has worked so hard and suffered so much for the Tamils in Sri Lanka. I do look forward to meeting with you personally the next time I lecture in Chennai. And I hope you have a wonderful 88th Birthday Celebration. STOLAT!

Francis A. Boyle (far left) on the floor of the International Court of Justice on 1 April 1993, squaring off against his adversary Shabtai Rosenne from Israel (far right) representing Yugoslavia, just before he argued and then won the first of his two World Court Orders overwhelmingly in favor of the Republic of Bosnia and Herzegovina against Yugoslavia to cease and desist from committing all acts of genocide in violation of the 1948 Genocide Convention. This was the flrst time ever that any Government or Lawyer had won two such Orders in one case since the World Court was founded in 1921. He also won an Article 74(4) Order from the World Court to the same effect. Under Article 74(4) of the Statute of the International Court of Justice, when the Full Court is not in Session, the President of the Court exercises the Full Powers of the Court and can issue an Order that is binding upon the states parties in a case.

Australia aiding and abetting Sri Lanka's war crimes—Prof. Boyle

[TamilNet, Saturday, 14 November 2009, 00:25 GMT]

"Australia is a contracting party to the 1951 Convention Relating to the Status of Refugees as well as to its related 1967 Protocol. Thereunder Australia has an absolute obligation to provide meaningful and humane asylum procedures, regulations and hearings to all Tamils fleeing from Sri Lanka," said Francis A. Boyle, professor of International Law at the University of Illinois College of Law, in a note sent to TamilNet Friday.

"To the contrary, this Australian agreement with the GOSL to cut-off Tamil Asylum seekers violates this 1951 Refugees Convention and its 1967 Refugees Protocol as well as the peremptory norm of customary international human rights law set forth in Article 14(1) of the 1948 Universal Declaration of Human Rights: 'Everyone has the right to seek and to enjoy in other countries asylum from persecution.'

"As such this 'Agreement' between GOSL and Australia is void ab initio. It is not entitled to any legal significance or recognition whatsoever.

"In addition, by means of implementing this agreement Australia will now become an aider and abettor to GOSL's war crimes, crimes against humanity and genocide against the Tamils in violation of Australia's own solemn legal obligations under the Genocide Convention, the Rome Statute for the International Criminal Court, the Four Geneva Conventions of 1949 and their Two Additional Protocols of 1977, among others," Professor Boyle said.*

"Of course it comes as no surprise that the White Racist Australian Government would criminally mistreat Tamils of Color after its longstanding history of criminal mistreatment of Australia's own Indigenous People of Color for which Australia has not yet properly atoned, rectified, and compensated," Boyle further said.

"This agreement between Australia and the GOSL is similar to the agreement between the United States and the military dictatorship then ruling Haiti to cut-off Haitian refugees then fleeing governmental persecution in Haiti by ship to the United States in gross violation of their international legal rights.

"That U.S.-Haiti agreement was condemned by every human rights body and human rights organization that considered the matter, which would be too numerous to list here. But that same body of international law and human rights decisions, jurisprudence, principles, and condemnations would also apply here," Professor Boyle added.

---

*See also Tony Iltis & Stuart Munckton, *Sri Lanka: Australian Complicity in Genocide*, International News, Green Left Weekly No. 818, November 18, 2009.

States financing Tamil internment, UN complicit in Crimes against Humanity—Boyle

[TamilNet, Friday, 16 October 2009, 02:36 GMT]

United Nations Organization and other Western States financing the Nazi-style concentration camps, where nearly 300,000 Tamil civilians are held against their wishes under Sri Lanka military supervision,* are complicit in Sri Lanka's genocide against Tamils, and also complicit in these crimes against humanity, said Francis A. Boyle, professor of International Law at the University of Illinois College of Law, in a note sent to TamilNet Thursday.

Prof. Boyle said: "Crimes against Humanity are a precursor to genocide. In this regard, Article II of the 1948 Genocide Convention provides in relevant part:

'In the present Convention, genocide means any of the following acts committed with intent to destroy, in whole or in part, a national, ethnical, racial or religious group as such:

... (b) Causing serious bodily or mental harm to members of the group;

(c) Deliberately inflicting on the group conditions of life calculated to bring about its physical destruction in whole or in part;...'

"For the Government of Sri Lanka (GoSL) to continue to imprison 300,000 Tamils "as such" within these Nazi-style concentration camps constitutes the international crime of genocide as defined by Articles II(b) and (c) of the 1948 Genocide Convention as quoted above," Boyle added.

"Furthermore, for the United Nations Organization and Western States to continue to finance these Nazi-style concentration camps renders them complicit in this instance of the GoSL's genocide against the Tamils in violation of Genocide Convention Article III(e) that criminalizes 'Complicity in genocide.'

"In addition, both the United Nations Organization and these financing Western States are also complicit in these Crimes against Humanity perpetrated by the GoSL against the Tamils," Professor Boyle said.

**See, e.g.*, Emily Wax, *In Sri Lanka, Anger over Detainees' Fate*, Washington Post, Nov. 11, 2009.

SLA war crimes eerily similar to Srebrenica Scorpions' terror, says Boyle

[TamilNet, Wednesday, 26 August 2009, 00:27 GMT]

Summary executions violate Common Article 3 to the Four Geneva Conventions of 1949, to which Sri Lanka is a Contracting Party, prohibiting in subsection I(d) "... the carrying out of executions without previous judgment pronounced by a regularly constituted court...." Violations of the Geneva Conventions are war crimes, said Professor Francis Boyle, after watching the video on the cold-blooded extra-judicial killings carried out by the Sri Lanka Army (SLA) soldiers published by a German-based group "Journalists for Democracy in Sri Lanka (JDS)," Tuesday.

"We have a video of the same being done to Bosnians at Srebrenica by Serbia's 'Scorpions,' which I viewed with one of the few male survivors while in the killing fields of Srebrenica itself," Boyle added, continuing: "Of course the Scorpion executions were just a small element of the Serbian genocide at Srebrenica."

Srebrenica massacre of 6 Bosnian Muslims

A video of Serb paramilitary soldiers Scorpions, caught in the act of murdering six Bosnian Muslim youths in July 17, 1995, near the town of Trnovo, Srebrenica, discovered 10 years later, shocked Serbia and led to the arrest and later conviction of the soldiers. The six Muslim men and boys were forced to lie down with their hands tied before being shot in the back by their captors. Two of the victims were 17, while the others were in their 20s and 30s. A Belgrade war-crimes court sentenced four Scorpions to a total of 58-years in prison.

The New York Times reporting on the story on the 6-person massacre by the Scorpions, said: "The faces of the perpetrators can be seen and their insults to the Muslims can be heard. The film was shot by a Scorpions member."

In remarkable eerie similarity with the SLA crimes, the SLA terror video was also obtained by an SLA soldier using a mobile-phone camera, and the SLA soldiers are also heard spewing insults to the naked Tamil prisoners.

"Scorpions, however, did not strip and then murder the Bosnians in the nude. But the GoSL Army did exactly that, which is even more akin to what the Nazis did to the Jews, depriving their victims of the last shred of their humanity before dying," Boyle observed.

Killings by SLA

German police ready to shoot dead Jewish men stripped naked

On the disappearances inside internment camps, the press release issued by the JDS said: "The Sri Lankan government justifies the internment of approximately 280,000 Tamil people, for over three months now, on the basis that they are 'screening' for LTTE cadres. These camps still remain out of bounds for independent media and human rights observers. Apart from these known camps, it is widely believed that there are over 10,000 Tamils held in undisclosed locations. Further, as a recent BBC report reveals the interned Tamils have to regularly experience the trauma of the appearance of the 'dolphin vans' in the camps—as these whisk away people—who then disappear."

Commenting on the disappearances, Boyle said, "when the enforced disappearances are 'widespread' or 'systematic' they become Crimes against Humanity under the Rome Statute for the International Criminal Court," adding: "Crimes against Humanity are the precursor to genocide, just as Hitler and the Nazis did to the Jews—I also visited Dachau."

The Scorpions (Škorpioni) were a Serbian paramilitary group which actively sought out the extermination of other ethnicities in the wars in Croatia, Bosnia and Herzegovina, and Kosovo. The unit was formed in 1991 in what was then the breakaway Croatian Serb Republic of Serbian Krajina. The Scorpion leader was Slobodan Medić.

Boyle: India a moral failure, Colombo's monstrosity matched only by Nazis

[TamilNet, Tuesday, 25 August 2009, 00:51 GMT]

"India's support to Rajapaksa Government is an atrocious crime. Tamils are undergoing unspeakable hardship, and the monstrosity is only matched by the Nazis terror on Jews. The world had simply closed its eyes....Failure to ensure safety to Sri Lanka Tamils is a moral disgrace to India and a stain in India's illustrious history," said Francis Boyle, expert in International Law and Professor at the University of Illinois College of Law, during an interview with Tamil Nadu magazine, Dalit Murasu.**

English translation of the Tamil article follows: (Note: The Tamil article is a translation of a recorded interview conducted in English):

Dalit Murasu: When more than 300,000 Tamils are held against their wishes in internment camps, do you think there remains any prospect of reaching a resolution to the conflict through intervention of International Rights Organizations including United Nations?

Prof. Francis A Boyle: It is imperative that these organizations should intervene. The 1948 Genocide Convention and the 1949 Geneva Conventions obligate the United Nations to engage in Sri Lanka's conflict and seek resolution. I have been consistently writing and advocating the urgent need for the UN and the International Community to intervene and save the Tamil people held by the Sri Lanka Government in the several internment camps. Reports indicate nearly 1400 people die in a week in these camps, and that the conditions within the camps are very similar to those in the Nazi internment camps.

DM: Even after Sri Lanka's military unilaterally declared that the "war was over in Sri Lanka," the International Community, various Rights Organizations, and the media have failed to expose the gross rights violations that occurred during and after the war. You have noted in several articles that the internment camps are nothing but "death camps." Do you think similar silence would have prevailed if the affected people are from Palestine or from a European country?

FAB: One cannot be certain how the International Community will react to your hypothetical scenarios. While the U.S. supported peace talks between the two adversaries in Sri Lanka, U.S.'s approach to mediating conflicts took a dramatic turn after the 9-11, when the Bush administration started to aggressively pursue the "war on terror" on all movements that used violence to achieve their goals. The President of India sending a congratulatory message to Sri Lanka's President is indeed a sad event. India has assured Sri Lanka of its cooperation, and India's position vis-a-vis Sri Lanka is totally unacceptable. India is ready and willing to continue support to Sri Lanka while standing on the bodies of 30,000 Tamils killed during the last several weeks of war. China and Pakistan both are collaborating with Sri Lanka.

The 65 million Tamils in Tamil Nadu should soon rise up to constrain India. The uprising in numbers and intensity should surpass the protests that occurred while Sri Lanka was slaughtering the Tamils. If India reconfigures its policy on Sri Lanka, US will likely support that. US will view with concern a friendly China-Sri Lanka relationship.

India's support to Rajapaksa Government is an atrocious crime. Tamils are undergoing unspeakable hardship, and the monstrosity is only matched by Nazis terror on Jews. The world had simply closed its eyes.

DM: The world was waiting to hear the details of the last weeks of the war from the doctors detained by the Sri Lanka Government. These Doctors were later paraded in front of the media and were forced to recant casualty figures. Do you think there is any chance for the truth to come out?

FAB: That depends on you, me, the other media, and is in the hands of the 65 millions Tamils in Tamil Nadu. Sri Lanka Government has been systematically destroying physical evidence after barring news organizations from visiting the crime area and imposing censorship on journalists reporting the details. US will have detailed evidence of what's happening, and of what has happened. While the world watches in silence atrocities are continuing.

DM: Why is the International Community not taking effective action to resettle the displaced people?

FAB: I don't think the International Community has any interest in the welfare of the Tamil people. That is why they kept silent during the slaughter of nearly 50,000 Tamils between February and May 2009. Finally the IMF loan is also going to be awarded. [was awarded early this month]. What happened in Sri Lanka is an attempt at extermination of a race, a racist war. Same thing happened in the 1930's against the Jews. Only after millions were killed the world began to know the truth of the atrocities. The world would not do anything.

DM: If the IC does not have an interest in Sri Lanka, why did they express their commendations to Sri Lanka after the war?

FAB: I only said they have no interest in Tamils. Countries certainly have geopolitical interest in creating conditions advantageous to them. Use of sea ports, and control of land mass in the Indian Ocean is certainly of interest to many powers.

DM: Will the Sri Lanka Government, which did not heed to the righteous demands of the Tamils when they had military power, attend to Tamils welfare now that Tamils appear defeated and powerless?

FAB: Definitely not. Sri Lankan state has set about to exterminate or, in the least, marginalize the Tamil people. The State inebriated with military victory have incarcerated the Tamil people in internment camps. For every 3 Tamils there are 14 Sinhala soldiers. This is violation of Geneva Conventions. What we witness in Sri Lanka is a clear attempt to destroy a race in whole or in part. All should identify this act as genocide.

DM: Why is the US unwilling to release satellite images it may have taken during the last stages of war?

FAB: US is cognizant of the serious repercussions that may result when the world sees the truth. These images will reveal the slaughter of Tamils with the use of heavy weapons, heavy artillery, and aerial bombardments by the Sri Lanka military. US's behavior was the same with respect to Bosnia. US is unlikely to reveal Sri Lanka images as truth may lead the civilized world to demand a solution that will be inimical to US's interest.

DM: What's the US position on Sri Lanka's Tamils? Has the US revealed its true policy?

FAB: I believe the US will continue to support Rajapaksa. The IMF loan is a clear indication of US's policy towards Sri Lanka. Earlier US supported peace talks. There is no more space for US to take that position. What's happening in Sri Lanka is a clear case of genocide. However, if the US accepts this, then Article I of the Genocide Convention will obligate the US to intervene to stop the genocide. US does not want to do that. Similar thing happened in Bosnia too.

DM: Tamils are contemplating the establishment of a transnational government. In the future if Tamils declare a State of Tamil Eelam either within Sri Lanka or outside, what will be US's position?

FAB: The US will not be disposed to supporting it.

DM: What do you think is a feasible political solution to the struggle waged by the Tamils for the last half a century?

FAB: The political solution has to be determined by the Tamils themselves. One of three solutions are possible. 1. Create a free, sovereign, separate state for themselves. 2. Form a confederation with another independent state. And 3. Any other solution agreed by a majority Tamil people. International laws dictate that Tamils are entitled to the right of self-determination. India, you, me or the Sri Lanka Government cannot dictate terms to what Tamils should do.

I want to emphasize one point here. Historically, peoples who have suffered through genocide-level atrocities like what the Tamil people have been through, assured their safety only after creating a separate state for themselves.

During the last few months when more than 50,000 Tamils were slaughtered in Vanni no country was able to stop the killings. All countries failed to execute their obligatory duty as required by the 1948 Genocide Convention. For Tamils to safeguard their lives from the Sri Lankan State, International Community should assist the Tamils to form their own separate state. International covenants declare that it is necessary and just that such peoples who have been affected by genocidal crimes to form their own state.

India's reason for not supporting Sri Lanka's Tamils is that a separate Tamil State in Sri Lanka will trigger fissiparous tendencies within Tamil Nadu. This is a lie and simply double talk. Failure to ensure safety to Sri Lanka Tamils is a moral disgrace to India and a stain in India's illustrious history.

The International Covenant on Civil and Political Rights (ICCPR) makes it clear that the Tamil people have the right to self-determination. Sri Lanka is a signatory to this covenant. Sri Lanka has accepted that Tamil people is a distinct race with their own language and have lived in areas of historical inhabitation.

Therefore, they have the right to exercise their right to self-determination, and as a free people they can then safeguard and nurture their social, economic, and cultural well-being.

Boyle debunks Kohona's war-crimes braggadocio

[TamilNet, Sunday, 23 August 2009, 03:17 GMT]

Debunking Sri Lanka's Foreign Secretary, Palitha Kohona's statement that "no winner of a war has been tried [for war crimes] before a Tribunal," Francis Boyle, Professor of International Law at the Illinois College of Law, said, as legal counsel for the Mothers of Srebrenica and Podrinja, he had convinced the Honorable Carla Del Ponte, the Prosecutor for the International Criminal Tribunal for the Former Yugoslavia (ICTY), to indict Yugoslav President Slobodan Milosevic for every crime in the ICTY Statute, including genocide, war crimes and crimes against humanity.

Palitha T. B. Kohona

Kohona told a Sri Lanka's local paper in an interview Thursday: "If you look at the history of war crimes there isn't one instance where a winner of a war has been tried before a Tribunal. They have always been set up for losers. And if you were to take winners then the start would have to be taken elsewhere. Sri Lanka did not drop atom bombs or destroy entire cities during the war."

Boyle mocked this statement pointing to the fate of Slobodan Milosevic, and added, "Milosevic died on trial before the ICTY for these international crimes, including the genocidal massacre at Srebrenica.

"Today, Milosevic's henchman Radovan Karadzic—self-styled President of the self-styled Republika Srpska—is on trial before the ICTY for every crime in the ICTY Statute, including the genocidal massacre at Srebrenica," Prof. Boyle said.

Boyle warned, "someday we shall hold to account the GoSL genocidaires as well, especially the Rajapaksa brothers and Fonseka, for their international crimes, including the genocidal massacre of Tamils on the Wanni Beach."

"Colombo bringing the war-crimes issue to public scrutiny reflects the nervousness the Sri Lanka's ruling administration feels on the potential fate of some high-level officials when the international legal spotlight turns on them. The evidence being collected from Satellite-witnessed massacres of Tamil civilians, and the eye-witness accounts that will soon be available from massacre escapees, will be haunting these officials," spokesperson of a US-based activist group TAG told TamilNet.

Boyle, Fein charge Sri Lanka with Genocide during Chennai seminar

[TamilNet, Tuesday, 09 June 2009, 02:20 GMT]

Francis Boyle, Professor of International Law at the University of Illinois College of Law, and Bruce Fein, a Washington D.C. Attorney, speaking at a seminar in Chennai organized by the International Tamil Center Monday, reiterated charges of Genocide against the Sri Lanka Government alleging massacre of more than 50,000 Tamil civilians, sources attending the event said. While Prof. Boyle urged India to file charges in International Court against Sri Lanka for violating the Genocide Convention, and to order Colombo "to cease and desist from all acts of genocide against Tamils," Fein stressed the urgent need for the Tamils to reach a "consensus on their political aspirations." The event was organized by Dr. Panchadcharam, a consultant physician from New York.

Full text of draft of Prof. Boyle's talk at the seminar follows:

THE RIGHTS OF THE TAMILS LIVING ON THE ISLAND OF SRI LANKA UNDER INTERNATIONAL LAW AND PRACTICE

Introduction

There are two basic points I want to make: First, the Tamils living on Sri Lanka have been the victims of genocide. Second, the Tamils living on Sri Lanka have the right to self-determination under international law and practice, including the right to establish their own independent state if they so desire. And the fact that the Tamils living on Sri Lanka have been victims of genocide only strengthens and reinforces their right to self-determination, including establishing their own independent State if that is their desire.

Genocide

Article I of the 1948 Genocide Convention requires all 140 states parties to immediately act in order "to prevent" the ongoing GoSL genocide against the Tamils. One of the most important steps the 140 contracting states parties to the Genocide Convention must take in order to fulfill their obligation under Article I is to sue Sri Lanka at the International Court of Justice in The Hague (the so-called World Court) for violating the 1948 Genocide Convention on the basis of Article IX thereto: "Disputes between the Contracting Parties relating to the interpretation, application or fulfillment of the present Convention, including those relating to the responsibility of a State for genocide or for any of the other acts enumerated in Article III, shall be submitted to the International Court of Justice at the request of any of the parties to the dispute."

Any one or more of the 140 states parties to the Genocide Convention (1) must immediately sue Sri Lanka at the International Court of Justice in The Hague; (2) must demand an Emergency Hearing by the World Court; and (3) must request an Order indicating provisional measures of protection against Sri Lanka to cease and desist from committing all acts of genocide against the 300,000 Tamils in Vanni. Such a World Court Order is the international equivalent to a domestic temporary restraining order and permanent injunction.

Once issued by the World Court, this Order would be immediately transmitted to the United Nations Security Council for enforcement under U.N. Charter article 94(2). So far the member states of the United Nations Security Council have failed and refused to act in order to do anything to stop the GoSL's genocide against the Tamils (1) despite the fact that the situation in Vanni constitutes a "threat to the peace" that requires Security Council action under article 39 of the United Nations Charter and (2) despite the fact that they are all obligated "to prevent" Sri Lanka's genocide against the Tamils under article I of the Genocide Convention. This World Court Order will put the matter on the Agenda of the Security Council and force the Security Council to take action in order "to prevent" the ongoing genocide against the Tamils by Sri Lanka.

Article II of the Genocide Convention defines the international crime of genocide in relevant part as follows:

> In the present Convention, genocide means any of the following acts committed with intent to destroy, in whole or in part, a national, ethnical, racial or religious group, as such:

> (a) Killing members of the group;
> (b) Causing serious bodily or mental harm to members of the group;
> (c) Deliberately inflicting on the group conditions of life calculated to bring about its physical destruction in whole or in part;

> ...

Certainly the Sinhala-Buddhist Sri Lanka and its legal predecessor Ceylon have committed genocide against the Hindu/Christian Tamils that actually started on or about 1948 and has continued apace until today and is now accelerating in Vanni in violation of Genocide Convention Articles II(a), (b), and (c).

For the past six decades, the Sinhala-Buddhist Ceylon/Sri Lanka has implemented a systematic and comprehensive military, political, and economic campaign with the intent to destroy in substantial part the different national, ethnical, racial, and religious group constituting the Hindu/Christian Tamils. This Sinhala-Buddhist Ceylon/Sri Lanka campaign has consisted of killing members of the Hindu/Christian Tamils in violation of Genocide Convention Article II(a). This Sinhala-Buddhist Ceylon/Sri Lanka campaign has also caused serious bodily and mental harm to the Hindu/Christian Tamils in violation of Genocide Convention Article II(b). This Sinhala-Buddhist Ceylon/Sri Lanka campaign has also deliberately inflicted on the Hindu/Christian Tamils conditions of life calculated to bring about their physical destruction in substantial part in violation of Article II(c) of the Genocide Convention.

Since 1983 the Sinhala-Buddhist Sri Lanka have exterminated approximately 100,000 Hindu/Christian Tamils. The Sinhala-Buddhist Sri Lanka have now added another 300,000 Hindu/Christian Tamils in Vanni to their genocidal death list. Humanity needs one state party to the Genocide Convention to fulfill its obligation under article I thereof to immediately sue Sri Lanka at the World Court in order to save the 300,000 Tamils in Vanni from further extermination. Time is of the essence!

Self-determination

This gets into the second point that I want to make concerning the Tamils as a group of people living on the Island of Sri Lanka—their right to self-determination under international law and practice. And here I wanted to quote from an international treaty to which the government of Sri Lanka is a party, thus explicitly recognizing that the Tamils living on the Island of Sri Lanka have a right of self-determination. This is from the International Covenant on Civil and Political Rights, to which the government of Sri Lanka is a party. They are bound by their own treaty, which says quite clearly in Article One: "All peoples have the right of self-determination."

And clearly, the Tamils living on the Island of Sri Lanka are a "people." The Tamils on Sri Lanka have a separate language, race, ethnicity, and religions, from the GoSL. The Tamils see themselves as a separate group of "people" and they are perceived to be such by the GoSL. For that precise reason the GoSL has attempted to exterminate the Tamils and ethnically cleanse their Homeland. So no better proof is needed than that. Both the objective criteria and the subjective criteria for establishing a "people" with a right of self-determination under international law and practice have been fulfilled by the Tamils living on Sri Lanka.

Let me continue enumerating a few more of the most basic self-determination rights of the Tamils living on Sri Lanka under international law that are recognized by this International Covenant that the GoSL is a party to: "By virtue of that right they freely determine their political status and freely pursue their economic, social and cultural development." Those are rights that the Tamils living on Sri Lanka have today even as recognized by the government of Sri Lanka. Those are group rights and not just individual rights. And those are group rights that must be protected because the government of Sri Lanka has attacked the Tamils as a group, not just as individuals. So, since Tamils have been victims as a group, they must be protected as a group. And one of the most basic rights of all that the Tamils have to protect themselves is this right of self-determination including determining their political status and pursuing their own economic, social and cultural development, as well as the establishment of an independent state of their own if that is what the Tamils decide is required for them to accomplish these objectives.

Another component of this right of self-determination for the Tamils living on Sri Lanka is set forth in paragraph (2) of this Article One of the International Covenant on Civil and Political Rights, to which the government of Sri Lanka is a party. Notice here I am only using the treaties the GoSL itself is a party to, including the Genocide Convention. I am not citing any principles of international law that the GoSL has not already recognized and indeed violated grievously with respect to the Tamils living on Sri Lanka: "All peoples may, for their own ends, freely dispose of their natural wealth and resources without prejudice to any obligations arising out of international economic cooperation, based upon the principle of mutual benefit, and international law. In no case may the people be deprived of its own means of subsistence."

Yet we all know for a fact that the GoSL has done everything humanly possible to deprive the Tamil people of their own means of subsistence to a level that now constitutes genocide, in violation of that provision I quoted before from the Genocide Convention prohibiting inflicting on a group conditions of life calculated to bring about their physical destruction in whole or in part. Notice these economic and political rights are related to each other. Both elements of the right to self-determination must protect the Tamils since they have been victims of genocide. We must protect their political rights as well as their economic rights, to freely dispose of their natural wealth and resources. The Tamil people, not the GoSL, must control their traditional Homeland in the North and the East of the Island, their farms, their mines, their plantations, their forests, their waters, their beaches etc. This is critical. Yet today we know that the GoSL is currently in the process of stealing, destroying and negating all these economic and political rights of the Tamils in their traditional Homeland in the North and the East of the Island of Sri Lanka. The GoSL is currently inflicting ethnic cleansing on the Tamils living there.

I have already established that the Tamil people living on Sri Lanka have a right of self-determination, even in accordance with the GoSL's own treaties themselves. What are some of the other political consequences of their right of self-determination? These are set forth in what is known as the Declaration on Principles of International Law Concerning Friendly

Relations and Co-operation Among States in Accordance with the Charter of the United Nations (1971). The government of Sri Lanka approved this Declaration in the United Nations General Assembly -- so I am not quoting here any provision of law that the GoSL has not already approved. And from the Declaration let me state what are the political alternatives that are open to the Tamil people, and they are set forth as follows: "[1] The establishment of a sovereign and independent State, [2] the free association or integration with an independent State, or [3] the emergence into any other political status freely determined by a people constitute the modes of implementing the right of self-determination by that people."

So again, it is not for the GoSL to determine what might be the ultimate political outcome here. It is for the Tamil people living on Sri Lanka to determine which of those three options they desire. I also want to make it clear that it is not for me to tell the Tamils on Sri Lanka which of these three options they should choose. Moreover, it is not for the Tamils of India to tell the Tamils on Sri Lanka which of these three options they should choose. This is for them to decide pursuant to their right of self-determination under international law and practice.

However I do want to note that historically the only way a people that has been subjected to genocide like the Tamils on Sri Lanka have been able to protect themselves from further extermination has been the creation of an independent state of their own. Indeed as the world saw for the last several months the government of Sri Lanka wantonly, openly, shamelessly, and gratuitously exterminated over 50,000 Tamils in Vanni; yet not one state in the entire world rose to protect them or defend them or help them as required by Article I of the 1948 Genocide Convention. Hence the need for the Tamils on Sri Lanka to have their own independent state in order to protect themselves from further annihilation by the GoSL. International law and practice establish that an independent state of their own is the only effective remedy as well as the only appropriate reparation for a people who have been the victims of genocide.

Now the Indian government has basically argued that if it were to recognize the right of the Tamils on Sri Lanka to self-determination and an independent state of their own, then the 65 million Tamils in Tamil Nadu would also assert that same right and proceed to secede from India. I submit this is a false dichotomy under international law and practice. It must not be used as an excuse for inaction by the government of India when it comes to protecting the Tamils living on Sri Lanka.

In this regard, let me return to the Declaration on Principles of International Law Concerning Friendly Relations and Cooperation Among States that was approved by both India and Sri Lanka and sets forth rules of customary international law interpreting the terms of the United Nations Charter itself as determined by the International Court of Justice in the *Nicaragua* case (1986). In particular let me draw to your attention the following language: "Nothing in the foregoing paragraphs shall be construed as authorizing or encouraging any action which would dismember or impair, totally or in part, the territorial integrity or political unity of sovereign and independent States conducting themselves in compliance with the principle of equal rights and self-determination of peoples as described above and thus possessed of a government representing the whole people belonging to the territory without distinction as to race, creed or color."

This paragraph of the Declaration sets forth the rules of customary international law when it comes to the right of a people to secede from another state by means of exercising their right of self-determination. As you can see from the above language secession is permitted only when a government does not conduct itself "in compliance with the principle of equal rights and self-determination of peoples" and thus does not represent "the whole people belonging to the territory without distinction as to race, creed or color."

From its very foundation in 1948 the government of Ceylon/Sri Lanka has never conducted itself "in compliance with the principle of equal rights and self-determination of peoples" with respect to the Tamils. Furthermore, the government of Ceylon/Sri Lanka has never represented "the whole people belonging to the territory without distinction as to race, creed or color" with respect to the Tamils. In fact the government of Ceylon/Sri Lanka has always discriminated against and persecuted the Tamils on grounds of race, creed, color, and language. This endemic pattern of criminal behavior by the Sinhala has now culminated in wholesale acts of genocide against the Tamils being inflicted by the government of Sri Lanka. So of course the Tamils have the right to secede from Sri Lanka under international law and practice and especially under the terms of this Declaration.

Conversely, the government of India does conduct itself "in compliance with the principle of equal rights and self-determination of peoples" with respect to the Tamils in Tamil Nadu and is thus "possessed of a government representing the whole people belonging to the territory without distinction as to race, creed or colour." India just had elections where the Tamils in Tamil Nadu participated on a basis of full equality with everyone else. The Tamils in India have full legal equality with all other peoples in India and indeed have their own state here in Tamil Nadu. Therefore in my opinion, the 65 million Tamils in Tamil Nadu do not have a right of secession under international law and practice according to this Declaration, which sets forth the basic rules of customary international law on this subject.

Conversely, however, the Tamils living on Sri Lanka do have a right of secession under international law and practice including this Declaration for which both India and Sri Lanka voted. So with all due respect to the position of the Indian government, it is a false dichotomy for it to assert that recognition of the right of self-determination with an independent state of their own for the Tamils living on Sri Lanka would lead to the same for the Tamils in Tamil Nadu. There is no basis in international law for this conclusion. Indeed, basic principles of international law including this Declaration would fully support the territorial integrity of India in the event the government of India were to recognize the right of the Tamils living on the Island of Sri Lanka to self-determination including an independent state of their own.

Conclusion

Be that as it may, even if out of an excess of caution the government of India is not prepared to go that far at this time, nevertheless at a minimum, since it is the original homeland for the Tamils, the government of India has the right, the obligation, and the standing under international law and practice to act as *parens patriae* for the Tamils living on Sri Lanka. Therefore, India must immediately sue the GoSL for genocide at the International Court of Justice in The Hague, demand an Emergency Hearing of the Court, and request that the World Court issue a Temporary Restraining Order against the GoSL to cease and desist from committing all acts of genocide against the Tamils living on Sri Lanka. The ghosts of Dachau, Auschwitz, Cambodia, Sabra and Shatilla, Srebrenica, Rwanda, Kosovo, and now Vanni demand no less!

Sinhala "lebensraum" in progress in Vanni, warns Prof. Boyle

[TamilNet, Wednesday, 03 June 2009, 03:15 GMT]

"The Government of Sri Lanka (GoSL) is continuing to inflict Nazi-type crimes and atrocities against the Tamils even after their alleged excuse of fighting a 'war against terrorism' has been exposed as a bogus pretext to annihilate the Tamils and to steal their lands and natural resources. This is what Hitler and the Nazis called 'lebensraum'— 'living space' for the Sinhala at the expense of the Tamils. The GoSL's 'ethnic cleansing' of the Tamil Homeland for the benefit of the Sinhala is now underway," warns Francis Boyle, professor of International Law at the University of Illinois College of Law.

"With the UN already under fire for withholding and downplaying the number of civilian casualties in Sri Lanka, another ongoing controversy has opened up concerning the number of internally displaced persons detained in the IDP camps in northern Sri Lanka. Between the May 27 and May 30 reports of the UN's Office for the Coordination of Humanitarian Affairs, over 13,000 IDPs simply disappeared from the camps," reported Inner City Press which is covering the affairs at the United Nations in New York.

"Concerning these missing 13,000+ genocide-survivors from the Safety Zone, Article 7(1)(i) of the Rome Statute for the International Criminal Court provides that the 'enforced disappearance of persons' is a Crime Against Humanity 'when committed as part of a widespread or systematic attack directed against any civilian population, with knowledge of the attack,'" Boyle said.

"Clearly the GoSL's enforced disappearances of these Tamils and other Tamils in the past has been both 'widespread' and 'systematic' as documented over the years by numerous human rights NGOs. The GoSL's widespread and systematic enforced disappearances of Tamils over the years constitutes a Crime Against Humanity," Boyle added.

"According to the Nuremberg Charter (1945), the Nuremberg Judgment (1946), and the Nuremberg Principles (1950), the paradigmatic example of a Crime Against Humanity is what Hitler and the Nazis did to the Jews. Historically, this Nuremberg Crime Against Humanity was the legal precursor to the International Crime of Genocide as defined by the 1948 Genocide Convention," Boyle said.

Lebensraum served as a major motivation for Nazi Germany's territorial aggression. Adolf Hitler believed that the German people needed Lebensraum —for a *Großdeutschland*, land, and raw materials—and that it should be taken in the East. It was the stated policy of the Nazis to kill, deport, Germanize or enslave the Polish, and later also Russian and other Slavic populations, and to repopulate the land with *reinrassig* (racially pure) Germanic peoples.

"The Sri Lanka Government's Nazi-type crimes in the Vanni appear motivated by the doctrine of lebensraum, and the future survival of Tamil culture in Sri Lanka is in peril," says Prof. Boyle.

UN Officials complicit in aiding, abetting GoSL's Nazi-type crimes—Prof. Boyle

[TamilNet, Saturday, 30 May 2009, 11:14 GMT]

Pointing to a report in the French paper Le Monde, which quoted Vijay Nambiar, Chief of Staff of UN Secretary General Ban Ki Moon, as telling UN representatives in Sri Lanka that the UN should "keep a low profile" and play a "sustaining role" that was "compatible with the government," Francis Boyle, professor of International Law at the University of Illinois College of Law said Saturday that both the United Nations Organization itself and its highest level officials are guilty of aiding and abetting Nazi-type crimes against the Tamils by the Government of Sri Lanka, in violation of international law. "Unless this Momentum is reversed and all these U.N. Officials fired, the United Nations Organization shall follow the League of Nations into the 'ashcan' of History," Boyle said.

**Vijay Nambiar
Chief of Staff of
Ban Ki Moon**

"Nambiar's statement was made while the GoSL inflicted genocide, crimes against humanity, war crimes and ethnic cleansing upon the Tamils in violation of the 1948 Genocide Convention, the Four Geneva Conventions of 1949 and their Two Additional Protocols of 1977, as well as the principles of Customary International Criminal Law set forth in the Nuremberg Charter (1945), the Nuremberg Judgment (1946) and the United Nation's own codification of the Nuremberg Principles (1950) for the trial and prosecution of the Nazis—all of which are now incorporated into the Rome Statute for the International Criminal Court," Boyle said.

"In other words, both the United Nations Organization itself and its highest level officials are guilty of aiding and abetting Nazi-type crimes against the Tamils by the GoSL.

"The United Nations Organization and its Highest Level Officials did the exact same thing to the Bosnians at Srebrenica in July of 1995—days that have lived in infamy and shame for the United Nations ever since then.

"By comparison, today the GoSL's genocidal massacre of the Tamils in Vanni could be about four times Serbia's genocidal massacre of the Bosnians at Srebrenica."

Further, *The Times* of the UK revealed Saturday, that the top aide to the United Nations Secretary-General Nambiar was told more than a week ago that at least 20,000 Tamil civilians were killed in the Sri Lankan Government's final offensive against the Tamil Tiger rebels this month.

"History is repeating itself with a Vengeance for the United

Nations. Unless this Momentum is reversed and all these U.N. Officials fired, the United Nations Organization shall follow the League of Nations into the 'ashcan' of History!," Boyle said.

Satish Nambiar

Paid military consultant

Adding further complicity to Vijay Nambiar's role as a special UN envoy to Sri Lanka is the involvement of his brother Satish Nambiar, a former Indian general as a consultant to the Sri Lankan government. Satish Nambiar "was quoted on the Sri Lankan military's web page praising the Army's and its commander's conduct of the war in the north, despite all the civilians killed. It is, the [unnamed Security Council] diplomat said bitterly, all a family affair," a report of 11th May in the Inner City Press, said.

Unprincipled, shameless, "Orwellian" UN resolution ever—Prof. Boyle

[TamilNet, Thursday, 28 May 2009, 23:31 GMT]

"This is one of the most unprincipled and shameless resolutions ever adopted by any body of the United Nations in the history of that now benighted Organization. It would be as if the U.N. Human Rights Council had congratulated the Nazi government for the 'liberation' of the Jews in Poland after its illegal and genocidal invasion of that country in 1939," said Francis Boyle, professor of International Law at the University of Illinois College of Law, referring to the resolution passed at the United Nations Human Rights Council on the Sri Lanka war.

"This Resolution simultaneously gives the imprimatur of the U.N. Human Rights Council to the ethnic cleansing, genocide, crimes against humanity and war crimes that the Government of Sri Lanka has already inflicted upon the Tamils in the past, as well as the Council's proverbial 'green light' for the GoSL to perpetrate and escalate more of the same international crimes against the Tamils in the future," Boyle said.

"The U.N. Human Rights Council and those member States that voted in favor of this Resolution have thereby become ACCESSORIES AFTER THE FACT to the GoSL's genocide, crimes against humanity, war crimes and ethnic cleansing against the Tamils in the past, as well as AIDERS AND ABETTORS to future acts of genocide, crimes against humanity, war crimes and ethnic cleansing that the GoSL will undoubtedly inflict upon the Tamils thanks to this Resolution—all in violation of the Genocide Convention, the Four Geneva Conventions of 1949 and their Two Additional Protocols of 1977 as well as the Rome Statute for the International Criminal Court.

"Sri Lanka, together with these other Council States, are contracting parties to some or all of these International Criminal Law Conventions and therefore must be held accountable for their violation and international crimes against the Tamils," Boyle added.

"History shall so judge them all!"

"Orwell stands vindicated by the U.N. Human Rights Council: WAR IS PEACE, FREEDOM IS SLAVERY, IGNORANCE IS FREEDOM, THE U.N. HUMAN RIGHTS COUNCIL LOVES BIG BROTHER," Boyle said, indicating he is deeply disturbed by the U.N. action.

"Glaring hypocrisy, blatant sophistry" Boyle slams Swiss UN Resolution

[TamilNet, Tuesday, 26 May 2009, 17:35 GMT]

Pointing out the twelfth operative paragraph of the Draft Resolution sponsored by Switzerland, that is currently pending before the U.N. Human Rights Council, Professor Boyle, expert in International Law and Professor at the University of Illinois College of Law, says this would be the same "as if the U.N. Human Rights Council had invited the Nazi government to investigate and prosecute itself for genocide, crimes against humanity and war crimes against the Jews instead of supporting the Nuremberg Charter and Tribunal."

The twelfth operative paragraph says, "12. The Council stresses the importance of combating impunity and calls on the government of Sri Lanka to investigate all allegations and bring to justice, in accordance with international standards, perpetrators of violations of human rights and of international humanitarian law, including hostage taking, torture, enforced disappearances and extrajudicial, summary or arbitrary executions, and to increase its efforts to further prevent such violations;"

Boyle said, " I am not going to waste my time here going through the hypocrisy and sophistry of the Draft Resolution sponsored by Switzerland that is currently pending before the U.N. Human Rights Council with the support of 25 other U.N. Member States. For operative paragraph 12 of the Swiss Resolution gives their entire Public Relations game away.

"It calls upon the Government of Sri Lanka to investigate and prosecute itself for war crimes and crimes against humanity, including hostage taking, torture, enforced disappearances and extrajudicial, summary or arbitrary executions.

"It would be as if the U.N. Human Rights Council had invited the Nazi government to investigate and prosecute itself for genocide, crimes against humanity and war crimes against the Jews instead of supporting the Nuremberg Charter and Tribunal.

"So in other words the Swiss Resolution is basically a continuation of the international whitewash and cover-up of the GoSL's genocide, crimes against humanity and war crimes against the Tamils," Professor Boyle said.

He added, "[t]he glaring hypocrisy and blatant sophistry of the Swiss Resolution is heightened by the fact that Switzerland is the Depositary for the Four Geneva Conventions of 1949 and their Two Additional Protocols of 1977 and therefore bears a special obligation under international law to promote, guarantee and ensure their effective enforcement rather than their negation and nullification, which this Swiss Resolution will do. Obviously, Switzerland knows exactly what it is doing. The same is true for the 25 other state Co-Sponsors of the Swiss Resolution.

"Instead of this meaningless and hypocritical and unprincipled Swiss Resolution, the U.N. Human Rights Council must establish an International Commission of Investigation to inquire into whether the GoSL has inflicted genocide, crimes against humanity and war crimes against the Tamils. Otherwise the U.N. Human Rights Council and its member states will simply and knowingly become part of the GoSL's propaganda campaign and cover-up against the Tamils.

"If adopted, History shall record for all time their cruel crocodile tears shed for the Tamils in this infamous Swiss Resolution," Boyle warned.

"Accessories after the fact to acts of Genocide"

[TamilNet, Saturday, 23 May 2009, 02:00 GMT]

Condemning the sponsorship, by twelve states, of a self-praising resolution submitted to the United Nations by the Government of Sri Lanka, before the scheduled UN Human Rights Council emergency session scheduled for Monday, Professor Boyle, an expert in International Law said Friday that these states have become accessories after the fact to the numerous acts of genocide, crimes against humanity and war crimes that the Government of Sri Lanka has perpetrated upon the Tamils.

Labeled "Assistance to Sri Lanka in the Promotion and Protection of Human Rights," Sri Lanka's proposed text is co-signed by Indonesia, China, Saudi Arabia, India, Pakistan, Malaysia, Bahrain, Philippines, Cuba, Egypt, Nicaragua, and Bolivia, reported UN Watch, a non-governmental organization based in Geneva whose mandate is to monitor the performance of the United Nations.

"Their sponsorship of this Resolution means that the above-mentioned states have thereby all become ACCESSORIES AFTER THE FACT to the numerous acts of genocide, crimes against humanity and war crimes that the Government of Sri Lanka has perpetrated upon the Tamils in violation of the 1948 Genocide Convention, the Four Geneva Conventions of 1949 and their Two Additional Protocols of 1977, as well as the rules of customary international criminal law, including humanitarian law and the laws of war," Prof. Boyle said.

"By definition, violations of international treaties, genocide, crimes against humanity and war crimes cannot possibly fall within the domestic jurisdiction of a State.

"That Principle goes back to the Nuremberg Charter of 1945 and the Nuremberg Judgment of 1946 concerning the prosecution of the Nazis," Boyle added.

"This Resolution constitutes a total debasement and perversion of everything the United Nations Charter and the U.N. Human Rights Council are intended to stand for," Boyle said.

By contrast, the upcoming Monday session was initiated by the Council's European Union members and supported by Argentina, Bosnia, Canada, Chile, Mexico, Mauritius, South Korea, Switzerland, Ukraine and Uruguay, UN Watch said.

"Sri Lanka's action today constitutes an outrageous abuse and show of contempt for the international human rights process," said Hillel Neuer, an international lawyer and the executive director of UN Watch, a Geneva-based human rights monitoring group.

300,000 Tamils held in Nazi-style concentration camps, says Prof. Boyle

[TamilNet, Friday, 22 May 2009, 12:30 GMT]

"These Nazi-style concentration camps that the Government of Sri Lanka is now forcibly imposing on at least 300,000 completely innocent Tamil civilians constitute acts of genocide within the meaning of Article II(c) of the 1948 Genocide Convention, to which Sri Lanka is a contracting party," Professor Boyle who is an expert international law and teaches at the University of Illinois College of Law said.

Article II(c) of the 1948 Genocide Convention criminalizes: "c) Deliberately inflicting on the group conditions of life calculated to bring about its physical destruction in whole or in part."

"All other contracting parties to the Genocide Convention such as the United States, Britain, France and India have an absolute obligation under Article I of the Genocide Convention 'to prevent' these acts of genocide against Tamils perpetrated by the GoSL under the guise of concentration camps," Professor Boyle said.

"Yet so far these other States have done nothing to alleviate the genocidal plight of the Tamils in Vanni.

"Unless these other states act immediately to rectify the genocidal humanitarian situation for the Tamils in Vanni, they will all become 'complicit' in these the GoSL's latest acts of genocide against the Tamils in violation of Genocide Convention Article III(e) that prohibits, condemns and criminalizes: '(e) Complicity in genocide,'" Boyle added.

"These states have already made a mockery out of history's post World War II emphatic injunction that motivated the drafting of the Genocide Convention: Never again!," Boyle said in a note to TamilNet.

Sri Lanka destroys evidence, prevents ICRC, UN access—Prof. Boyle

[TamilNet, Wednesday, 20 May 2009, 04:20 GMT]

Noting that the slow genocide of Tamils in Sri Lanka accelerated to more than 10,000 killed in the last few months, far exceeding the horrors of Srebrenica, Professor Boyle in conversation with Los Angeles KPFK radio host, Michael Slate, Tuesday, accused Sri Lanka Government of bulldozing and destroying evidence of massacres in the Safety Zone while preventing access to the Red Cross and UN agencies. Boyle added that the United States Government with spy satellites would be knowing exactly what Sri Lanka's actions are in the Safe Zone, and stand implicated along with UK, France, and India in allowing the genocide to happen.

"Today ICRC still does not have access when the area should be flooded with food and medicine to urgently attend to the 300,000 Internally Displaced Tamils held in Sri Lanka Army (SLA) supervised camps," Boyle said, adding, survivors from the Safety Zone, from starvation, resembled escapees from Nazi death camps.

The situation was similar to what happened in Gaza, Boyle said, but in Gaza people had access to food via under ground tunnels, whereas the Tamils holed up in the Safety Zone were completely cutoff from the outside and were entirely dependent on food transported by the ICRC ships.

Tracing the history of the conflict, Boyle and Slate agreed that Sri Lanka was an apartheid state from the very beginning of independence, and pointed to the violent elements of the Buddhist clergy, and the India's Dravidian-oriented racism as elements that exacerbated the deterioration of the conflict towards genocide.

Peace processes failed, Boyle argued, because Sri Lankan Governments, instead engaging in good faith negotiation, "wanted control, domination, and elimination of the Tamil population."

"We may be at the beginning of a humanitarian catastrophe for the Tamil people in Sri Lanka which would fit the ultimate objective of the Government motivated by chauvinist, violent racism," Boyle said, adding "my experience in working in genocidal situations says once the government and the people are possessed of this genocidal mentality it's very difficult to stop."

Slate added, "Tamil people are a severely oppressed nation. Anyone of conscience must stand up and support their resistance."

"Klerk risks repeating Netherland's criminality on Srebrenica genocide"

[TamilNet, Wednesday, 13 May 2009, 23:06 GMT]

By dismissing the horrendous rights violations of Sri Lanka in the safety zone of Mullaiththeevu as "not applicable" to providing favorable tariff treatment to Sri Lankan textiles under the GSP Plus Program, Pieter de Klerk, Netherland's Acting Permanent Representative to the UN, is in danger of repeating Netherland Government's history of criminality on Srebrenica genocide again on the genocide currently taking place in Vanni, Sri Lanka, a legal scholar in the U.S. pointed out. Inner City Press which carried the Dutch Representative's statement, mused, "[i]f the killing of thousands of civilians, hundreds in the last weekend alone, does not implicate the EU's [European Union] notions of human rights, perhaps these notions are bankrupt."

At a panel discussion Tuesday on the European Union and Human Rights, at the United Nations in New York, Inner City Press asked the Netherlands' acting Permanent Representative, Piet de Klerk, what the EU is doing about following up on its favorable tariff treatment to Sri Lankan textiles under the GSP Plus program, on which the EU purportedly considers human rights. DPR de Klerk said he didn't think that human rights were "applicable to this sort of situation."

"The Dutch Government was criminally responsible for the genocidal massacre of 8000 Bosnian Muslims at Srebrenica in July of 1995 by Serbia. So of course it comes as no surprise that the Dutch Government has no problem with the Srebrenica-style genocidal massacre of 10,000 Tamils in Vanni by Sri Lanka in 2009. History is repeating itself," said University of Illinois law professor, Francis Boyle, who was a key player in bringing indictment against Slobodan Milosevic for committing genocide, crimes against humanity, and war crimes in Bosnia and Herzegovina.

The criminal complaint for the Srebrenica massacre included the Dutch nationals, Joris Voorhoeve, Dutch Minister of Defense, Dutch General Cees Nicolai, in the UN Chain of Command and reporting to Voorhoeve as well, and the Dutch Colonel Thomas Karremans, in charge of Srebrenica at the time of the massacre.

The Dutch government resigned on 16 April 2002, a week after a report on the 1995 fall of Srebrenica held political leaders partly responsible for failing to protect Muslims in a UN "safe haven" in Bosnia.

Full text of the criminal complaint against United Nations' officials follows:

MOTHERS OF SREBRENICA
AND PODRINJA ASSOCIATION

v

UNITED NATIONS OFFICIALS AND OTHERS
(CRIMINAL COMPLAINT FOR
THE SREBRENICA MASSACRE)

UNITED NATIONS, THE HAGUE, NETHERLANDS.

The Mothers of Srebrenica and Podrinja Association, headquartered in Vogosca, Bosnia and Herzegovina file a Criminal Complaint with the Prosecutor for the International Criminal Tribunal for the Former Yugoslavia (ICTY), Madame Carla Del Ponte, on Friday, February 4 against the following Officials of the United Nations Organization and

**Piet de Klerk
Netherland's
Acting Permanent
Representative
to the UN**

others for the role they played in the fall and genocidal massacre at Srebrenica in July of 1995: BOUTROS BOUTROS-GHALI, KOFI ANNAN, YASUSHI AKASHI, BERNARD JANVIER, RUPERT SMITH, HERVÉ GOBILLIARD, JORIS VOORHOEVE, CEES NICOLAI, THOMAS KARREMANS, ROBERT FRANKEN, THORVALD STOLTENBERG, CARL BILDT, DAVID OWEN, MICHAEL ROSE, THEIR SUBORDINATES, SLOBODAN MILOSEVIC, RADOVAN KARADZIC, AND RATKO MLADIC.

The genocidal massacre at Srebrenica was the single greatest human rights atrocity perpetrated in Europe since the genocidal horrors inflicted by the Nazis during the Second World War. Approximately 10,000 Bosnian Muslim men and boys were systematically exterminated during just a few days by the Bosnian Serb Army under the direct command of Milosevic, Karadzic, and Mladic. During this time, the above-named United Nations Officials and their subordinates deliberately and maliciously refused to do anything to stop this genocidal massacre at the U.N.-declared "safe area" of Srebrenica despite having the legal obligation, the legal and political authority, and the military power to do so.

The Complaint accuses the above-named United Nations Officials and their subordinates of planning, preparing, conspiring, instigating, complicity, and otherwise aiding and abetting, in the planning, preparation, conspiracy, complicity, and execution of crimes referred to in articles 2 to 5 of the ICTY Statute: Article 2—Grave Breaches of the Geneva Conventions of 1949; Article 3—Violations of the Laws or Customs of War; Article 4—Genocide; and Article 5—Crimes against Humanity.

Under ICTY Statute article 18(1), this Complaint establishes a "sufficient basis to proceed" toward the investigation and indictment of the above-named United Nations Officials and their subordinates by the Prosecutor. Pursuant to article 18(4) of the Statute, the Complaint requests that the Prosecutor prepare the appropriate indictments against the above-named United Nations Officials and their subordinates, and transmit these indictments to a Judge of the ICTY Trial Chamber for confirmation. If confirmed by the Judge, the Complaint requests that pursuant to Statute article 19(2), the Prosecutor request the Judge to issue international warrants calling for the arrest, detention, surrender and transfer to the Tribunal of the above-named United Nations Officials and their subordinates. The Complaint also requests that the Prosecutor ask the confirming Judge to freeze the worldwide financial assets of the above-named United Nations Officials and their subordinates so that the Mothers of Srebrenica and Podrinja Association might receive some small degree of reparations for the terrible harm that the above-named United Nations Officials and their subordinates deliberately and maliciously inflicted upon them and their deceased next-of-kin at Srebrenica and its environs during July of 1995.

WE WILL NOT REST UNTIL JUSTICE IS DONE!

Mothers of Srebrenica & Podrinja
Sakiba ðere 9
Vogosca
Bosnia & Herzegovina
Professor Francis A. Boyle
Attorney for the
Mothers of Srebrenica & Podrinja

Prof. Boyle: Hold Emergency Meeting of UNSC to stop Tamil genocide

[TamilNet, Tuesday, 12 May 2009, 23:20 GMT]

Pointing out that, under the current circumstances, the Provisional Rules of Procedure of the United Nation's Security Council (UNSC) provide at least three ways to convene a formal meeting of the Security Council in order to terminate the Genocide against Tamils by the Government of Sri Lanka (GoSL), Prof. Francis A. Boyle, professor of International Law at the Illinois University College of Law, says, failure of the Secretary General, Governments of the United States, U.K, France, and India to hold a UNSC Emergency meeting indicates that they are all quietly supporting the GoSL genocide against the Tamils from behind the scenes, despite their crocodile tears in public.

Professor Boyle provides the legal framework for the possible three ways to convene a UN Security Council Emergency meeting:

First, Rule 2 provides: "The President {of the Security Council} shall call a meeting of the Security Council at the request of any member of the Security Council." So in other words, any member of the Security Council can convene a meeting of the Security Council despite the opposition of Russia and China. Why have not the United States, Britain or France so far convened a meeting of the Security Council to terminate the GoSL's genocide against the Tamils? Clearly, any one of these states can do so immediately if they really cared about the Tamils in Vanni. The fact that they have not indicates that they are quietly supporting the GoSL genocide against the Tamils from behind the scenes despite their crocodile tears in public.

Second, Rule 3 provides in relevant part: "The President {of the Security Council} shall call a meeting of the Security Council...if the Secretary-General brings to the attention of the Security Council any matter under Article 99." Article 99 of the U.N. Charter provides that: "The Secretary-General may bring to the attention of the Security Council any matter which in his opinion may threaten the maintenance of international peace and security." 10,000 Tamils exterminated by the GoSL during the past 3 months certainly threatens international peace and security in relations between India--which serves as *parens patriae* for these Tamils under international law-- and Sri Lanka as well as the peace and security of the northern Indian Ocean. Why has the U.N. Secretary-General refused to exercise his powers under U.N. Charter Article 99 and Rule 3 to convene an Emergency Meeting of the Security Council in order to terminate the GoSL's genocide against the Tamils? Is Ban Ki-moon going to wait until the GoSL exterminates another 10,000 Tamils in the so-called No Fire Zone, which is really a

Genocide Zone for the Tamils in Vanni? The fact that he has not exercised his powers under Article 99 indicates that he is quietly supporting the GoSL genocide against the Tamils from behind the scenes despite his crocodile tears in public and those shed by other officials in the U.N. Secretariat.

Third, Rule 3 also provides in relevant part: "The President {of the Security Council} shall call a meeting of the Security Council if a dispute or situation is brought to the attention of the Security Council under Article 35..." Article 35(1) of the U.N. Charter provides in relevant part: " Any Member of the United Nations may bring any dispute, or any situation of the nature referred to in Article 34, to the attention of the Security Council..." Article 34 of the U.N. Charter provides in relevant part: "The Security Council may investigate any dispute, or any situation which might lead to international friction or give rise to a dispute..." For some reason, the Government of India does not consider the recent extermination of 10,000 Tamils--for whom India is the *parens patriae* under international law--by the GoSL to constitute a "dispute" between India and Sri Lanka. Why not?

Boyle adds, "but certainly the GoSL's recent extermination of 10,000 Tamils, for whom India serves as *parens patriae* under international law 'might lead to international friction or give rise to a dispute' between India and Sri Lanka. Indeed according to the statements by the Prime Minister and other government officials of India and numerous trips by the latter to Sri Lanka and by GoSL officials to India, the GoSL's recent extermination of 10,000 Tamils has created 'international friction' between India and Sri Lanka. Therefore India has an obligation to bring this matter to the attention of the Security Council under U.N. Charter Article 35 and to demand an immediate, emergency meeting of the Security Council under its Rule of Procedure No. 3 in order to terminate the GoSL's genocide against the Tamils in Vanni. Failure by the Government of India to do so would only render India guilty of 'complicity' in the GoSL's genocide against the Tamils under Article III(e) of the 1948 Genocide Convention.

"Shall India—the Home of Gandhi—turn and look away from the Tamils in Sri Lanka as they are being exterminated by the GoSL without doing all in its power at both the Security Council and the International Court of Justice (as previously explained by this author) to save these Tamils for whom it serves as *parens patriae* under international law? Today the Tamils in Sri Lanka have now become Gandhi's Harijans. Yet so far the Government of India has treated the Tamils of Sri Lanka as if they were 'untouchables,'" Boyle says.

Ba Ki Moon
UN Secretary
General

Dr. Susan Rice
US Ambassador
to the UN

David Miliband
British Foreign
Secretary

Bernard Kouchner
French Minister
of Foreign and
European Affairs

Manmohan Singh
India's Prime Minister

US violates the Genocide Convention by permitting Sri Lanka to commit slow-motion genocide—Prof. Boyle

[TamilNet, Tuesday, 12 May 2009, 04:26 GMT]

Pointing to the statement issued by the U.S. Department of State that after an informal meeting at the United Nations that "[t]he United States is deeply concerned by the continued unacceptably high levels of civilian casualties," expert in International Law, Professor Francis A. Boyle said, the Obama administration is violating the 1948 convention for continuing to give "green light" to the Government of Sri Lanka to destroy the LTTE no matter what the cost to innocent Tamil civilians. Lawrence Christy, the head of Tamils Rehabilitation Organization (TRO) Field Office on Monday put the death toll of civilians at more than 3,200 killed during the weekend.

Boyle explains: "[t]he implication of this official Statement by the United States Government is that there exists an acceptable level of civilian casualties to be inflicted by the Government of Sri Lanka upon completely innocent Tamils in Vanni.

"Yet under international humanitarian law civilians can never be made the object of a military attack--as just happened in the GoSL 'massacre on the beach' of Tamils over the weekend. So 2000 murdered Tamil civilians in one operation is 'unacceptably high' in the opinion of the Obama administration.

"The conclusion is obvious that the Obama administration continues to give the proverbial 'green light' to the GoSL to destroy the LTTE no matter what the cost to innocent Tamil civilians so long as their death and destruction and genocide transpire in increments of somewhat fewer than 2000 Tamil civilians at a time.

"Slow- motion genocide indeed here being advocated by the United States government in violation of the 1948 Genocide Convention, to which it is a contracting party," warns Prof. Boyle.

India should sue Sri Lanka in ICJ for massacre of 2000 Tamils—Prof. Boyle

[TamilNet, Sunday, 10 May 2009, 14:00 GMT]

"In light of the latest atrocity by the Government of Sri Lanka that overnight exterminated 2000 Tamils, at a minimum the Government of India must sue Sri Lanka for violating the 1948 Genocide Convention before the International Court of Justice in The Hague, request an Emergency Hearing by the World Court, and win an Order of Provisional Measures of Protection --the international equivalent of a temporary restraining order-- against the GoSL to cease and desist from committing all acts of genocide against the Tamils," said Professor Boyle, professor of International Law at the University of Illinois College of Law, in a note sent to TamilNet Sunday. "I stand ready to file this World Court Lawsuit immediately upon receipt of the appropriate authorization from the Government of India," Boyle further said.

"This ICJ Order would be immediately transmitted to the United Nations Security Council for enforcement under the terms of the United Nations Charter and thus would place the GoSL genocide against the Tamils on the formal agenda of the Security Council for action despite the wishes of some of its Permanent Members such as Russia and China," Boyle said.

"In the event these two Permanent Members were to veto enforcement measures by the Security Council against the GoSL under U.N. Charter Chapter VII, then the entire matter can be turned over to the U.N. General Assembly for action pursuant to the terms of the Uniting for Peace Resolution (1950) in order to terminate the ongoing GoSL genocide against the Tamils," Boyle added.

"I stand ready to file this World Court Lawsuit immediately upon receipt of the appropriate authorization from the Government of India.

"The GoSL genocide against the Tamils has now exceeded the horrors of Srebrenica. India must act now before Vanni becomes another Rwanda," Professor Boyle warned the International Community.

UN violating Charter obligation to promote, encourage human rights—Prof. Boyle

[TamilNet, Friday, 08 May 2009, 00:45 GMT]

Dithering in the halls of the human rights apex body, the United Nations, culminating in the recent uncharacteristic pronouncement that the Secretary General Ban Ki-moon is "too-busy" to visit Sri Lanka, has prompted a legal scholar to point out that "where an individual such as the U.N. Secretary General has an obligation to act to prevent criminal activity and either refuses or fails to do so, that would render him 'complicit' with the underlying criminal activity—in this case genocide." Prof. Francis Boyle said Thursday that "[t]he U.N. Secretary General must immediately travel to Sri Lanka and do all in his power 'to prevent' the Government's genocide against the Tamils."

In a Thursday story, Inner City Press (ICP), which covers the developments within the United Nations, said that while there was earlier speculation that the Secretary General "will definitely consider" visiting Sri Lanka if he "feels that it can save lives," the ICP has learnt that "such a trip, for now, is unlikely."

Prof. Boyle of University of Illinois College of Law and an expert in International Law, pointed out that "[u]nder Chapter XV of the United Nations Charter, the U.N. Secretariat, headed-up by the U.N. Secretary General, is one of six independent Organs of the United Nations Organization itself. As such the U.N. Secretary General is obligated to implement the "Purposes of the United Nations" set forth in Article 1 of the Charter.

"Article 1(3) of the Charter provides that one of these "Purposes of the United Nations" is: "To achieve international co-operation in solving international problems of an economic, social, cultural or humanitarian character, and in promoting and encouraging respect for human rights and for fundamental freedoms for all without distinction as to race, sex, language or religion."

Boyle added, "[i]n other words, the U.N. Secretary General has a U.N. Charter obligation 'in promoting and encouraging respect for human rights and for fundamental freedoms for' the Tamils in Sri Lanka. Consequently, the U.N. Secretary General has a Charter obligation to immediately visit Sri Lanka and do all in his power 'to prevent' the Government's on-going genocide against the Tamils as required by the peremptory norm of international law set forth in Article I of the 1948 Genocide Convention.

"Not to visit Sri Lanka immediately for this Purpose would constitute a violation of the United Nations Charter by the U.N. Secretary General himself.

"In addition, where an individual such as the U.N. Secretary General has an obligation to act to prevent criminal activity and either refuses or fails to do so, that would render him 'complicit' with the underlying criminal activity—in this case genocide. Article III(e) of the 1948 Genocide Convention prohibits, criminalizes and calls for the punishment of: 'Complicity in genocide.'

"The U.N. Secretary General must immediately travel to Sri Lanka and do all in his power 'to prevent' the Government's genocide against the Tamils. For the U.N. Secretary General to fail or to refuse to discharge this U.N. Charter obligation would render him complicit in the Government of Sri Lanka's genocide against the Tamils," Prof. Boyle said.

Matthew Lee   **Ban Ki Moon**
of Inner City Press   **UN Secretary General**

Green light to rid Tigers while 50,000 lives at risk, Boyle faults US, UK

[TamilNet, Thursday, 07 May 2009, 04:33 GMT]

"US. UK, France and India appear to have given green light to Sri Lanka to get rid of the Tigers no matter what the cost is to the 50,000 lives of innocent Tamils at risk now. Let's get back to the need to change that green light to a red light, and let's solve the humanitarian crisis first, and then talk about some sort of solution," said Francis Boyle, professor of International Law at the University of Illinois College of Law, during an interview with Aljazeera network Wednesday. Eric Solheim, key architect of the 2002 peace process in Sri Lanka, and Nirj Deva, a Member of European Parliament and of Sri Lankan origin also participated in the discussions.

Dismissing talks of who holds the military upper hand as "petty and insulting," Boyle stressed the need for immediate humanitarian intervention.

"50,000 people are bombarded, killed and are starving to death. We need to act immediately to remedy the situation. Immediate ceasefire, and massive humanitarian help via air, sea and land, is what's needed," Boyle said.

Mr Solheim said both sides must act to resolve the crisis, the Tigers should allow the civilians to leave the area, and Colombo to allow humanitarian aid to go in and permit UN relief agencies to engage in relief effort.

Mr Deva took the official line of the Sri Lanka Government, describing the unfolding humanitarian crisis as one of "largest ever evacuation of hostages."

Slow-motion genocide to exceed horrors of Srebrenica, warns Prof. Boyle

[TamilNet, Tuesday, 05 May 2009, 18:52 GMT]

Professor Boyle of University of Illinois College of Law, an international expert on Bosnia and crimes of Genocide said Tuesday, "[s]ince the outset of this latest crisis in January, the GoSL has exterminated about 7000 Tamils in Vanni, certainly a 'substantial part' of the Tamil population in Vanni and Sri Lanka. If not stopped now, the GoSL's toll of genocide against the Tamils could far exceed the recent horrors of Srebrenica." Prof. Boyle's call for urgent food drop to the civilians close to starvation in the Safe Zone, has gathered momentum, and international media are seeking his comment on the urgency of humanitarian support.

In a note sent to TamilNet, Prof. Boyle says, "[t]he slow-motion genocide by the Government of Sri Lanka against the Tamils in Vanni is now accelerating to the point of outright extermination in violation of Genocide Convention Articles I, II(a), II(b) II(c), inter alia.

"Every state in the world has the obligation 'to prevent' this GoSL genocide against the Tamils as required by the jus cogens, erga omnes rule of customary international law set forth in Article I of the Genocide Convention. These peremptory norms of international law apply to every state in the world, including the Member States of the United Nations Security Council, and especially its Permanent Members such as the United States, Britain and France, as well as to India. They must all exert maximum political, economic and diplomatic pressure upon the GoSL for an immediate cease-fire in conjunction with the massive provision of food, water, medicine and other humanitarian relief supplies by land, sea and air to the dying Tamils in Vanni.

"A generation ago the world turned away from the Nazi genocide against the Jews—and lived to regret it. Humanity is at a similar crossroads today. A generation ago the world designed the Genocide Convention to prevent a repetition of what Hitler and the Nazis had done to the Jews even 'in part,' according to Article II of the Genocide Convention. In the Bosnian case I convinced the World Court that the proper interpretation of this term taken from Article II of the Genocide Convention meant a 'substantial part.' The World Court later found that the Serbian extermination of 8000 Bosnian Muslim men and boys at Srebrenica was genocide in violation of the Genocide Convention.

"Since the outset of this latest crisis in January, the GoSL has exterminated about 7000 Tamils in Vanni, certainly a 'substantial part' of the Tamil population in Vanni and Sri Lanka. If not stopped now, the GoSL's toll of genocide against the Tamils could far exceed the recent horrors of Srebrenica," Boyle warns.

India obligated to bring Sri Lanka's genocide to UN Security Council—Prof. Boyle

[TamilNet, Monday, 04 May 2009, 21:36 GMT]

Pointing to India's Prime Minister, Manmohan Singh's statement that the lack of peace and stability in Sri Lanka can also "affect security situation in our country [India]," as reported in the Press Trust of India Monday, Francis Boyle, professor of International Law at University of Illinois College of Law said that "[i]n light of this latest statement by the Prime Minister of India, the Government of India must immediately bring the Government of Sri Lanka's genocide against the Tamils to the attention of the United Nations Security Council for remedial action," as allowed by the Article 35(1) of the UN Charter.

PTI in a report published Monday said: "The Prime Minister expressed concern over the developments in the neighboring nations including Pakistan, Nepal and Sri Lanka and said it could affect the security situation in the country. 'Today, there is lack of peace and stability in our neighboring nations, be it Nepal, Pakistan and Sri Lanka. It (the developments) can also affect security situation in our country,' he said, claiming that only Congress was capable of dealing with such critical issues."

Professor Boyle added, "Article 35(1) of the United Nations Charter clearly states: 'Any Member of the United Nations may bring any dispute, or any situation of the nature referred to in Article 34, to the attention of the Security Council or of the General Assembly.'

"Article 34 refers in relevant part to: 'any situation which might lead to international friction or give rise to a dispute.'

"Clearly, according to the Indian Prime Minister's own statement, the GoSL genocide against the Tamils has already 'lead to international friction' between India and Sri Lanka, and it very well could and should 'give rise to a dispute' between the two countries.

"India must lead the way at the United Nations Security Council to assemble the requisite number of member states to take action against Sri Lanka under Chapter VI and/or Chapter VII of the U.N. Charter," Boyle said.

Prof. Boyle calls for humanitarian airdrop to starving civilians in "safety zone"

[TamilNet, Thursday, 30 April 2009, 19:10 GMT]

Francis Boyle, professor of International Law at the University of Illinois College of Law, on Thursday called on India, the United States, Britain and France to fulfill their obligations under the Geneva Conventions and Protocol, and under the Genocide Convention by launching an immediate humanitarian air-drop relief operation for the starving Tamil civilians within the so-called safety zone, who are suffering without adequate humanitarian supplies for weeks. In a note sent to TamilNet, Prof. Boyle said starvation of civilians, as a method of warfare, can also constitute an act of genocide as defined by Article II (c) of the 1948 Genocide Convention.

"Article 54(1) of Additional Protocol I to the Four Geneva Conventions of 1949 sets forth a rule of customary international humanitarian law that obligates every state in the world: 'Starvation of civilians as a method of warfare is prohibited.' Starvation of civilians as a method of warfare is a war crime. Every contracting party to the Geneva Conventions and Protocol has the obligation under Common Article 1 thereof 'to respect' the Conventions and Protocol themselves and 'to ensure respect' for the Conventions and Protocol 'in all circumstances' by other contracting parties such as Sri Lanka.

"Furthermore, starvation of civilians as a method of warfare can also constitute an act of genocide as defined by Article II (c) of the 1948 Genocide Convention: 'Deliberately inflicting on the group {in this case Tamils} conditions of life calculated to bring about its physical destruction in whole or in part.' Every contracting state party to the Genocide Convention has the obligation 'to prevent' genocide by Sri Lanka against the Tamils as required by Article I thereof.

"Therefore, every state party to the Geneva Conventions and Protocols as well as to the Genocide Convention have the solemn obligation to terminate GoSL's starvation of Tamils as a method of warfare. Under the current 'circumstances' one of the most effective means this can be done is for those states with the capability (e.g., India, United States, Britain, France) to immediately undertake an airdrop of food and other humanitarian relief supplies to the starving Tamils in Vanni.

"I hereby call upon these states and in particular India, the United States, Britain and France to fulfil their obligations under the Geneva Conventions and Protocol as well as under the Genocide Convention by launching an immediate humanitarian air-drop relief operation for the benefit of the starving Tamils in Vanni, Sri Lanka."

Miliband's statement obligates UK to take immediate UN action—Prof. Boyle

[TamilNet, Thursday, 30 April 2009, 03:42 GMT]

Pointing to the latest statement during the visit to Sri Lanka by British Foreign Minister, David Miliband that "[t]his is a civil war that does have regional and wider ramifications...," Professor Francis Boyle, professor of International Law at the University of Illinois College of Law, said that Miliband's statement obligates Britain, as a Permanent Member of the Security Council, under U.N. Charter Article 35(1) to bring this "civil war" and genocide in Sri Lanka "to the attention of the Security Council" for the purpose of obtaining remedial action under Chapters VI and/or VII of the Charter.

During a BBC interview when asked whether it is time for a UN Security Council resolution as Sri Lanka is paying no attention to international opinion, Miliband responded: "Well this is the first delegation that's been allowed in, media are not being allowed in to the north east of the country which only adds to the concern.

David Miliband British Foreign Secretary

"I think that we were right; Britain, France, the US, to raise this issue at the United Nations last Friday this does belong on the United Nations Security Council agenda. This is a civil war that does have regional and wider ramifications and, obviously, a massive civilian emergency as well."

Professor Boyle says, "[u]nder Article 24 of the United Nations Charter, the United Nations Security Council has 'primary responsibility for the maintenance of international peace and security.'

"According to U.N. Charter Chapter VII, Article 39: 'The Security Council shall determine the existence of any threat to the peace, breach of the peace or act of aggression and shall make recommendations, or decide what measures shall be taken in accordance with Articles 41 and 42, to maintain or restore international peace and security.'

Prof Boyle adds, according to this latest statement by British Foreign Minister David Miliband: "This is a civil war that does have regional and wider ramifications...."

In other words, the GoSL "civil war" and genocide against the Tamils constitutes a "threat to the peace" for which the Security Council has "primary responsibility" to rectify.

"Therefore it can no longer be argued by other Security Council Member States such as China and Russia that this is an 'internal matter' or a 'domestic concern' for which the Security Council does not have jurisdiction to act.

"Indeed, in light of this recent statement by their Foreign Minister Miliband, Britain—as a Permanent Member of the Security Council—has an obligation under U.N. Charter Article 35(1) to bring this 'civil war' and genocide in Sri Lanka 'to the attention of the Security Council' for the purpose of obtaining such remedial action under Chapters VI and/or VII of the Charter," Boyle said in a note to TamilNet.

Stalling, obfuscation mirror UN's actions before Srebrenica genocide

[TamilNet, Wednesday, 22 April 2009, 16:19 GMT]

"This same type of deliberate stalling, delaying and obfuscation by United Nations Officials preceded and occurred during the course of the genocidal massacre at Srebrenica. Of course these UN Officials were then (and are still today) acting at the behest of the Permanent Members of the Security Council, who supported Serbia taking over the Srebrenica 'safe-haven' as designated by the Security Council, no matter what the cost to the innocent civilians seeking refuge there," said Prof. Francis Boyle, professor of International Law at the University of Illinois College of Law, in a note sent to TamilNet, commenting on the denial at the United Nations to have Security Council hearings on the humanitarian situation in Sri Lanka.

"Today, they are all guilty of aiding and abetting Sri Lanka's genocide against the Tamils in violation of the 1948 Genocide Convention.

"History will hold them all accountable, including and especially the United Nations and its Highest Level Officials such as Ban Ki-moon, Nambiar and Holmes.

"Under the terms of the United Nations Charter Chapter XV, the UN Secretariat and thus these UN Officials are legally independent of the United Nations Security Council. These UN Officials have a separate and independent obligation to uphold the Purposes and Principles of the UN Charter no matter what the U.N. Security Council Members might tell them to do.

"Article 1(3) of the UN Charter provides in relevant part that one of the 'Purposes of the United Nations' is 'promoting and encouraging respect for human rights and for fundamental freedoms for all without distinction as to race, sex, language or religion.'

"Within Chapter XV of the Charter, article 99 expressly provides:'The Secretary-General may bring to the attention of the Security Council any matter which in his opinion may threaten the maintenance of international peace and security.'

"UN Secretary-General Ban Ki-moon must immediately convene an Emergency Meeting of the Security Council in order 'to prevent' the ongoing genocide against the Tamils by Sri Lanka as required by the 1948 Genocide Convention," Prof. Boyle said.

US should intervene directly with GoSL, LTTE to protect civilians—Professor Boyle

[TamilNet, Tuesday, 14 April 2009, 16:42 GMT]

With Norway's ouster as a third-party engaging with the Liberation Tigers of Tamil Eelam (LTTE), the role of the United States in having direct access with the Liberation Tigers has become critical to negotiating a ceasefire and bring relief to the more than 250,000 Tamil civilians caught in the war. Ambassador Lunstead points out that legal restrictions imposed by US domestic laws do not prevent the U.S. taking that role, and Professor Boyle further asserts that Geneva Conventions of 1949 makes it an obligation for the U.S. to intervene directly with both the Government of Sri Lanka (GoSL) and the LTTE in order to protect these innocent Tamil civilians.

Professor Boyle, professor of International Law at the University of Illinois College of Law, in a note sent to TamilNet said: "Both the United States and Sri Lanka are contracting parties to the Four Geneva Conventions of 1949. Common article 1 thereof provides: 'The High Contracting Parties undertake to respect and to ensure respect for the present Convention in all circumstances.' The United States government has an absolute obligation 'to ensure respect' for the Geneva Conventions 'in all circumstances.' With respect to the current situation in Vanni where the lives and well-being of 250,000 Tamils are at risk and in grave danger, the United States government has an absolute obligation to intervene directly with both the Government of Sri Lanka (GoSL) and the LTTE in order to protect these innocent Tamil civilians and to terminate the massive war crimes that are currently being inflicted upon them by the GoSL in violation of the Geneva Conventions. The same arguments apply to every state that is a contracting party to the Geneva Conventions, which includes almost every state in the world. In other words, almost every state in the world has both the right, the standing, and the obligation to intervene directly with both the GoSL and the LTTE in order to terminate war crimes from being inflicted upon the completely innocent Tamil civilians currently living in Vanni."

Jeffrey Lunstead, former US Ambassador to Sri Lanka, had earlier traced the legal and policy implications of the U.S. officials engaging directly with the LTTE. He makes the following point, "the legal restrictions were clear: the U.S. government could not provide material assistance to the LTTE, and had to block LTTE funds. LTTE officials could not obtain visas to visit the U.S. unless a waiver was granted by the Attorney General based on a recommendation by the Secretary of State. It should be noted that there is no legal proscription against meeting with LTTE officials. A decision not to meet with LTTE officials is a policy decision, not a legal one," indicating that the US's domestic laws do not bar the US officials from engaging directly with the LTTE.

On the question if "direct U.S. contact with the LTTE have made this [U.S.] position clearer and perhaps induced a change in behavior [of the LTTE]," Ambassador responds: "This question is of course unanswerable. As many participants have noted, direct U.S. contact with the LTTE, a designated Foreign Terrorist Organization (FTO), was difficult in the aftermath of September 11, 2001. One potential advantage of direct U.S. communication with the LTTE, had it occurred, would have been the ability of the U.S. to hear LTTE."

US support to IMF's Sri Lanka loan illegal— Prof. Boyle

[TamilNet, Thursday, 19 March 2009, 00:17 GMT]

"Concerning the proposed loan to Sri Lanka by the International Monetary Fund, United States domestic law makes it quite clear that the Obama Administration is obligated to oppose the loan. And given the weighted voting system for the IMF Board of Directors, a United States vote against the loan would be tantamount to a veto," said Prof. Boyle, Professor at Illinois College of Law, adding, "for the Obama Administration to violate the Statute [22 USC 262d] and vote in favor of the proposed IMF loan to support the GoSL's 'policy goals' would render the United States government 'complicit' with Sri Lanka's genocide."

Meg Lundsager who spent several years with the Treasury department in various capacities and also served as a member of the National Security Council staff, was confirmed by the US Senate in April 2007, and is now the official US Executive Director at the IMF. In the weighted voting arrangement of the IMF, US holds 16.77% of votes.

Title 22 of the United States Code, Chapter 7, Section 262d, "Human Rights and United States Assistance policies with international financial institutions" says quite clearly in relevant part:

(a) Policy goals

The United States government, in connection with its voice and vote in...the International Monetary Fund shall advance the cause of human rights, including by seeking to channel assistance towards countries other than those whose governments engage in—

(1) a pattern of gross violations of internationally recognized human rights, such as torture or cruel, inhumane, or degrading treatment or punishment, or prolonged detention without charges, or other flagrant denial to life, liberty, and the security of person....

"Most Human Rights Organizations, including and especially Human Rights Watch and Amnesty International, have determined that the Government of Sri Lanka (GoSL) has historically perpetrated 'a pattern of gross violations of internationally recognized human rights' against the Tamil population living there, including and especially the 300, 000 Tamils now besieged and subjected to genocide, crimes against humanity and war crimes by the GoSL Army in Vanni," Prof. Boyle asserts.

Furthermore, subsection (f) of the above statute mandates:

"(f) Opposition by United States Executive Directors of institutions to financial or technical assistance to violating countries

The United States Executive Directors of the institutions listed in subsection (a) of this section {which includes the IMF} are authorized **AND INSTRUCTED** to oppose any loan, any extension of financial assistance, or any technical assistance to any country described in subsection (a)(1) or (2) of this section, unless such assistance is directed specifically to programs which serve the basic human needs of the citizens of such country." [Emphasis added.]

"It is also clear from the IMF's own statement that the proposed IMF loan to GoSL will NOT be used to 'serve the basic human needs of the citizens of such country,' but in fact will be used to support 'the government's policy goals': 'IMF spokesman David Hawley said the loan funds would be used for "the government's policy goals."'"

"Of course the GoSL 'policy goals' currently include waging warfare, war crimes, crimes against humanity and genocide against the Tamils, including and especially the 300,000 Tamil Civilians now besieged by the GoSL Army in Vanni," says Prof. Boyle.

UN Rights chief, Navi Pillay recently said that "[c]ertain actions being undertaken by the Sri Lankan military and by the LTTE [Tigers] may constitute violations of international human rights and humanitarian law," and RSF and HRW reports allege that Sri Lanka has committed war crimes.

Prof. Boyle adds: "Consequently the Obama Administration is **MANDATED** by this law to vote against the proposed IMF loan to Sri Lanka. Indeed, for the Obama Administration to violate this Statute and vote in favor of the proposed IMF loan to support the GoSL's 'policy goals' would render the United States government 'complicit' with Sri Lanka's genocide, crimes against humanity, and war crimes against the Tamils, including and especially the 300,000 Tamils currently besieged by the GoSL Army in Vanni, in violation of Genocide Convention Article III (e) and the Four Geneva Conventions of 1949, as well as the U.S. Genocide Convention Implementation Act and the U.S. War Crimes Act.

"Therefore we must prevent this from happening by mobilizing as much public pressure as possible upon the Obama Administration to vote against this proposed IMF loan to the GoSL, which would be tantamount to a veto. In addition, for similar legal reasons, all people of good faith and good will around the world must pressure their governments to vote against the proposed IMF loan to Sri Lanka," appeals Prof. Boyle.

AFP in a report Wednesday on Sri Lanka's bailout talks with IMF said: "The island turned to the International Monetary Fund after pouring an unprecedented 1.6 billion dollars into financing the military drive against Tamil Tiger rebels that the government says it is close to winning. Economists say the economic woes caused by the high defence spending have been compounded by the global economic meltdown and the government's policy of halting privatisation of state-run enterprises," further clarifying that the reason for loan request is the expenditure due to the "genocidal" war against the Tamils.

Boyle warns UN repeating Srebrenica debacle in Vanni

[TamilNet, Monday, 16 March 2009, 03:41 GMT]

Pointing out that "in 1995 the United Nations Organization as a whole was fully complicit in Serbia's genocidal massacre of 8000 Bosnian Muslim men and boys at Srebrenica in violation of Article III (e) of the 1948 Genocide Convention that prohibited, criminalized and required the punishment of: 'Complicity in genocide'," Professor Francis Boyle, an expert in international law and a professor at Illinois College of Law, said that it looks as if "the United Nations is now repeating one of the most shameless and disgraceful debacles in its entire history in today's Vanni Pocket by becoming complicit in Sri Lanka's genocide against the Tamils there."

"Indeed, at the time Srebrenica was designated a United Nations 'safe area' supposedly under the protection of the United Nations Security Council, whose member states refused to lift even one finger to save these Bosnians from Serbian genocide," says Prof. Boyle who won two World Court Orders on the basis of the 1948 Genocide Convention that were overwhelmingly in favor of the Republic of Bosnia and Herzegovina against the rump Yugoslavia to cease and desist from committing all acts of genocide against the Bosnians.

Professor Boyle pointed to the Inner City Press (ICP) report which stated that "[t]he UN on Monday acknowledged that it is funding camps in Sri Lanka from which people cannot leave."

ICP has been asking for two weeks at the UN whether international aid funds will be used for detention camps in which those fleeing the conflict zone in Sri Lanka will be detained, until the end of 2009 or longer. Holmes confirmed that the UN has "offered to assist transit camps" or "semi-permanent camps," and as to funding as so far "make no links between the two."

U.N. human rights chief warned Friday that "civilian casualties could reach "catastrophic" proportions if the two sides do not suspend their fighting," and that the Sri Lankan military and the Tamil rebels may have committed war crimes.

Pillay also said the "army has repeatedly shelled inside safe 'no-fire' zones set up for the civilians, and that 'a range of credible sources' showed that more than 2,800 civilians had been killed and more than 7,000 wounded since January 20."

Stopping Sri Lanka's genocide at ICJ, UN— Prof. Boyle

[TamilNet, Wednesday, 11 March 2009, 12:14 GMT]

"Any one or more of the 140 states parties to the Genocide Convention (1) must immediately sue Sri Lanka at the International Court of Justice in The Hague; (2) must demand an Emergency Hearing by the World Court; and (3) must request an Order indicating provisional measures of protection against Sri Lanka to cease and desist from committing all acts of genocide against the 350,000 Tamils in Vanni," says Professor Francis Boyle, an expert in international law and a professor at University of Illinois College of Law, outlining the steps for the Tamil diaspora to take to bring Sri Lanka to International Court of Justice (ICJ).

How to Stop Genocide by Sri Lanka Against the Tamils at the International Court of Justice and the U.N. Security Council

On 8 April 1993 and 13 September 1993 the author single-handedly won two World Court Orders on the basis of the 1948 Genocide Convention that were overwhelmingly in favor of the Republic of Bosnia and Herzegovina against the rump Yugoslavia to cease and desist from committing all acts of genocide against the Bosnians.*

Today the Government of Sri Lanka (GoSL) has trapped three hundred and fifty thousand Tamils in a forty square mile area of the Vanni region where it is mercilessly, deliberately, and systematically exterminating them by means of artillery shells, cluster bombs, rockets, jet fighters, tanks, and other weapons of mass and indiscriminate slaughter. The GoSL Defense Minister Rajapaksa has determined that this entire area now inhabited by 350,000 Tamils is nothing more than a free fire-zone in violation of the most fundamental requirements of International Humanitarian Law. The GoSL defense minister has ordered all doctors and medical personnel out of Vanni on pain of being murdered by the GoSL army, including the International Committee of the Red Cross. The GoSL defense minister has also compiled a death list of Tamil civilians to be massacred in Vanni. If the states of the world do not act immediately and effectively to stop GoSL, they will soon be witnessing serial massacres of Tamils along the lines of Srebrenica, Sabra and Shatilla, Rwanda, and Kosovo.

Article I of the 1948 Genocide Convention requires all 140 states parties to immediately act in order "to prevent" this ongoing GoSL genocide against the Tamils. One of the most important steps the 140 contracting states parties to the Genocide Convention must take in order to fulfill their obligation under Article I is to sue Sri Lanka at the International Court of Justice in The Hague (the so-called World Court) for

---

* See Appendix I below.

violating the 1948 Genocide Convention on the basis of Article IX thereto: "Disputes between the Contracting Parties relating to the interpretation, application or fulfillment of the present Convention, including those relating to the responsibility of a State for genocide or for any of the other acts enumerated in Article III, shall be submitted to the International Court of Justice at the request of any of the parties to the dispute."

Any one or more of the 140 states parties to the Genocide Convention:

1. must immediately sue Sri Lanka at the International Court of Justice in The Hague;

2. must demand an Emergency Hearing by the World Court; and

3. must request an Order indicating provisional measures of protection against Sri Lanka to cease and desist from committing all acts of genocide against the 350,000 Tamils in Vanni.

Such a World Court Order is the international equivalent to a domestic temporary restraining order and injunction. Once issued by the World Court, this Order would be immediately transmitted to the United Nations Security Council for enforcement under U.N. Charter article 94(2). So far the member states of the United Nations Security Council have failed and refuse to act in order to do anything to stop the GoSL's genocide against the Tamils

1. despite the fact that the situation in Vanni constitutes a "threat to the peace" that requires Security Council action under article 39 of the United Nations Charter and

2. despite the fact that they are all obligated "to prevent" Sri Lanka's genocide against the Tamils under article I of the Genocide Convention. This World Court Order will put the matter on the Agenda of the Security Council and force the Security Council to take action in order "to prevent" the ongoing genocide against the Tamils by Sri Lanka.

Article II of the Genocide Convention defines the international crime of genocide in relevant part as follows:

> In the present Convention, genocide means any of the following acts committed with intent to destroy, in whole or in part, a national, ethnical, racial or religious group, as such:
>
> (a) Killing members of the group;
> (b) Causing serious bodily or mental harm to members of the group;
> (c) Deliberately inflicting on the group conditions of life calculated to bring about its physical destruction in whole

or in part;

...

Certainly the Sinhala-Buddhist Sri Lanka and its legal predecessor Ceylon have committed genocide against the Hindu/Christian Tamils that actually started on or about 1948 and has continued apace until today and is now accelerating in Vanni in violation of Genocide Convention Articles II(a), (b), and (c).

For at least the past four decades, the Sinhala-Buddhist Ceylon/Sri Lanka has implemented a systematic and comprehensive military, political, and economic campaign with the intent to destroy in substantial part the different national, ethnical, racial, and religious group constituting the Hindu/Christian Tamils. This Sinhala-Buddhist Ceylon/Sri Lanka campaign has consisted of killing members of the Hindu/Christian Tamils in violation of Genocide Convention Article II(a). This Sinhala-Buddhist Ceylon/Sri Lanka campaign has also caused serious bodily and mental harm to the Hindu/Christian Tamils in violation of Genocide Convention Article II(b). This Sinhala-Buddhist Ceylon/Sri Lanka campaign has also deliberately inflicted on the Hindu/Christian Tamils conditions of life calculated to bring about their physical destruction in substantial part in violation of Article II(c) of the Genocide Convention.

Since 1983 the Sinhala-Buddhist Sri Lanka have exterminated approximately 70,000 Hindu/Christian Tamils. The Sinhala-Buddhist Sri Lanka have now added another 350,000 Hindu/Christian Tamils in Vanni to their genocidal death list. Time is of the essence!

Humanity needs one state party to the Genocide Convention to fulfill its obligation under article I thereof to immediately sue Sri Lanka at the World Court in order to save the 350,000 Tamils in Vanni from extermination. The ghosts of Dachau, Auschwitz, Cambodia, Sabra and Shatilla, Srebrenica, Rwanda, and Kosovo demand no less.

Evacuation would constitute U.S. "complicity in genocide"—Prof Boyle

[TamilNet, Tuesday, 10 March 2009, 05:59 GMT]

"For the United States government to 'evacuate' Tamils from Vanni and then turn them over to the genocidal Government of Sri Lanka would constitute 'Complicity in genocide' by the United States to the genocide that GoSL is currently inflicting on the Tamils in violation of Genocide Convention Article III (e) and the United States's own Genocide Convention Implementation Act as amended. Such a turn-over could very well create personal criminal responsibility for United States government officials involved in this process under both international criminal law and United States domestic criminal law," warns Prof. Boyle, an expert in international law and a professor at University of Illinois College of Law.

In a note sent to TamilNet, Prof Boyle adds: "The United States government is a party to the 1948 Genocide Convention, which has been implemented as internal United States domestic criminal law by means of the Genocide Convention Implementation Act as currently amended. Article III (e) of the Genocide Convention prohibited, criminalized and requires the punishment of 'Complicity in genocide.'"

Note that the 2007 Genocide Accountability Act (GAA) amended the Genocide Convention Implementation Act of 1987 signed by President Ronald Reagan.

An article that appeared in *Telegraph* edition of 8th March said that "[t]he Obama administration will sound out foreign secretary Shiv Shankar Menon on Monday on India's support for a US-led invasion of Sri Lanka to evacuate nearly 200,000 Tamil civilians trapped inside territory controlled by the Liberation Tigers of Tamil Eelam with precariously declining stocks of food or medicine.

"'We had some people there to look at the situation to identify what the possibilities might be. We would do whatever we can to help these people,' assistant secretary of state for South and Central Asian affairs Richard Boucher told a group of South Asian journalists yesterday," the *Telegraph* report added.

Forced starvation constitutes an act of Genocide—Prof. Boyle

[TamilNet, Friday, 06 March 2009, 04:53 GMT]

Commenting on recent reports that Colombo is withholding food supplies forcing into starvation the more than 300,000 Tamil civilians trapped in the war-zone, Prof. Boyle, an expert in international law and a professor at University of Illinois College of Law, in a note sent to TamilNet said, "[I]n the context of longstanding Sri Lankan genocide against the Tamils, this recent GoSL atrocity also constitutes an act of genocide as defined, prohibited and criminalized by Genocide Convention Article II (c):'Deliberately inflicting on the group conditions of life calculated to bring about its physical destruction in whole or in part.'

"The United States government has an obligation to prosecute U.S. Citizen Defense Minister Rajapaksa and U.S. Resident General Fonseka for violating the Genocide Convention Implementation Act and the U.S. War Crimes Act," Prof. Boyle added.

Boyle quoted sections of the 1949 Geneva Conventions to substantiate his claim, saying: "Additional Protocol I of 1977 to the Four Geneva Conventions of 1949 provides in relevant part as follows: Article 54.-Protection of objects indispensable to the survival of the civilian population:

1.   Starvation of civilians as a method of warfare is prohibited.

2.   It is prohibited to attack, destroy, remove or render useless objects indispensable to the survival of the civilian population, such as foodstuffs, agricultural areas for the production of foodstuffs, crops, livestock, drinking water installations and supplies and irrigation works, for the specific purpose of denying them for their sustenance value to the civilian population or to the adverse Party, whatever the motive, whether in order to starve out civilians, to cause them to move away, or for any other motive.....

"This basic rule of International Humanitarian Law constitutes customary international law, the violation of which is a war crime," Boyle added.

Britain trying to dodge obligations to prevent Genocide of Tamils—Prof. Boyle

[TamilNet, Monday, 02 March 2009, 04:05 GMT]

Commenting on British Foreign Secretary David Miliband's statement in the British Parliament that "a failed [UN] resolution—one that faces a veto—is worse than no resolution at all," Prof Boyle, an expert in international law and a professor at University of Illinois College of Law, said that "Uniting for Peace Resolution of 1950" allows a vetoed resolution to be turned over to United Nations General Assembly for action. "The General Assembly can and must do the same with respect to the genocidal plight of the Tamils in Sri Lanka [...] Britain is simply trying to dodge its own obligation under Article I of the Genocide Convention 'to prevent' the genocide against the Tamils by Sri Lanka," Prof Boyle added.

The British Foreign Secretary David Miliband was questioned in the British Parliament Wednesday by Liberal Democrat MP Edward Davey as to why Britain's representative in UN earlier failed to support a briefing on Sri Lanka while ministers in London call for ceasefire.

Miliband replied: "I am sorry to hear the Hon. Gentleman talk in that way, because he knows that a failed resolution—one that faces a veto—is worse than no resolution at all, and it would strengthen precisely the forces that he and I oppose. I can assure him that our diplomats, whether in New York or in the region, are all working off the same script, which is one that has been set by the Prime Minister and me."

Professor Boyle said "[w]ith all due respect to the British Foreign Secretary, this statement is double-talk and he must know it. Under the terms of the U.N.'s Uniting for Peace Resolution of 1950, in the event one or more permanent members were to exercise a veto at the United Nations Security Council concerning a matter related to international peace and security, the matter can then be turned over to the United Nations General Assembly for action.

"Thereunder the General Assembly can take effective action by means of a two-thirds vote. The United Nations General Assembly has repeatedly acted under the Uniting for Peace Resolution with respect to the genocidal plight of the Palestinians.*

"The General Assembly can and must do the same with respect to the genocidal plight of the Tamils in Sri Lanka. Invoking the Uniting for Peace Resolution is the well-known way to overcome threatened vetoes by Russia and China. Britain is simply trying to dodge its own obligation under Article I of the Genocide Convention 'to prevent' the genocide against the Tamils by Sri Lanka, Professor Boyle said in a note sent to TamilNet.

---

* See Francis A. Boyle, *Breaking All the Rules* 31-32 (2008).

Britain legally obliged to prevent Genocide in Sri Lanka: Prof. Boyle

[TamilNet, Thursday, 26 February 2009, 20:27 GMT]

Since the British Foreign Minister has now publicly admitted on behalf of his Government that Government of Sri Lanka (GoSL) is "quite prepared to go ahead with acts of genocide," then under Article I of the Genocide Convention, the British government has a legal obligation "to prevent" this expected genocide of the Tamils by GoSL, said Professor Boyle, professor of international law at the University of Illinois College of Law, in a note sent to TamilNet.

"Britain also has domestic implementing legislation for the Genocide Convention that leads to the same legal conclusion," Prof. Boyle added.

Reporting from the transcript of the discussion on Sri Lanka in Parliament from Hansard, TamilNet earlier said, "Britain's Foreign Secretary, David Miliband, agreed Tuesday with parliamentarians who said that the Sri Lankan government is 'quite prepared to go ahead with acts of genocide.'

"Responding to Mr. Elfyn Llwyd, MP, Mr. Miliband said 'the resolution of [a] terrorist problem cannot be achieved at the expense of the rights of minority communities in Sri Lanka, and that is what we are trying to work on.' Britain was encouraging Sri Lanka's government to work with London's newly appointed Special Envoy to Sri Lanka, former defence minister and Secretary of State for Scotland, Des Browne, the Foreign Secretary said."

India legally obliged to prevent GoSL's genocide against Tamils—Prof. Boyle

[TamilNet, Thursday, 05 February 2009, 05:02 GMT]

Emphasizing that under Common Article 1 to the Four Geneva Conventions of 1949, India has the obligation "to respect and to ensure respect" for these Conventions "in all circumstances," Professor Francis Boyle, professor of international law at the University of Illinois College of Law, in a communiqué sent to TamilNet says, "India must demand that the United States government prosecute Rajapaksa immediately for violating the U.S. Genocide Convention Implementation Act as well as the U.S. War Crimes Act," and appeals to the Tamils worldwide and people of good faith and goodwill to mobilize behind the legal agenda set forth above [in the communique] and to pressure the Governments of India and the United States to fulfill their solemn obligations under the Genocide Convention and the Four Geneva Conventions of 1949.

Full text of the communiqué follows:

The Government of Sri Lanka (GoSL) is currently inflicting acts of genocide against the Tamils in violation of the 1948 Genocide Convention, and war crimes against them in violation of the Four Geneva Conventions of 1949. India is a party to all five of these Conventions. Therefore, under Article 1 of the Genocide Convention India has an obligation to do everything in its power "to prevent" GoSL's genocide against the Tamils.

Furthermore, under Common Article 1 to the Four Geneva Conventions of 1949, India has the obligation "to respect and to ensure respect" for these Conventions "in all circumstances." This requirement means that India has an obligation to prevent the GoSL from inflicting war crimes against the Tamils. Similar principles of analysis likewise apply to all 140 states that are parties to the Genocide Convention and to all states that are parties to the Four Geneva Conventions, which is almost every state in the world.

In addition, as the original homeland for the Tamils, India has the right, the obligation, and the standing under international law to act as *parens patriae* for the Tamils in Sri Lanka. Therefore, India must immediately sue the GoSL for genocide at the International Court of Justice in The Hague, demand an Emergency Hearing of the Court, and request that the World Court issue a Temporary Restraining Order against the GoSL to cease and desist from committing all acts of genocide against the Tamils. Time is of the essence!

GoSL Defense Minister Rajapaksa has determined that a quarter-million Tamils are nothing more than a free-fire zone, which constitutes an act of genocide as well as a war crime. Since he is a United States Citizen, India must demand that the United States government prosecute Rajapaksa immediately for violating the U.S. Genocide Convention Implementation Act as well as the U.S. War Crimes Act. Under Article 1 of the Genocide Convention the United States government has an obligation "to prevent and to punish" genocide. This treaty obligation requires the United States government to institute criminal proceedings against U.S. Citizen Rajapaksa in order "to punish" his genocide against the Tamils.

India must use its newly founded special relationship with the United States government to do just that. Both the United States and India have a joint and several obligation "to prevent" the GoSL from committing genocide against the Tamils and "to punish" U.S. Citizen Rajapaksa for committing genocide against the Tamils. The Four Geneva Conventions also require that India demand that the United States government prosecute U.S. Citizen Rajapaksa for violating the U.S. War Crimes Act, which the United States government is obligated to do under both the Geneva Conventions and that Act.

I call upon all Tamils around the World and all people of good faith and good will to mobilize behind the legal agenda set forth above and to pressure the Governments of India and the United States (as well as your own Governments) to fulfill their solemn obligations under the Genocide Convention and the Four Geneva Conventions of 1949.

As an internationally recognized expert, Professor Boyle serves as counsel to Bosnia and Herzegovina. On 8 April 1993 and 13 September 1993 the author single-handedly won two World Court Orders overwhelmingly in favor of the Republic of Bosnia and Herzegovina against the rump Yugoslavia to cease and desist from committing all acts of genocide against the Bosnians.

A scholar in the areas of international law and human rights, Professor Boyle received a J.D. degree, and A.M. and Ph.D. degrees in political science from Harvard University. Prior to joining the faculty at the College of Law, he was a teaching fellow at Harvard and an associate at its Center for International Affairs.

Gotabaya should be prosecuted for Genocide, war crimes—Prof. Boyle

[TamilNet, Tuesday, 03 February 2009, 22:47 GMT]

Commenting on the interview to the BBC and to the Sky TV by Sri Lanka's Defence Secretary, Professor Francis Boyle, professor of international law at the University of Illinois College of Law, told TamilNet that "the deliberate targeting of Hospitals and Civilians by the Government of Sri Lanka (GoSL) violates the Geneva Conventions and is thus a war crime," and that "as a United States Citizen, Defense Secretary Rajapaksa, should be prosecuted by the United States government for violating the US Genocide Convention Implementation Act and the US War Crimes Act."

Full text of the comment by Prof Boyle follows:

The deliberate targeting of Hospitals and Civilians by the Government of Sri Lanka (GoSL) violates the Geneva Conventions and is thus a war crime. The GoSL Defense Secretary Rajapaksa has publicly admitted that they have turned the Tamil North of the country into a so-called free-fire zone, which is clearly illegal and criminal under International Humanitarian Law.

It is the culmination of the long-standing GoSL policy to inflict genocide upon the Tamils in violation of the 1948 Genocide Convention, to which Sri Lanka is a contracting party. As a United States Citizen Defense Secretary Rajapaksa should be prosecuted by the United States government for violating the US Genocide Convention Implementation Act and the US War Crimes Act.

As an internationally recognized expert, Professor Boyle serves as counsel to Bosnia and Herzegovina. He also represents two associations of citizens within Bosnia and has been instrumental in developing the indictment against Slobodan Milosevic for committing genocide, crimes against humanity, and war crimes in Bosnia and Herzegovina. A scholar in the areas of international law and human rights, Professor Boyle received a J.D. degree, and A.M. and Ph.D. degrees in political science from Harvard University. Prior to joining the faculty at the College of Law, he was a teaching fellow at Harvard and an associate at its Center for International Affairs.

Sri Lanka fully intends to destroy Tamil Homeland, says Boyle

[TamilNet, Thursday, 26 November 2009, 02:17 GMT]

Responding to Sri Lanka's President Rajapakse's statement to heads of media Tuesday ruling out the re-merger of Northern and Eastern provinces, Professor Boyle said, "[o]bviously, the Government of Sri Lanka fully intends to carve-up, destroy, and dismantle the Tamil Homeland on the Island of Sri Lanka for all time, and towards that end inflict even more acts of genocide against the Tamils living there. Historically, the only way for this to be counteracted is to establish an Independent State for the Tamils on Sri Lanka."

• Text of Boyle speech at Chennai seminar available at http://www.tamilnet.com/img/publish/2009/11/BoyleChennaiSeminar.pdf

Boyle pointed out that his Chennai speech in June this year provides the legal basis for the Tamils to establish an Independent State.

"For the reasons argued therein, I would encourage the Tamil People on a worldwide basis to give the most serious consideration to the adoption of a Unilateral Declaration of Independence and the establishment of a Provisional Government for Tamil Eelam," Boyle said.

"This would be similar to what the Palestinians did in their own Declaration of Independence dated 15 November 1988, as I have detailed in my book *Palestine, Palestinians and International Law*.*

"Today the State of Palestine is recognized de jure by about 126 other states. Palestine has Observer State status at the United Nations, and has all the rights of a U.N. Member State but the right to vote. Recently, the Palestinian leadership announced that it will apply for Membership in the United Nations Organization. Palestine is also a member state of the League of Arab States and the Islamic Conference Organization. The World Court also invited Palestine to participate in its proceedings," Boyle added.

"Certainly history cannot guarantee the same type of results for Tamil Eelam. But what is the alternative?"

* http://www.claritypress.com/files/BoyleII.html

Rajapakse brothers, Brigadier Silva, presumptive war criminals, says Boyle

[TamilNet, Tuesday, 15 December 2009, 04:18 GMT]

Former Sri Lanka Army (SLA) Commander General Sarath Fonseka's statement to the effect that the Rajapaksa Brothers, Gotabhaya Rajapakse and Basil Rajapakse, and Brigadier Shavendra Silva ordered the murder of surrendering LTTE leaders protected by a White Flag pursuant to a prior agreement to surrender that way sets forth a prima facie "war crime" under the customary international laws of war as codified into and exemplified by U.S. Army Field Manual 27-10 "The Law of Land Warfare" (1956), paragraph 504, said Professor Francis A. Boyle, University of Illinois College of Law, and an expert in International Law, in a note sent to TamilNet.

Boyle said, the prima facie war crimes culpability attaches for the following three reasons, at least :

504. Other Types of War Crimes In addition to the "grave breaches" of the Geneva Conventions of 1949, the following acts are representative of violations of the law of war ("war crimes"):
...
e. Abuse of or firing on the flag of truce.
...
l. Killing without trial spies or other persons who have committed hostile acts.
...
n. Violation of surrender terms.

Consequently the Rajapakse Brothers and Brigadier Silva are presumptive war criminals. Every State in the world has both the right and the obligation to prosecute them should they leave Sri Lanka and enter into the territorial jurisdiction of another State, Boyle said.

Professor Boyle added, this War Crime also constituted a gross violation of Common Article 3 to the Four Geneva Conventions of 1949, to which Sri Lanka is a party and also constitutes customary international law:

Persons taking no active part in the hostilities, including members of armed forces who have laid down their arms... shall in all circumstances be treated humanely, without any adverse distinction founded on race, colour, religion or faith, sex, birth or wealth, or any other similar criteria.

To this end the following acts are and shall remain prohibited at any time and in any place whatsoever with respect to the above-mentioned persons:

> (a) violence to life and person, in particular murder of all kinds...
>
> ....
>
> (d) ...the carrying out of executions without previous judgment pronounced by a regularly constituted court affording all the judicial guarantees which are recognized as indispensable by civilized peoples."

Every State in the World is a Contracting Party to the Four Geneva Conventions of 1949. Therefore, every State in the World has both the right and the duty to prosecute the Rajapakse Brothers and Brig. Silva for this War Crime, Professor Boyle asserted.

"Legally, they are like unto Pirates--Hostes humani generis, the enemies of all humankind! The International Community has acted effectively to suppress and to punish Pirates coming from Somalia.

"That same International Community must now act effectively to suppress and to punish War Criminals coming from Sri Lanka," Boyle said.

Fonseka revelations mandate independent probe into UN's role, says Boyle

[TamilNet, Thursday, 24 December 2009, 01:11 GMT]

Former Sri Lanka Army Commander, Sarath Fonseka's revelations of Gotabhaya Rajapakse ordering executions of surrendering LTTE leaders and their families, and UN chief of Staff Vijay Nambiar's reported role in the deadly surrenders "require a formal Investigation of the entire role played by the United Nations Organization and its Officials throughout the course of this latest irruption of the GOSL genocide against the Tamils starting in January of 2009 until today," said Professor Francis Boyle, professor of international law at the University of Illinois. "The U.N. Secretary General has the power to order and publish such an investigation," Boyle added.

"The previous U.N. Secretary General Kofi Annan so ordered two separate investigations concerning the roles played by the United Nations during the genocides in Rwanda and Srebrenica, respectively," Boyle noted.

* Independent Report on Rwanda genocide (5Mb)
  <http://www.tamilnet.com/img/publish/2009/12/Rwanda-UNreport.pdf>

* UN report on Srebrenica Genocide (11Mb)
  <http://www.tamilnet.com/img/publish/2009/12/UNSrebrenicaReport.pdf>

"The U.N. Rwanda Report was conducted by a body of credible, professional and outside independent experts and was thus first-rate.

* Annan on Rwanda, Srebrenica
  <http://www.tamilnet.com/img/publish/2009/12/AnnanOnRwnada.pdf>

"By comparison, the U.N. Srebrenica Report was specifically designed to be an in-house cover-up by the U.N. Bureaucracy of their and its Complicity in the genocidal massacre of 8000 Bosnian Muslims at Srebrenica by Serbia, and thus was not worth the paper it was written on," Boyle cautioned of the lack of credibility in UN's internal investigations.

"So the world must demand that the U.N. Secretary General Ban Ki-moon appoint an investigative committee of outside, independent experts to examine the role played by the United Nations Organization during the GOSL's genocidal massacre of about 30,000 Tamils on the Vanni Beaches and the continued incarceration of about 250,000 Tamils in GOSL concentration camps," Boyle said in a note sent to TamilNet.

Weeratunge statement proves India's complicity in Sri Lanka's genocide, says Prof. Boyle

[TamilNet, Sunday, 17 January 2010, 17:16 GMT]

If the statement of Lalith Weeratunga, a top aide to Sri Lanka's President Mahinda Rajapakse, that Sri Lanka's use of heavy weapons was eventually stopped as part of a political deal with the Indian government, was true, "then it proves India's complicity in the GOSL's [Government of Sri Lanka's] genocide against the Tamils," says Professor Boyle, expert in International Law in a note sent to TamilNet. "The Government of India temporarily stopped the GOSL's genocide against the Tamils, thus proving it could do so.... India therefore violated its obligation under article 1 of the Genocide Convention "to prevent" the GOSL genocide against the Tamils," asserts Prof. Boyle.

Full text of the statement from Prof. Boyle follows:

Lalith Weeratunge

If this report is correct on the facts, then it proves India's complicity in the GOSL's genocide against the Tamils. Under basic principles of criminal law that are recognized and applied internationally, when there is an obligation to act to prevent the death of a human being that is incumbent upon a person in a position of trust with respect to that human being such as a policeman, fireman, medical doctor, lifeguard etc., and that person fails or refuses to act to prevent the death of that human being, that person becomes legally responsible for the homicide of that human being.

In this case we are talking about 50,000 dead Tamils on Sri Lanka who were exterminated by the GOSL.

India had an absolute obligation "to prevent" this ongoing GOSL genocide against the Tamils in Sri Lanka under article 1 of the 1948 Genocide Convention, to which both India and Sri Lanka are contracting parties. In addition, the Government of India (GOI) serves as the Tamil's parens patriae under international law and thus occupies a position of trust with respect to the Tamils in Sri Lanka. The Government of India recognized the existence of this "trust" when it asked the GOSL for the temporary cease-fire against the Tamils, which India obtained.

The Government of India temporarily stopped the GOSL's genocide against the Tamils, thus proving it could do so. But only for the demented purpose of getting itself re-elected, not for the purpose of terminating the GOSL's genocide against the Tamils, which India obviously could have done and so did temporarily. India therefore violated its obligation under article 1 of the Genocide Convention "to prevent" the GOSL genocide against the Tamils.

Furthermore, India also thereby became complicit in the GOSL's genocide against the Tamils in violation of article 3(e) of the Genocide Convention that prohibits and criminalizes "complicity" in genocide. The Government of India failed and refused to terminate the GOSL genocide against the Tamils despite the facts (1) that the GOI obviously had the capability to do so and (2) that the GOI obviously recognized it occupied a position of trust with respect to the Tamils in Sri Lanka.

For these reasons, both the Government and the State of India are legally responsible for the commission of the international crime of Complicity in Genocide in violation of the 1948 Genocide Convention. India has an obligation to pay reparations for this international crime to the Tamils on Sri Lanka—both severally and jointly with the GOSL. Indeed, the Government of India and the GOSL conspired together to commit genocide against the Tamils in violation of article 3(b) of the 1948 Genocide Convention prohibiting and criminalizing "conspiracy" to commit genocide.

The same is true for those Highest Level Indian Government Officials who made these reprehensible, condemnable, unprincipled and criminal decisions. They had the mens rea (criminal intent) necessary to constitute the international crimes of Complicity in and Conspiracy to Commit Genocide. These Highest Level Officials of the Indian Government are personally culpable for the commission of the international crimes of Complicity in Genocide and Conspiracy to Commit Genocide. These Highest Level Officials of the GOI must be prosecuted for these crimes—both in India and elsewhere. How low they have sunk from India's glory days of Gandhi and Nehru. Sic transit gloria mundi!

Gotabhaya opens door for UN investigations of Sri Lanka war crimes—Prof. Boyle

[TamilNet, Friday, 05 February 2010, 04:51 GMT]

Referring to Gotabhaya Rajapakse's interview to the BBC Tuesday where Mr Rajapakse said that he would not allow any war crimes investigation in Sri Lanka, Professor Francis Boyle, an expert in International Law and a professor of Law at the University of Illinois College of Law said, "Defense Secretary Rajapakse has now publicly and definitively ruled out any investigation of war crimes by the Government of Sri Lanka. And he is a government official acting within the scope of his official duties so that his statement binds the State of Sri Lanka under international law. Hence the basic requirement of international law mandating "complementarity" has been satisfied.

"In other words, a sovereign state must first be given the opportunity to investigate and prosecute war crimes committed by its own armed forces. Only if the sovereign state fails or refuses to do so, can international bodies step in to conduct those investigations and prosecutions such as the International Criminal Court," Prof. Boyle said.

"In this case, U.N. Special Rapporteur Philip Alston has called for such an investigation. U.N. Secretary General Ban Ki-moon has indicated that he would be prepared to consider such an investigation.

"Now that Defense Minister Rajapakse has rejected such an investigation by the GOSL itself, under international law the onus is now upon U.N. Secretary General Ban Ki-moon to appoint a war crimes investigation body with respect to Sri Lanka as he has recently done in Africa," Prof. Boyle added.

"The Governments of the United States and the United Kingdom must pressure Ban Ki-moon to do the right thing here for the Tamils on Sri Lanka," Professor Boyle further said of the role of the U.S. and U.K. in applying pressure to the U.N. to begin investigations of war crimes allegedly committed by the Sri Lanka Army against Tamil civilians.

Boyle's book added to World Court library

[Tamilnet, Sunday, 07 February 2010, 03:16 GMT]

The Peace Palace Library (PPL), the main library of the World Court, the popular name for the International Court of Justice (ICJ), has acquired *The Tamil Genocide by Sri Lanka*, a recent publication by Clarity press authored by Francis A. Boyle, professor of International Law at University of Illinois College of Law, Marianne Brouwer, principal catalog librarian for the PPL, confirmed. "The book has made it to the World Court. Now we just need to file the lawsuit [against Sri Lanka for Genocide/war-crimes]," commented Boyle.

The International Court of Justice acts as a world court. The Court has a dual jurisdiction: it decides, in accordance with international law, disputes of a legal nature that are submitted to it by States (jurisdiction in contentious cases); and it gives advisory opinions on legal questions at the request of the organs of the United Nations or specialized agencies authorized to make such a request (advisory jurisdiction).

World Court catalogue entry

"The huge building is called the Peace Palace, donated by Andrew Carnegie to house the Permanent Court of Arbitration (PCA), established at the First Hague Peace Conference in 1898. When the Permanent Court of International Justice was founded in 1921, it moved in to take over the Grand Courtroom there since everyone had assumed it would supplant the PCA, though the PCA still survives today," Boyle said of the history of the World Court.

"I joined their library at the time I became Bosnia's Ambassador to the ICJ in 1993. The Registrar took me down to get enrolled. The entire complex is still owned by the Carnegie Endowment and leased to the UN. All is explained in my book *Foundations of World Order* (Duke U Press: 1999)," Boyle told TamilNet.

"When I showed up on a Saturday to file Bosnia's World Court lawsuit for genocide, the Registrar told me he would have to track down the janitor for the Carnegie Center in order to open the place up and receive my Application. It took him a while to do that in The Sleepy Hague on a Saturday," Boyle recounted his early days of his fight for Bosnia in the World Court.

French UN comments wrong, misleading, says Prof. Boyle

[TamilNet, Saturday, 06 March 2010, 00:12 GMT]

Responding to United Nation's France Ambassador, Gerard Araud's, comment on UN inaction on Sri Lanka's civilian slaughter that the UN Secretary General cannot intervene against the wishes of a UN member state, Professor Boyle, an expert in International Law and a professor at the University of Illinois College of Law, told TamilNet that the French statement is "simply wrong and deliberately misleading," and explained that "article 100 of the UN charter made it quite clear that UN Secretariat, including the Secretary General, was completely independent of the Member States of the United Nations."

Gerard Araud,French Ambassador to UN

Professor Boyle said, "[t]he French Ambassador to the U.N. is simply wrong and deliberately misleading when it comes to the requirements of the United Nations Charter. Thereunder, the United Nations Secretariat including the United Nations Secretary General are one of six Independent Organs of the United Nations Organization itself, as recognized by Chapter XV of the United Nations Charter, together with the Security Council, the General Assembly, the International Court of Justice, the Trusteeship Council, and the Economic and Social Council. When the United Nations Charter itself was drafted, it was made clear that no one of these Organs had any authority to direct or command any other Organ what to do. Each Organ was given its own independent powers and responsibilities under the terms of the United Nations Charter.

"Furthermore, article 100 of the Charter made it quite clear that the U.N. Secretariat, including the Secretary General, was completely independent of the Member States of the United Nations," Professor Boyle added.

Article 100 of Chapter XV, titled "The Secretariat," states:

1.In the performance of their duties the Secretary-General and the staff shall not seek or receive instructions from any government or from any other authority external to the Organization. They shall refrain from any action which might reflect on their position as international officials responsible only to the Organization.

2. Each Member of the United Nations undertakes to respect the exclusively international character of the responsibilities of the Secretary-General and the staff

and not to seek to influence them in the discharge of their responsibilities.

"The U.N. Secretariat and the U.N. Secretary General have an absolute and independent U.N. Charter obligation to investigate war crimes, crimes against humanity and genocide against Tamils by the Government of Sri Lanka irrespective of the wishes of the U.N. Member States, including France," Boyle said.

Time for International Criminal Tribunal on Sri Lanka, says Boyle

[TamilNet, Sunday, 07 March 2010, 22:03 GMT]

Dismissing the response by Colombo that Ban Ki-moon had not appointed panel of experts on other countries where there are "continuing armed conflicts on a large scale, involving major humanitarian catastrophes and causing the deaths of large numbers of civilians due to military action," as "simply untrue nonsense," Francis A. Boyle, professor at the University of Illinois College of Law, said that during the past year alone UN Human Rights Council had authorized Goldstone Commission investigation into Israel war crimes against Palestinians in Gaza. Noting that the "United Nations is just beginning to do the right thing for the Tamils," Prof Boyle urged that "Tamils around the world could do the same thing for establishing an International Criminal Tribunal for Sri Lanka (ICTSL)."

"Of course this statement by the Government of Sri Lanka (GoSL) is simply untrue nonsense, and the GOSL knows it. During the past year alone the UN Human Rights Council authorized the so-called Goldstone Commission investigation into Israel war crimes and crimes against humanity perpetrated against the besieged 1.5 million Palestinians in Gaza. The Goldstone Report ultimately found that Israel had indeed inflicted war crimes and crimes against humanity against the Palestinians—just short of genocide," Boyle pointed out.

"Any appointment of such a panel as intended, would compel Sri Lanka to take necessary and appropriate action in that regard," Sri Lanka's President had told the UN Secretary General, local media in Colombo reported. The reports did not clarify what the "necessary and appropriate" actions are likely to be.

Professor Boyle said, "the UN Human Rights Council has so far done the right thing for the Palestinians. Unfortunately, the GoSL was able to manipulate anti-Western sentiments there in order to block similar action by the Human Rights Council when it came to the investigation of the GoSL's own international crimes against the Tamils. So now one year after the GoSL's genocidal massacre against the Tamils, the United Nations is just beginning to do the right thing for the Tamils. But better late than never," Boyle added.

"I already have a proposal for the establishment of an International Criminal Tribunal for Israel (ICTI) that is currently pending before the United Nations General Assembly," Professor Boyle pointed out, and added, "Tamils around the world could do the same thing for establishing an International Criminal Tribunal for Sri Lanka (ICTSL). The UN General Assembly would have the power to establish an ICTSL as a "subsidiary organ" under U.N. Charter Article 22. That way, the concerned GoSL members (e.g., Rajapakses, Fonseka, General Staff et al) could be held accountable for their international crimes against the Tamils without needing any prior reference by the U.N. Security Council to the International Criminal Court, which would be subject to a likely Great Power Veto—for example by China.

"But there is no veto in the U.N. General Assembly. We would just need a majority vote in the UN General Assembly to set up an ICTSL. Concerned Tamils around the world should contact their respective governments of current nationality or legal residence and ask them to sponsor my proposal for establishing an International Criminal Tribunal for Sri Lanka by the United Nations General Assembly," Boyle said.

UN investigation can serve as leverage to establish ICTSL, says Prof. Boyle

[TamilNet, Thursday, 11 March 2010, 03:28 GMT]

Commenting on the United Nations report that UN Secretary General, Ban Ki-moon's appointed experts will establish standards for Sri Lanka's accountability concerning "possible breaches of international humanitarian law...," Professor Francis A. Boyle of University of Illinois College of Law said, "[t]his language of "international humanitarian law" means that the United Nations will be getting into investigating war crimes and crimes against humanity committed by the GOSL against the Tamils, which is an encouraging sign. In other words, the United Nations will be investigating international criminal responsibility by the Rajapakses, Fonseka, the General Staff, et al," Boyle added.

"We need to keep the pressure on Ban Ki-moon and the United Nations Secretariat and the most powerful States such as the United States and the United Kingdom to go through with this investigation. The final results of this investigation can then be used as leverage for the U.N. General Assembly to establish an International Criminal Tribunal for Sri Lanka (ICTSL) as a "subsidiary organ" under U..N. Charter article 22," Professor Boyle told TamilNet.

"The United Nations Security Council established the International Criminal Tribunal for the former Yugoslavia (ICTY) and the International Criminal Tribunal for Rwanda (ICTR). But China would undoubtedly exercise its Veto Power at the United Nations Security Council to prevent the Council from establishing the ICTSL.

"China would also veto any attempt by Security Council members to refer the GOSL crimes against the Tamils to the International Criminal Court (ICC). And unfortunately, the ICC Prosecutor has publicly stated that he does not believe he has jurisdiction to open an investigation into GOSL crimes on his own accord because Sri Lanka is not a party to the Rome Statute for the International Criminal Court.

"Therefore, the creation of the ICTSL by the U.N. General Assembly is the one option we have to establish some degree of international criminal accountability for the atrocities against the Tamils perpetrated by the GOSL's highest level officials," Prof. Boyle said.

"When in March of 1993 as the Lawyer for the Republic of Bosnia and Herzegovina I personally went after Slobodan Milosevic in the International Court of Justice in The Hague for committing genocide, war crimes and crimes against humanity against the Bosnians, nobody else realistically expected they would ever see him on trial for anything.

"Yet Milosevic died in March of 2006 while being tried before the ICTY in The Hague for committing every crime in the ICTY Statute, including genocide at Srebrenica.

"Based upon my personal experience in bringing Milosevic to justice, that is about the time-frame we are looking at for doing the same to the Rajapakses, Fonseka, the GOSL General Staff, et al.

"The time for the Tamil Diaspora to get organized for this task is now!" Professor Boyle reiterated.

Demand that US reveal more inculpatory war crimes evidence, urges Boyle

[TamilNet, Saturday, 13 March 2010, 18:13 GMT]

While applauding the U.S. Government for revealing significant amount of details that point to complicity of Sri Lanka Government in committing war crimes and crimes against humanity, Professor Francis A. Boyle of University of Illinois College of Law, urged American Tamils to "pressure the relevant agencies of the United States government to produce as much evidence in public as they possibly can against the Rajapakses, Fonseka, the GOSL General Staff, etc." Prof. Boyle noted that "[t]he United States government did this once before against the Serbian genocidaires Milosevic, Karadzic et al. for what they did to the Bosnians and the Kosovars. The United States government can certainly do the same against the GOSL genocidaires against the Tamils," Prof. Boyle said.

Hillary Rodham Clinton,
U.S. Secretary of State

Madeleine K. Albright

Acting U.S. Secretary of State under Bush Jr.,
Larry Eagleburger

While informed sources in Europe said that the Office of War Crimes Issues (S/WCI) of the U.S. State Department is collecting evidence from eye-witnesses who escaped from the battle-zones in the Northeast, Boyle said, more detailed imagery from defense satellites will be in possession of the U.S. Government. Some of the latest commercial imagery has finer resolutions of 9.75 inches, but these images are controlled by the Defense Department, according to reports.<http://www.dodbuzz.com/2009/04/07/president-approves-new-satellite-system/>

"For example, during the Serbian War/Genocide against the Bosnians, President Bush Sr.'s Acting U.S. Secretary of State Larry

Eagleburger publicly condemned Radovan Karadzic—now on trial in The Hague before the International Criminal Tribunal for the Former Yugoslavia (ICTY)—for committing international crimes against the Bosnians and provided public evidence to the United Nations in order to back up those charges.

"The same could be done to the Rajapakses, Fonseka, the GOSL General Staff Members, etc.," Prof. Boyle said.

"Later on, during Slobodan Milosevic's genocidal rampage against the Kosovars, then U.S. Secretary of State Madeleine Albright met with then ICTY Prosecutor Louise Arbour (<http://secretary.state.gov/www.statements/1999/990430a.html>) and promised to provide the ICTY with U.S. intelligence information on atrocities being committed by Serbia in Kosovo.

"With that promise and information, Arbour was able to indict Milosevic for war crimes and crimes against humanity under the ICTY Statute for what he did to the Kosovars. Milosevic died while on trial before the ICTY for the commission of international crimes in Kosova, Bosnia (for genocide, war crimes and crimes against humanity) and Croatia (for war crimes and crimes against humanity)," Prof Boyle said.

Acting U.S. Secretary of State Larry Eagleburger publicly condemns Karadzic.

"The United States agencies will respond to public pressure by Tamil American Citizens and Members of the United States Congress. The time to get organized for this is now," exhorted Prof. Boyle.

While promising U.S's assistance in providing war crimes evidence against Milosevic and Serb Military commanders, Albright said in April 1999, "[t]here should be no misunderstanding. When it comes to the commission of war crimes or crimes against humanity, "just following orders" is no defense. These are crimes for which individuals are responsible and for which individuals will be held accountable. Justice Arbour has rightly indicated that the Tribunal will follow the evidence no matter where it leads. In that, it has the full support of the United States. American personnel are assisting in the difficult work of documenting refugee charges, and doing what they can to gather supporting accounts.

"Justice Arbour and I today discussed how the United States can provide more information to the Tribunal, and how to speed up delivery of potential evidence to The Hague. I assured her that we are asking Congress for additional resources for the Tribunal to meet new demands for investigations in Kosovo. And we discussed other needs of her investigations, which I am not going to get into, but which I assure you that the United States will do everything we possibly can to meet.

"The Tribunal now needs real-time support for its Kosovo investigations, and the United States is determined to give it. The world needs to know exactly what is happening there, and we are committed to helping discover it. Milosevic's victims, and those everywhere who love justice, need to know that there will be no impunity for those who commit these heinous offenses. And we're committed to helping the Tribunal ensure that those responsible are held accountable."

Cutting UN ties will earn Sri Lanka rogue status, says Prof. Boyle

[TamilNet, Friday, 19 March 2010, 00:28 GMT]

"If the Government of Sri Lanka ruptures relations with the United Nations, then it will turn itself into a pariah state along the lines of apartheid South Africa or the genocidal rump Yugoslavia, both of which the United Nations General Assembly suspended from participation in the activities of the United Nations for their criminal behavior. In fact and in law, the same principles should apply here." said Professor Boyle, commenting on Colombo's recent warning that "ties with the United Nations (UN) is in danger of going sour if the present conflict with UN Secretary General Ban Ki-moon over his move to appoint a panel on Sri Lanka is not resolved."

To U.N. Secretary General Ban Ki-moon's stated intention to appoint an expert committee to advise Ban on "the standards, benchmarks and parameters, based on international experience, that must guide any accountability process [for addressing violations of international humanitarian and human rights laws]," Sri Lanka's Foreign Minister responded that the proposed UN measure can only be construed as an "intrusive unilateral initiative" by the UN Secretary General, and that "if not resolved taking into consideration Sri Lanka's unique context and rising public anger against the UN Chief's proposed move, it has the potential to dent or sour the excellent partnership Sri Lanka."

Professor Boyle added that in addition to the suspension from the UN activities, "[t]he United Nations General Assembly should also suspend Sri Lanka from participation in the activities of the entirety of the United Nations Organization and its Subsidiary Bodies and Affiliated Organizations because of the genocide, war crimes and crimes against humanity that the GOSL inflicted on the Tamils in Vanni a year ago.

"Materially, there is no difference between apartheid South Africa and the genocidal rump Yugoslavia, on the one hand, and the genocidal, apartheid Sri Lanka, on the other. For that reason, Sri Lanka deserves to be treated as a pariah state by the United Nations Organization itself and by its 192 member states," Prof. Boyle added.

In earlier commentaries on the U.N.-Sri Lanka issue, Prof. Boyle repeatedly rejected Government of Sri Lanka's allegations that this [investigations into war crimes] is an "internal" matter of "domestic concern" that is beyond the competence of the UN.

Prof. Boyle, who is also a leading expert in International Law, asserted that "the U.N. Secretary General has the power to order and publish not only investigations into the violations of member countries in the conduct of war, but also the "entire role played by the United Nations Organization and its Officials," during the wars.

Prof. Boyle: PCIJ precedent brings GoSL's war crimes within UN jurisdiction

[TamilNet, Saturday, 20 March 2010, 20:58 GMT]

Quoting a landmark 1923 decision on rules governing international agreements by the Permanent Court of International Justice (PCIJ), Professor Boyle, an expert in international law, referred to Colombo's claim that UN is infringing on the sovereignty of a member state, and said, "I am not going to spend a lot of time here refuting this erroneous and disingenuous interpretation of international law and the requirements of the United Nations Charter by the GoSL (Government of Sri Lanka) and its Foreign Minister. There is one definitive answer to their objection. Namely, the GoSL Army undoubtedly inflicted numerous violations of the Four Geneva Conventions of 1949 upon the Tamils in Vanni a year ago, and in particular but not limited to gross violations of Common Article 3 thereof, which constituted war crimes. Sri Lanka is a contracting party to the Four Geneva Conventions of 1949."

The Government of Sri Lanka through its Foreign Minister government reiterated its position Thursday that the proposed move by the UN Secretary General to appoint a Panel of Experts to advise him on accountability issues relating to Sri Lanka is an infringement on the sovereignty of an independent Member State, without prejudice to the application of enforcement measures under Chapter VII.

Professor Boyle said, "according to the famous holding of the Permanent Court of International Justice (PCIJ) in the Tunis-Morocco Nationality Decrees Case of 1923, the moment a state concludes an international agreement on any subject, that subject is no longer a matter of exclusively internal or domestic or sovereign concern but thereafter becomes a matter of international concern. Under the terms of the United Nations Charter, the Permanent Court of International Justice is the predecessor in law to the current International Court of Justice, the so-called World Court. Hence PCIJ decisions are still valid as a matter of public international law as of today.

"For these reasons, the GoSL's gross violations of the Four Geneva Conventions inflicted upon the Tamils in Vanni do not fall within the domestic jurisdiction or sovereign concern of Sri Lanka alone, but also fall within the jurisdiction of international law and of the United Nations itself. For this reason alone, the U.N. Secretary General has the legal authority under the terms of the United Nations Charter to appoint a Committee of Experts to advise him upon all war crimes and crimes against humanity that were inflicted by the GOSL against the Tamils in Vanni a year ago. The sooner the better for the integrity of the U.N. Secretary General, the United Nations Organization, the Geneva

Conventions, and International Law, Prof Boyle said.

Professor Boyle added, that "[t]he same arguments also apply pari passu to the GoSL's violation of the 1948 Genocide Convention against the Tamils in Sri Lanka. Sri Lanka is a contracting party to the Genocide Convention. The U.N. Secretary General must give his proposed U.N. Committee of Experts terms of reference that would include the Geneva Conventions and Protocols, the Genocide Convention, as well as war crimes and crimes against humanity under customary international criminal law.

"The Statutes for the International Criminal Tribunal for the former Yugoslavia and/or for the International Criminal Tribunal for Rwanda and their respective U.N. investigations would be excellent models to apply to the GoSL: The International Criminal Tribunal for Sri Lanka (ICTSL)," Boyle said.

The spokesperson for US-based pressure group, Tamils Against Genocide (TAG), said, "Professor Boyle's opinion on the legality, based on international law, of Secretary General's (UNSG's) intent to form an advisory committee provides a firm legal basis for the UNSG to urgently to take the first step towards investigating war-crimes widely believed to be committed by both protagonists in Sri Lanka's conflict. TAG, in parallel, will use judicial systems in countries that allow extra-territorial jurisdiction to prosecute Sri Lanka officials responsible for the dastardly crime of slaughtering more than 40,000 Tamil civilians," the spokesperson added.

Meanwhile, Inner City Press reported that when asked of the war-crimes and NAM's letter, UK Permanent Representative to the UN Mark Lyall Grant said "the Secretary General does have a mandate through the UN Charter to uphold human rights and humanitarian international law, and therefore he is entirely within his rights to set up a group of experts who will advise him on taking forward his concerns about some of the allegations that have been made in the recent months in Sri Lanka."

Ambassador Grant added that "[UK has] made it very clear that we always want to see an end to impunity, that we want to see allegations of war crimes, human rights violations, human rights abuses, thoroughly investigated."

Appoint Prof. Boyle to UN advisory panel, Tamil Groups urge Ban Ki-moon

[TamilNet, Sunday, 28 March 2010, 22:56 GMT]

Key expatriate Tamil organizations, the US-based Tamil Political Action Council (USTPAC), and Global Tamil Forum (GTF), in a press release issued Sunday following the announcement by UN Secretary General to appoint an advisory panel on Sri Lanka's war-crime issues, said "[w]e appeal to the Secretary General, that in the interests of fairness to the victims that the Secretary General consults the Tamils also in appointing the advisory panel," adding, "the USTPAC and the Global Tamil Forum strongly recommend Professor Francis A. Boyle to the advisory panel."

• USTPAC supports UN Secretary General's move creating advisory panel <http://www.tamilnet.com/img/publish/2010/03/Appeal_to_UN_Sec_General_032810.pdf>

Referring to a report by the the Inner City Press that the Secretary General has entrusted that the panel's terms of reference and its membership to be worked out by his chief of staff Mr. Vijay Nambiar and the Sri Lankan Ambassador to the UN, Dr. Palitha Kohena, the expatriate Tamil Groups appeared to raise concern that both candidates are favorable to Colombo.

"Currently a professor of law at the University of Illinois, Professor Boyle has been instrumental in developing indictment against Slobodan Milosevic for committing genocide, crimes against humanity, and war crimes in Bosnia and Herzegovina. As well known scholar in international law and human rights, Professor Boyle is eminently qualified to advise the UN Secretary General on war-crime investigations by parties to the conflict in Sri Lanka," the press release said.

The Tamil expatriate organizations unanimously welcomed UN Secretary General's initiative, and said the initiative deserves the full support of the international community, and should proceed without delay.

The terms of reference need to be broad enough to ensure full accountability," said a spokesperson for the USTPAC. The Secretary General's action follows calls by UN High Commissioner for Human Rights, Navi Pillai, and the UN Special Rapporteur on extrajudicial, summary or arbitrary executions, Philip Alston, urging international investigations based on credible reports of war crimes, the press release noted.

A spokesperson for US-based activist group, Tamils Against Genocide (TAG), welcomed the unanimous call of support by global Tamil organizations for Professor Boyle, and said, "however, the appointment of the chief of staff Mr. Nambiar and the Sri Lankan Ambassador Mr Kohona to the serious matter of assembling committee to advise of war crime issues is astonishing and alarming.

"Clearly the panel should consist of independent minded persons who have the requisite international experience, and their selection should be a totally transparent process, and free of any bias. The expert panel should also be empowered to receive and hear testimony from experts as well as witnesses with knowledge of the alleged war crimes in Sri Lanka.

"Since the Sri Lanka Government has strongly opposed the appointment of the panel from the beginning, its Ambassador has every reason to render the panel ineffective. Mr. Nambiar, for his part, was the point man for the UN on Sri Lanka when the alleged war crimes occurred, and has been the subject of strong criticism for his role.

"TAG appeals to the international community, especially the US, EU, UK, and other democracies, to press the UN Secretary General ensure that the declared determination to establish full accountability as an essential ingredient for national harmony, and as called for under international human rights and humanitarian laws, will indeed be realized," TAG spokesperson added.

Colombo adopts failed Sudanese ruse to deflect war crimes charges—Prof. Boyle

[TamilNet, Sunday, 09 May 2010, 14:38 GMT]

Commenting on Sri Lanka's President Rajapakse's announcement that Colombo will appoint a 7-person commission to "search for any violations of internationally accepted norms of conduct in such conflict situations, and the circumstances that may have led to such actions [in Sri Lanka], and identify any persons or groups responsible for such acts," Francis A Boyle, professor of International Law at the University of Illinois College of Law said "after it was announced that the ICC was going after Sudan, they hired a British lawyer to advise them on setting up some type of fake internal procedure of investigation/ prosecution in order to head off the ICC, pretending to satisfy the requirement of complementarity. It miserably failed, and Sudan's Al Bashir is now under ICC's arrest warrant."

"It is clear that this new commission will not have authority to prosecute anyone.* Therefore, the requirements of "complementarity" would be satisfied and Ban Ki-moon must move forward with the appointment of his committee of experts. This is just another effort by GoSL to stall the war-crimes moves by the United Nations. So far Ban Ki-moon has gone along with it. But it has now reached the end of its road. It is time for him to act," Professor Boyle said.

* Complementarity of the jurisdiction of the ICC
  <http://www.tamilnet.com/img/publish/2010/05/ICC-manual-en-p100-143.pdf>

* On complementarity
  <http://www.tamilnet.com/img/publish/2010/05/SSRN-id907404.pdf>

The doctrine of complementarity establishes the foundation that the International Criminal Court will complement national courts so that they retain jurisdiction to try genocide, crimes against humanity and war crimes. If a case is being considered by a country with jurisdiction over it, then the ICC cannot act unless the country is unwilling or unable genuinely to investigate or prosecute.

A country may be determined to be "unwilling" if it is clearly shielding someone from responsibility for ICC crimes. A country may be "unable" when its legal system has collapsed.

* http://www.msnbc.msn.com/id/36982383

According to Professor Boyle, Sri Lanka has clearly demonstrated its unwillingness to conduct an internationally acceptable unbiased investigation. The commission has no authority to prosecute, and the Defense Secretary Gotabhaya Rajapakse has threatened with death to eye witnesses who come forward to provide war-crimes testimony.[1]

"The Defense Secretary has also publicly rejected such an investigation by the GOSL itself, and therefore, under international law the onus is now upon U.N. Secretary General Ban Ki-moon to appoint a war crimes investigation body with respect to Sri Lanka as he has recently done in Africa," Prof. Boyle reiterated his earlier call for urgent UN action.

Colombo's efforts to derail UN's plans to conduct independent war crimes investigations are remarkably similar to Sudan's (failed) attempts to stall UN efforts to proceed with indicting Al-Bashir on war crimes charges.

Sudanese President Omar Hassan al-Bashir

First, in August 2008 Sudan's Justice Minister announced[2] a special "internal prosecutor" to look into rights abuses committed in war ravaged region of Darfur since 2003, three weeks after Moreno Ocampo, prosecutor of the International Criminal Court (ICC), announced that he is seeking an arrest warrant for the Sudanese president Omar Hassan Al-Bashir.

Second, Sudan had lobbied Non-Aligned Movement (NAM), as did Colombo to stall and condemn UN's efforts to proceed with war crimes investigations. Sudan lobbied NAM to condemn Ocampo's request and called on the UN Security Council (UNSC) resolution deferring Al-Bashir's indictment.

But ICC's appointed defense counsel for Darfur case rebuffed Sudanese efforts as "too late," and added, "[t]here can be no internal proceedings and it will not be acceptable anyways. As a starter it will not guarantee the rights of the victims. I am not questioning the integrity of Sudanese judiciary but things have changed today. Sudan could have moved to prosecute war criminals a long time ago," the ICC's counsel said.

A spokesperson for US-based activist group Tamils Against Genocide (TAG), said, "rogue states adopt different strategies to deflect

---

[1] http://www.island.lk/2010/05/06/news2.html
[2] http://www.sudantribune.com/spip.php?article28166

blame, even when there is overwhelming evidence of egregious conduct against their own civilians. Recently, Guinea's military junta hired two former war-crimes specialists as consultants to downplay violence after Guinea's soldiers were accused of massacring civilians. TAG believes that Sri Lanka's subterfuges are running out of steam, and as HRW recently pointed out, the International Community will have to soon take assertive action against Sri Lanka's game of smoke and mirrors. Additionally, Sri Lanka president's plan to bring the Attorney General's department under his control shatters whatever judicial independence that remained after 17th amendment was violated, and this situation may be legally argued as a "constructive" collapse of judiciary, thereby enabling complementarity under the "unable" doctrine, also," TAG's spokesperson added.

Treaty discussion, reminder for appointing Sri Lanka War Crimes panel, says Boyle

[TamilNet, Saturday, 29 May 2010, 21:53 GMT]

While Secretary General Ban Ki-moon extolled the contributions of the UN's International Criminal Court (ICC) as an effective instrument to uphold peace, justice and human rights, in a Washington Post article, as UN's member nations convene Monday in Kampala to formally review the Rome Treaty, Professor Francis A. Boyle criticized Ban for delaying action on establishing accountability for Sri Lanka's "massacre of about 50,000 Tamils" and urged Ban to "immediately appoint the International War Crimes Committee for Sri Lanka that he had already promised to do several weeks ago."

Between 31st May and 11 June, the first formal review of the Rome Statute[1] is to take place in Kampala, Uganda. In addition to State parties (signed and ratified Rome treaty), others who have signed but not ratified have been invited with observer status. The Secretariat has also invited non-signatory nations to attend without observer status.

• Ban Ki-moon on ICC
<http://www.tamilnet.com/img/publish/2010/05/MoonOnICC-WP.pdf>

In the Saturday edition of *Washington Post,* Ban said, "[s]o far, the ICC has opened five investigations. Two trials are underway; a third is scheduled to begin in July. Four detainees are in custody. Those who thought the court would be little more than a paper tiger have been proved wrong. To the contrary, the ICC casts an increasingly long shadow. Those who would commit crimes against humanity have clearly come to fear it."

Ban Ki-moon says in the article, "I will do my best to help advance the fight against impunity and usher in the new age of accountability. We must never forget that crimes against humanity are just that—crimes against us all."

Prof. Francis Boyle commented: "U.N. Secretary General Ban Ki-moon is certainly correct in his conclusion that crimes against humanity are "crimes against us all."

"For obvious reasons, the Government of Sri Lanka has refused to become a party to the Rome Statute for the International Criminal Court and thus ipso facto to incriminate itself for the genocidal massacre of about 50,000 Tamils in Vanni a year ago. So that leaves it up to Ban Ki-moon to "do my best to help advance the fight against impunity and usher in the new age of accountability," as he has just solemnly promised the entire world to do in the pages of the Washington Post. Hence, pursuant to this promise, Ban Ki-moon must immediately appoint the International War Crimes Committee for Sri Lanka that he had already promised to do several weeks ago.

"Time is of the essence! Evidence is being destroyed. Witnesses are being disappeared. Ethnic cleansing of Tamils in the Tamil Homeland in the North and the East of the Island is already underway."

Commenting on Ban Ki-moon's statement that "Women, children and the elderly are at the mercy of armies or militias who rape, maim and kill; who devastate towns, villages, crops, cattle and water sources -- all as a strategy of war. The more shocking the crime, the more effective it is as a weapon," Professor Boyle said:

"This is exactly what the GOSL did to about 50,000 Tamils a year ago in Vanni. Right now is the "occasion to strengthen our collective determination that crimes against humanity cannot go unpunished— the better to deter them in the future." In accordance with this his own logic and rationale, Ban Ki-moon must immediately appoint his proposed International War Crimes Committee for Sri Lanka if he is to have any credibility at all."

The ICC has jurisdiction over only the signatories of the Rome Treaty.

- Rome Statute
  <http://www.tamilnet.com/img/publish/2010/02/rome_statute.pdf>

- ICC Member States (110) as of 21 July 2009
  <http://www.tamilnet.com/img/publish/2010/03/ICCMemberStates.
  pdf>

- Non-signatories of Rome Statute
  <http://www.tamilnet.com/img/publish/2010/03/Signatures-
  Non_Signatures_and_Ratifications_of_the_RS_in_the_World_
  November_2009.pdf>

- Sri Lanka campaign for Rome ratification

In March this year Bangladesh became the first country in the South Asian sub-region to ratify the Rome Statute becoming the 111th member of the group of Nations to abide by the laws of the International Criminal Court (ICC), and thereby, actively cooperate in areas such as providing evidence of war-crimes and crimes against humanity, surrendering indicted individuals and holding national trials.

Sri Lanka has been refusing to ratify the Rome Statute.

In a 2005 appeal, Bhavani Fonseka, with the Center for Policy Alternatives in Colombo, said, "Sri Lanka's accession would not only help the whole of Asia to have a stronger voice in the decision-making processes of the ICC, it would also serve as a powerful way to promote peace domestically within Sri Lanka. Sri Lanka has a great tool for sustainable peace in the ICC treaty and acceding to it would signal that the country as a whole accepts the highest standards of human rights that the ICC treaty represents."

Only 7 countries in the Asian continent, Afghanistan, Bangladesh, Cambodia, Mongolia, the Republic of Korea, East Timor and Japan, have ratified the Rome Statute.

A spokesperson for US-based activist group Tamils Against Genocide (TAG), said, "rogue states adopt different strategies to deflect blame, even when there is overwhelming evidence of egregious conduct against their own civilians. Recently, Guinea's military junta hired two former war-crimes specialists[2] as consultants to downplay violence after Guinea's soldiers were accused of massacring civilians. TAG believes that Sri Lanka's subterfuges are running out of steam, and as HRW recently pointed out, the International Community will have to soon take assertive action against Sri Lanka's game of smoke and mirrors. Additionally, Sri Lanka president's plan to bring the Attorney General's department under his control shatters whatever judicial independence that remained after 17th amendment was violated, and this situation may be legally argued as a "constructive" collapse of judiciary, thereby enabling complementarity under the "unable" doctrine, also," TAG's spokesperson added.

[1]<http://www.icc-cpi.int/Menus/ASP/ReviewConference/>
[2]<http://turtlebay.foreignpolicy.com/posts/2010/02/24/guinea_s_junta_hires_ex_war_crimes_prosecutors_and_gets_a_favorable_report

Boyle: Independent Eelam will be a bulwark for India

[TamilNet, Sunday, 06 June 2010, 00:02 GMT]

Professor Francis A. Boyle, an expert in international law at the University of Illinois College of Law, said that an independent state of Tamil Eelam south of the Indian border will add to India's security, and therefore, India should actively intervene in the Tamil struggle and facilitate the formation of Tamil Eelam. Boyle was talking to the popular Tamil Nadu Tamil biweekly magazine Junior Vikatan in an exclusive interview given to the magazine's US correspondent Prakash M Swamy early part of May.

Text of the translation of the interview published in Vikatan follows (Note: original interview to Vikatan was in English):

Vikatan: One year has passed since the defeat of the Liberation Tigers of Tamil Eelam (LTTE). Do you think birth of Tamil Eelam is still a possibility?

Boyle: Faith propels life; in recent times, terrorism label was stamped on those who led and supported Tamil Eelam struggle. Now, since Tiger leadership has disappeared, Rajapakse is on his mission to destroy the Tamil people. Sri Lanka has no respect for any international law. India [as a regional super-power] has failed to contrain Sri Lanka's conduct. Transnational Government of Tamil Eelam (TGTE) will reflect the conscience of Tamil people. Counselors elected for TGTE will determine their future. Many directives will be taken at their first meeting.

Vikatan: Opponents claim that TGTE have only web presence. Can you comment?

Boyle: After the genocide, where is the space for Tamil leadership to operate or even emerge in Sri Lanka? Surviving leadership are all outside of Sri Lanka. Can these leaders visit Sri Lanka? Under these circumstances Tamils only option is the formation of Transnational Government. The counselors are elected democratically. Liberation struggle is taking its step in an entirely new direction. Let us wait to see the impact.

Vikatan: You support Palestinians, who have a state. Tamil people do not have a state.

Boyle: Not quite true. Tamil homeland is occupied by Sri Lankan state. This is sad! Tamils are enslaved in their own state. Rajapakse is supported by Israel, which is occupying Palestinian land. Wars for Palestinian independence and Tamil Eelam independence are similar. Both struggles are labelled as terrorism, illegal occupation. Currently, 127 out of 195 members of the United Nation have recognized Palestine. President Obama has recently said that an independent Palestine should be allowed to exist without security threats.

Vikatan: US, while fully engaged in Palestinian-Israel conflict refuses to play an active role in Tamil Eelam struggle. Why?

Boyle: Israel is the reason. Israel fully supports Sri Lanka. Obama supports Rajapakse administration because of China. America is concerned by the increasing Chinese influence in Sri Lanka, and that China may even be allowed to build a military base in Sri Lanka. U.S. even supported the dud committee set up by Sri Lanka to investigate the rights violations in Sri Lanka. This committee is useless, and without teeth. This committee will not dare investigate Rajapakse brothers. What is troubling is the UN ambassador to UN [and later Secretary of State Clinton] have extended their support to this committee.

Vikatan: What types configurations are possible for a future Tamil Eelam state?

Boyle: First, Tamil Eelam can be an independent sovereign state – this is the wish of Tamil people. Second, Tamil eelam can be similar to that of Commonwealth of Puerto Rico – Puerto Rico is a sovereign state, at the same time, comes under America's confederation. Third, it can be an independent province within a sovereign Sri Lankan state.

Vikatan: Could you comment on Indian government's refusal to issue visa to Prabhakaran's mother?

Boyle: Your central government has directed its anger against Prabhakaran on his mother. Is Ms. Parvathi an extremist? Is she scheming to over throw your government? She is eighty years old; she does not even have the strength to stand on her own. This is a serious violation of human rights. India has capable lawyers. Do you have honest and independent courts? Why have not this act been challenged in a court of justice in India? In the U.S., many lawyers and rights organizations would have immediately filed challenges in US Courts. India should not have politicized a humanitarian matter. Other than India getting a fleeting satisfaction by refusing visa to Prabhakaran's mother, no other useful purpose was served by India's act. Is India trying to punish Prabhakaran who is dead and gone?

Vikatan: What should be India's approach to dealing with Tamil Eelam struggle?

Boyle: I am not qualified to advise India. As an American who loves India,

I can share some thoughts. Tamils worldwide are connected culturally and emotionally to Eelam Tamils, and therefore, to their struggle. In this context, recognize that Prabhakaran era is over. Do not continue to show vengeance on Tamils and their struggle. India should change the way it views struggle for Tamil independence. In the changing geo-political structure, close alliance between China and Sri Lanka will be a danger to everyone. Independent Tamil Eelam will add security, and will be a bulwark to India's security. I am not a politician; an attorney, of Irish descent. I am not even a Tamil, but I feel their pain. India should actively intervene to facilitate the birth of Tamil Eelam.

Note: Professor Boyle extends his apology, and his congratulations to Mr Karuppan for his heroic legal action on behalf of Mr. Prabhakaran's Mother. Prof Boyle regrets that he had not read about the legal action at the time he gave this interview.

Mr Karuppan, in a communication to Prof Boyle following this article, noted that "Prabhakaran's mother was not refused visa. She was deported forcibly in the same plane back to the orgination Kaula Lampur. Although she had a valid visa issued by the High Commission of India in Malaysia on her valid Sri Lankan Passport.

- Karuppan v. Govt. of India
  <http://www.tamilnet.com/img/publish/2010/06/Karuppan_v._
  Govt._of_India.doc>

  "I had challenged the same up to the Supreme Court of India[1] from the High Court stating that deportation without any reason is illegal, when refugees without visa were not deported. Sought directions from the High Court to ask the Govt of India to send a special plane and bring her back and continue treatment at State Expense."

---

[1] <http://tamilnet.com/art.html?catid=13&artid=31587>

Boyle urges divestment-disinvestment campaign against "apartheid" Sri Lanka

[TamilNet, Friday, 23 July 2010, 00:07 GMT]

Speaking at the Federation of Tamil Sangams of North America (FeTNA) convention during the US Independence day weekend, Professor Boyle, an expert in International Law, said that Sri Lanka is a violator of the Apartheid Convention, and that Tamils across the world should, without delay, intensify a divestment and disinvestment campaign against Sri Lanka "in the same lines and for the same reason the world did this against the criminal apartheid regime in South Africa." The July event held in Waterbury, Connecticut, is traditionally the largest event of the Tamil speaking people in the US every year, and the Connecticut event this year drew more than 2000 Tamils.

Article I of the Apartheid Convention, more formally known as the International Convention on the Suppression and Punishment of the Crime of Apartheid (ICSPCA), labels the crime of Apartheid as a "crime against humanity," and declares that "inhuman acts resulting from the policies and practices of racial segregation and discrimination are crimes violating the principles or international law..."

Prof. Boyle said the long history of discriminatory policies instituted by successive governments of Sri Lanka against Tamils and the conduct of the Goverment of Mahinda Rajapakse on internment of Tamil civilians, continued colonization of Tamil lands, desecration of cemeteries and cultural symbols of Tamils overwhelmingly qualify Sri Lanka as an apartheid regime, and therefore, Sri Lanka should be prosecuted as a violator of the Apartheid Convention.

Prof. Boyle added that with the exception of one category of crime listed in Article II of the Apartheid Convention, that is the prohibition of mixed marriages, Sri Lanka has violated almost all other categories of crimes that qualify as "crime of Apartheid." Article II crimes include:

• Denial of the right to life and property;

• Deliberate imposition on a racial group of living conditions calculated to cause physical destruction of the group in whole or in part;

• Denying to a group basic human rights and freedom, right to freedom of movement and residence, the right to freedom of opinion and expression;

• Expropriation of land and property;

• Exploitation of labor of the members of a racial group; and

• Persecution of organizations or persons who oppose apartheid.

- Text of Apartheid Convention
  http://www.tamilnet.com/img/publish/2010/07/
  ApartheidConvention.pdf

- Rome Statute
  http://www.tamilnet.com/img/publish/2010/02/rome_statute.pdf

- Text of Genocide Convention
  http://www.tamilnet.com/img/publish/2010/07/
  GenocideConvention.pdf

Prof. Boyle pointed out that there is some degree of overlap between Apartheid Treaty and the Rome Statute of the International Criminal Court (ICC). He added that while Sri Lanka has avoided becoming signatory to the Rome Statute, the crimes against humanity fall into the category of peremptory norms, and the international laws are binding on Governments even when the countries are not signatories to the conventions.

Demand that US provide war crimes evidence to UN Panel, urges Boyle

[Tamilnet, Saturday, 13 November 2010, 20:45 GMT]

Pointing to the recent news stories on UN Sri Lanka Advisory Panel's willingness to review incriminating photographic evidence of graphic scenes with dead bodies blindfolded, hands bound and shot through the head, exposing alleged war crimes of Sri Lanka soldiers, Professor Boyle of University of Illinois, College of Law, said: "there is some precedent here in what happened to Milosevic. The Americans have all the intelligence the Tamils need. Tamil activists have to figure out a strategy to get the US Government to act."

Professor Boyle said, "[a]fter Milosovic started his campaign of aggression and genocide against the Kosovars, US Secretary of State Madeleine Albright met with the ICTY [International Criminal Tribunal - Yugoslavia] Prosecutor Louise Arbour and offered her US intelligence information to get him prosecuted. Arbour later prosecuted him for his crimes in Kosovo.

Acting U.S. Secretary of State Larry Eagleburger publicly condemns Karadzic

U.S. urges trials for Serb leaders

By Elaine Sciolino

The New York Times   17th Dec 1992

GENEVA — The United States named President Slobodan Milosevic of Serbia and other Serbian and Croatian political and military figures Wednesday as possible war criminals who should be tried someday by a "second Nuremberg" tribunal.

"We know that crimes against humanity have occurred, and we know when and where they occurred," Secretary of State Lawrence S. Eagleburger told delegates at a conference on the fighting in the Balkans. "We know, moreover, which forces committed those crimes, and under whose command they operated. And we know, finally, who the political leaders are and to whom those military commanders were — and still are — responsible."

Although once known for his close ties to Serbian leaders, in recent months Eagleburger has become the Bush administration's leading spokesman for war-crimes trials, calling for such a tribunal since August.

Eagleburger is a former American ambassador to Belgrade. This was the first time that the United States has made public a list of those who it argued should be tried for the crimes.

The call for a war-crimes tribunal to resemble the trial of major Nazi figures in Nuremberg after World War II was endorsed by Cyrus R. Vance and Lord Owen, the heads of a joint U.N.-European Community mediation effort.

Eagleburger

But the two mediators, who appealed for more time to negotiate a settlement to the war that has killed more than 17,000 and forced one million people from their homes, were clearly unenthusiastic about the American and French-backed campaign for a U.N. resolution enforcing a ban on Serbian flights over independent Bosnia and Herzegovina.

The mediators shared the British view that enforcement could endanger the lives of U.N. peacekeeping troops deployed on the ground and jeopardize the humanitarian effort. And they added their voices to the chorus of those who oppose lifting the U.N. arms embargo on all parties in the Balkan fighting.

The Bosnian government has sought an exemption from the embargo on the ground that it favors the Bosnian Serbs, who have continued to be well supplied by the Serbian-dominated Yugoslav army. Eagleburger had said he favored exempting the Bosnian government.

"Then I later convinced her successor Carla del Ponte to prosecute Milosevic for his crimes in Bosnia, on the grounds that her predecessor had indicted him for allegedly killing ten thousand in Kosovo and he had killed around ten thousand at Srebrenica alone. Del Ponte later expanded her investigation and indictment to include his crimes in Croatia as well. In Bosnia she indicted him for genocide, as I had requested," Professor Boyle said of his experience as the Counsel for the Mothers of Srebrenica and Podrinja

"United States Defense Department will have all the evidence necessary to indict Sri Lanka officials who were responsible for the 2009 May massacre. Expatriate Tamils have to keep working until they find a way to have this information accessible to UN prosecutors," Boyle said.

Michael Posner, Assistant Secretary of State for Human Rights, Harold Koh, US Legal Advisor for the State Department, Samantha Power, National Security Advisor for President Obama and who has done a lot of good work in Bosnia are key individuals who will be charting the US's policy on these matters, according to political sources in Washington.

With China, India rivalry escalating in the Indian Ocean, China's domination in Sri Lanka may open political space for India-US to take a more assertive course to the benefit of Tamils, Boyle speculated.

UN must produce a Congo-type war crimes report on Sri Lanka, says Prof. Boyle

[TamilNet, Friday, 19 November 2010, 05:12 GMT]

Reviewing the recently released 550-page United Nations Report of the Mapping Exercise Documenting the Most Serious Violations of Human Rights and International Humanitarian Law Committed Within the Territory of the Democratic Republic of the Congo (DRC), an article in the American Society of International Law (ASIL) said, "[t]he report detailing killings, rapes, destruction, and other violent attacks is alarming, not least because similar crimes continue to be committed in the DRC, where impunity still reigns large." Professor Boyle of Illinois College of Law, an expert in international law, commenting on the UN report said, "Tamils worldwide must demand the same "UN Mapping Report" of war crimes, crimes against humanity and genocide committed by the Government of Sri Lanka against the Tamils."

•   UN Report on Congo (6Mb)
    http://www.tamilnet.com/img/publish/2010/11/DRC_MAPPING_
    REPORT_Congo.pdf

•   UN maps Congo's serious crimes (150Kb)
    http://www.tamilnet.com/img/publish/2010/11/CongoMapsUN.pdf

The mapping exercise which began in July 2008, under the leadership of Luc Cote, a Canadian attorney experienced in investigating and prosecuting international crimes interviewed over 1,280 witnesses and gathered more than 1,500 documents throughout the DRC between October 2008 and May 2009, the article said.

The Report, submitted in June 2009 to the UN High Commissioner for Human Rights, was finalized in August 2010. After being leaked to the media, it was officially released two months later, in October 2010.

"The alleged killings of more than 40,000 Tamil civilians in Sri Lanka, and the atrocities committed by the Sri Lanka Security forces are eerily similar to or worse than the information unearthed by the UN Report on Congo that points to the perpetration of war crimes, crimes against humanity, and possible genocide within parts of the Republic of Congo," a spokesperson for Tamils Against Gencide (TAG), a US-based activist group said.

The ASIL article noting that "the prevailing impunity for yesterday's crimes often makes today's crimes possible, as those responsible are frequently the same perpetrators," concludes that "[i]n such circumstances, holding criminals accountable would help abate the cycle of violence."

"Even with an uncooperative Sri Lankan Government, using the Satellite technology available with the United States Defense Department and the United Nation's internal UNOSAT program, an International Investigative Panel should have at its disposal sufficient independent capacity to build a legally enforceable war-crimes charge sheet against Sri Lanka," TAG spokesperson added.

Admitting Rajapakse into US criminally similar to allowing in genocidaire Karadzic, says Boyle

[TamilNet, Thursday, 20 January 2011, 02:30 GMT]

Comparing alleged war-criminal and Sri Lanka's current President Rajapakse's reported admission into the United States to the Clinton administration's providing entry visa to genocidaire Radovan Karadzic to enter the U.S in order to attend the Vance-Owen Peace Negotiations in New York City, Professor Francis Boyle, expert in international law at the College of Law, University of Illinois, told TamilNet that Obama administration is obligated to apprehend, investigate and prosecute alleged genocidares for violating Geneva Convention and Genocide Convention. Obama administration giving Rajapakse visa to enter US and allowing him free movement is "Machiavellian Realpolitik at its worst," said Boyle.

"Why did the Obama administration give Rajapakse a Visa to enter the USA in the first place? Arguably if he were going only to UN Headquarters in New York, he would have a right to enter the country in order to do work at the U.N. under the terms of the U.N. Headquarters Agreement," said Boyle, adding, "But he has no right under international law to enter the USA itself.

"Indeed, the Conservative Reagan administration put Austrian President Kurt Waldheim on the Watch List and barred him from entering the country for mere alleged complicity in World War II war crimes—not ordering and supervising them like Rajapakse.

"Where are Michael Posner, Harold Koh, and Samantha Power?" Boyle asked in disbelief. Michael Posner is the Assistant Secretary, Bureau of Democracy, Human Rights, and Labor, Department of State, Samantha Power is in the National Security Council Staff, where she serves as a Special Assistant to the President and runs the Office of Multilateral Affairs and Human Rights, and Harold Koh is the Legal Adviser of the Department of State.

"Somewhat ironically and tragically, the Reagan administration had more respect for the Geneva Conventions than the allegedly "liberal" Obama administration. This is Machiavellian Realpolitik at its worst," said Boyle accusing the Obama administration for allowing Rajapakse to enter the U.S.

In a recent leak of US diplomatic cable, US Ambassador in Colombo, Ambassador Butenis, has openly acknowledged the complicity of Rajapakses in war-crimes in Sri Lanka.

"This reminds me of when the Clinton administration gave a Visa to the mass murderer, war criminal and genocidaire Radovan Karadzic to enter the country in order to attend the so-called Vance-Owen Peace Negotiations in New York City. Instead, the moment he set foot into the country the Clinton administration had an obligation to apprehend, investigate and prosecute Karadzic for violating the Geneva Conventions and the Genocide Convention. The same should be done by the Obama administration to Rajapakse," Boyle added.

Professor Francis A. Boyle was also a member of Board of Directors, Amnesty International USA (1988-1992).

The United States should investigate Sri Lankan President Mahinda Rajapkse, when he arrives on a surprise visit to the US this week, for his alleged role in perpetrating torture and war crimes, Amnesty International said Wednesday.

Spokesperson for US-based activist group Tamils Against Genocide (TAG) told TamilNet: "In the U.S. only the Justice Department can file criminal charges against individuals for war crimes. TAG's indictment document against Sri Lanka officials is already with the Justice Department. This document, together with the information collected by the State Department's war crimes division, and the recently made public contents of US diplomatic cables attaching culpability for war crimes on Rajapakses provide sufficient evidence that should exceed required "probable cause" standard to initiate investigations.

"Also, private citizens can file civil suit asking compensation for damages resulting from war-crimes. TAG intends to use this approach if the Justice Department does not act, or delays acting on, war crime charges," said the spokesperson.

Boyle reacts to UN report: "Creating Tamil Eelam the only remedy"

[TamilNet, Saturday, 16 April 2011, 23:25 GMT]

Reacting to the contents of the UN expert panel's report on Sri Lanka's war-crimes, Professor Boyle, expert in International Law, and Professor at the University of Illinois College of Law, told TamilNet, "there is absolutely no way the GOSL [Government of Sri Lanka] is going to implement any of them [panel's recommendations], and the GOSL has already rejected all of them, according to published reports. Therefore, under these circumstances of longstanding and ongoing genocide against them [the Tamils], the only effective remedy the Tamil People now have is to create the State of Tamil Eelam and move to have the International Community recognize it."

Professor Boyle added:

These excerpts support the worst conclusions that many of us drew during the course of the GOSL genocide against the Tamils in Vanni, which continues even today.

All Tamils must support Recommendation 1 (B) (ii) of the Report, that the U.N. Secretary General set up an International Commission of Inquiry on Sri Lanka to investigate GOSL war crimes, crimes against humanity, and genocide against the Tamils, by reference to and in accordance with the Statute of the International Criminal Court.

The U.N. Human Rights Council just recently established such a Commission on Libya. But given the Council's notorious bias in favor of Sri Lanka and against the Tamils, as recognized by this Report, the Council is not a viable mechanism for the establishment of that GOSL Commission.

The U.N. Secretary General must do it himself on behalf of the United Nations Organization itself. As for the rest of these Recommendations, there is absolutely no way the GOSL is going to implement any of them, and the GOSL has already rejected all of them, according to published reports.

Therefore, under these circumstances of longstanding and ongoing genocide against them, the only effective remedy the Tamil People now have is to create the State of Tamil Eelam and move to have the International Community recognize it. CREATE THE STATE OF TAMIL EELAM!

In Recommendations 4(A) the report states: The [UN] Human Rights Council should be invited to reconsider its May 2009 Special Session Resolution (A/HRC/8-11/L. 1/Rev. 2) regarding Sri Lanka, in light of this report.

Boyle had earlier commented[1] on the resolution: "This is one of the most unprincipled and shameless resolutions ever adopted by any body of the United Nations in the history of that now benighted Organization. It would be as if the U.N. Human Rights Council had congratulated the Nazi government for the "liberation" of the Jews in Poland after its illegal and genocidal invasion of that country in 1939."

---

[1] <http://tamilnet.com/art.html?catid=13&artid=29434>

Ban Ki-moon Accessory After the Fact to Sri Lanka war crimes, says Boyle

[TamilNet, Tuesday, 26 April 2011, 22:56 GMT]

Faulting UN Secretary General Ban Ki-moon for his continued "pattern and practice of criminal behavior by rejecting the recommendation of his own Panel that he appoint a Commission of Inquiry into GOSL war crimes and crimes against humanity against the Tamils," Professor Francis Boyle, expert in International Law and Professor at the University of Illinois School of Law, told TamilNet that "Ban Ki-moon is an absolute disgrace to the lofty standards of the United Nations Charter and the U.N. Declaration of Human Rights," and that Moon should be prevented from being elected for a second term.

Full text of the comment received from Prof. Boyle follows:

As documented in my book *The Tamil Genocide by Sri Lanka*, U.N. Secretary General Ban Ki-moon and many of his Staff aided and abetted and facilitated the GOSL genocide against around 50,000 Tamils in Vanni two years ago—about six times the number of victims of the genocidal massacre at Srebrenica.

He has now continued his pattern and practice of criminal behavior by rejecting the recommendation of his own Panel that he appoint a Commission of Inquiry into GOSL war crimes and crimes against humanity against the Tamils.

For that reason, Ban Ki-moon has now become an Accessory After The Fact to the GOSL war crimes, crimes against humanity and genocide against the Tamils.

Therefore, all Tamils around the world and the Government of India must actively work and do all in their power to make sure that Ban Ki-moon does not get a second term as U.N. Secretary General.

We need to put into power a new U.N. Secretary General who will implement the recommendations of the U.N. Panel and appoint a Commission of Inquiry into GOSL's international crimes against the Tamils.

He must go!

The sooner the better for all humanity!

Boyle: Word "Genocide" missing in UN Panel's war crimes report

[TamilNet, Saturday, 30 April 2011, 12:09 GMT]

Pointing out the instances where the criminal allegations on Sri Lanka made in the UN's war crimes report support the charge of genocide on Sri Lanka, Professor Francis Boyle, expert in International Law and Professor at the University of Illinois College of Law, told TamilNet, "[f]or obvious political reasons, no one wants to use the word "genocide." And that is because it then raises the question why did no one stop the genocide as required by article I of the Genocide Convention. The same phenomenon happened in Bosnia. No one would use the word "genocide" until afterwards, and it was too late to do anyone any good—they were all dead."

- Report of UN Secretary-General's Panel of Experts on Accountability in Sri Lanka (9Mb)
  <http://www.tamilnet.com/img/publish/2011/04/POE_Report_Full.pdf>

Boyle points to the accusation of "persecution" against Government of Sri Lanka (GoSL), in para 251, pg. 69: "The credible allegations supporting a finding of the crime against humanity of persecution insofar as the other acts listed here appear to have been committed on racial or political grounds against the Tamil population of the Vanni... "

This would support a genocide charge. And yet they (the members of UN panel) fail to get into genocide, Boyle says.

"Concerning their estimate that about 40,000 Tamils were exterminated by the GOSL in Vanni, that is about 5 times the 7000+ Bosnians exterminated at Srebrenica in 1995," and Prof Boyle provided the following analysis:

In its final Judgment on the merits in the Bosnia case that was issued in 2007, the World Court definitively agreed with me once and for all time that in order to constitute genocide, a state must only intend to destroy a "substantial part" of the group "as such":

198. In terms of that question of law, the Court refers to three matters relevant to the determination of "part" of the "group" for the purposes of Article II. In the first place, the intent must be to destroy at least a substantial part of the particular group. That is demanded by the very nature of the crime of genocide: since the object and purpose of the Convention as a whole is to prevent the intentional destruction of groups, the part targeted must be significant

enough to have an impact on the group as a whole. That requirement of substantiality is supported by consistent rulings of the ICTY and the International Criminal Tribunal for Rwanda (ICTR) and by the Commentary of the ILC to its Articles in the draft Code of Crimes against the Peace and Security of mankind (e.g. Krstić, IT-98-33-A, Appeals Chamber Judgment, 19 April 2004, paras. 8-11 and the cases of Kayishema, Byilishema, and Semanza there referred to; and Yearbook of the International Law Commission, 1996, Vol. II, Part Two, p. 45, para. 8 of the Commentary to Article 17).[1]

Furthermore, in paragraphs 293 and 294 of its 26 February 2007 Bosnian Judgment, the World Court found that you did not need six million exterminated people in order to constitute genocide. Rather, even the seven thousand murdered Bosnian Muslim men and boys at Srebrenica were enough to constitute genocide. These victims constituted about one-fifth of the Srebrenica community.

In this regard, I still serve as Attorney of Record for the Mothers of Srebrenica and Podrinja who constitute one of the primary groups of women survivors of that genocidal massacre still living in Bosnia today. I have personally toured the Killing Fields of Srebrenica with my Bosnian clients. I know genocide when I see it!

"The Report says nothing about genocide or the Genocide Convention. But I have already set forth the appropriate test from the ICJ's judgment in the Bosnian case and have discussed this at great length in my book *The Tamil Genocide by Sri Lanka*. So I am not going to repeat any of that analysis here," Prof Boyle said.

Commenting on the "para 229, p. 63 ...the State inexplicably excluded the ICRC, with its highly skilled family tracing services...," Professor Boyle explained, "the reason the ICRC was excluded and expelled was for the GOSL to better engage in enforced disappearances. Once registered with the ICRC, it becomes much harder to disappear someone."

For setting up these No Fire Zones, luring civilians in there, and then pouring artillery fire in there were clearly acts of treachery and thus war crimes, Prof Boyle said, "all those generals (detailed in pp 16-17) should be listed as presumptive war criminals."

US attaché clarification a linguistic legerdemain, accuses Boyle

[TamilNet, Monday, 06 June 2011, 00:03 GMT]

Response from the US State Department on the comments made this week by US defence attaché Lt. Col. Lawrence Smith in Colombo at the controversial 3-day seminar organised by the Sri Lankan military to expound on its defeat of the LTTE earlier this week that the remarks "reflected his personal opinions," and that "[t]hey [the comments] do not reflect the policy of the United States Government," was "all linguistic legerdemain by the United States Government," accused Professor Francis Boyle, an expert in International Law and a professor at the University of Illinois School of Law.

US defence attaché Lt. Col. Lawrence Smith

"This Defense Attaché is high-level Diplomatic Agent for the United States government protected by diplomatic privileges and immunities under international law and relevant treaties. He acts only pursuant to Instructions by his Government. Thus the United States government did accept the invitation by the GOSL to attend and participate in this Conference and to make this Statement," asserts Prof. Boyle.

"His [attaché's] Statement was made acting pursuant to Instructions by the United States government and represents the Official Position of the United States Government. In this case, he could have been acting pursuant to Instructions by the Pentagon and not by the State Department, which proves who really is conducting the foreign policy of the United States Government," Boyle explained, alerting the Tamil expatriate activists of the likely policy underpinning of US diplomatic behavior viś-a-viś Sri Lanka.

"As for the substance of his Statement, I see no point here in trying to establish precisely what happened during the denouement of the GOSL's genocidal massacre of about 50,000 Tamils in Vanni two years ago.

"That is why we need the U.N. Secretary General Ban Ki-moon to establish an International War Crimes Investigation Commission to look into it, which he has admitted he has the power to do unilaterally. Whatever these circumstances of surrender by LTTE leaders might have been, so long as they were waiving a White Flag or its functional Equivalent—and all reports indicate they were—they were not legitimate targets of attack. Killing someone waiving a White Flag or its Equivalent during armed combat is a serious war crime," Boyle said.

"Why did this US Defense Attaché, probably acting pursuant to Instructions by the Pentagon, want to muddy the waters and confuse the legal situation to the benefit of the GOSL?" Boyle further questioned the motivation behind the US Defense Attaché's conduct.

Boyle: Tamils safety possible only under separate state

[TamilNet, Sunday, 18 December 2011, 23:17 GMT]

Asserting that the "Tamils on the Island known as "Sri Lanka" have been the victims of genocide as defined by the 1948 Convention on the Prevention and Punishment of the Crime of Genocide," Francis A. Boyle, an expert in International Law, and a professor at the School of Law, University of Illinois, argues using the "remedial sovereignty" doctrine in support, and noting that "[h]istorically the only way a people who have been subjected to genocide like the Tamils on Sri Lanka have been able to protect themselves from further extermination has been the creation of an independent state of their own," and concludes, "[h]ence the need for the Tamils on Sri Lanka to create their own independent state in order to protect themselves from further extermination and total annihilation by Sri Lanka."

Full text of the article written by Boyle follows:

- Tamil Genocide by Sri Lanka
  <http://www.tamilnet.com/img/publish/2011/12/TGSL.pdf>

On 8 April 1993 and 13 September 1993 the author single-handedly won two World Court Orders on the basis of the 1948 Genocide Convention that were overwhelmingly in favor of the Republic of Bosnia and Herzegovina against Yugoslavia to cease and desist from committing all acts of genocide against the Bosnians.

The Tamils on the Island known as "Sri Lanka" have been the victims of genocide as defined by the 1948 Convention on the Prevention and Punishment of the Crime of Genocide.

I say that as the first person to have ever won anything from the International Court of Justice in The Hague (the so-called World Court of the United Nations System) on the basis of the Genocide Convention. And the fact that the Tamils living on "Sri Lanka" have been victims of genocide only strengthens and reinforces their right to self-determination under international law, including establishing their own independent State of Tamil Eelam if that is their desire.

Article II of the Genocide Convention defines the international crime of genocide in relevant part as follows: In the present Convention, genocide means any of the following acts committed with intent to destroy, in whole or in part, a national, ethnical, racial or religious group as such:

- (a)Killing members of the group;

- (b)Causing serious bodily or mental harm to members of the group;
- (c) Deliberately inflicting on the group conditions of life calculated to bring about its physical destruction in whole or in part; ....

Certainly the Sinhala-Buddhist Sri Lanka and its legal predecessor Ceylon have committed genocide against the Hindu/Christian Tamils that actually started on or about 1948 and has continued apace until today in violation of Genocide Convention Articles II(a), (b), and (c).

For the past six decades, the Sinhala-Buddhist Ceylon/Sri Lanka has implemented a systematic and comprehensive military, political, and economic campaign with the intent to destroy in substantial part the different national, ethnical, racial, and religious group constituting the Hindu/Christian Tamils. This Sinhala-Buddhist Ceylon/Sri Lanka campaign has consisted of killing members of the Hindu/Christian Tamils in violation of Genocide Convention Article II(a). This Sinhala-Buddhist Ceylon/Sri Lanka campaign has also caused serious bodily and mental harm to the Hindu/Christian Tamils in violation of Genocide Convention Article II(b). This Sinhala-Buddhist Ceylon/Sri Lanka campaign has also deliberately inflicted on the Hindu/Christian Tamils conditions of life calculated to bring about their physical destruction in substantial part in violation of Article II(c) of the Genocide Convention.

Since 1983 the Sinhala-Buddhist Ceylon/ Sri Lanka has exterminated approximately 150,000 Hindu/Christian Tamils. Nevertheless, apologists for Sri Lanka have argued that since these mass atrocities are not tantamount to the Nazi Holocaust against the Jews, therefore they do not qualify as "genocide." Previously, I had encountered and refuted this completely disingenuous, deceptive and bogus argument against labeling genocide for what it truly is, when I was the Lawyer for the Republic of Bosnia and Herzegovina arguing their genocide case against Yugoslavia before the International Court of Justice. There the genocidal Yugoslavia was represented by Shabtai Rosenne from Israel as their Lawyer against me. Rosenne proceeded to argue to the World Court that since he was an Israeli Jew, what Yugoslavia had done to the Bosnians was not the equivalent of the Nazi Holocaust against the Jews and therefore did not qualify as "genocide" within the meaning of the 1948 Genocide Convention.

I rebutted Rosenne by arguing to the World Court that you did not need an equivalent to the Nazi Holocaust against the Jews in order to find that wholesale atrocities constitute "genocide" in violation of the 1948 Genocide Convention. Indeed the entire purpose of the 1948 Genocide Convention was to prevent another Nazi Holocaust against the Jews. That is why Article I of the Genocide Convention clearly provided: "The Contracting Parties confirm that genocide, whether committed in time of peace or in time of war, is a crime under international law which they undertake *to prevent* and to punish." (Emphasis supplied.) You did not need six million dead human beings in order to constitute "genocide."

Furthermore, in support of my 1993 genocide argument to the World Court for Bosnia, I submitted that Article II of the 1948 Genocide Convention expressly provided: "In the present Convention, genocide means any of the following acts committed with the intent to destroy, in whole or *in part*, a national, ethical, racial or religious group, as such..." (Emphasis supplied.) In other words, that to be guilty of genocide a government did not have to intend to destroy the "whole" group as the Nazis intended to do with the Jews. Rather, a government can be guilty of genocide if it intends to destroy a mere "part" of the group. Certainly Yugoslavia did indeed intend to exterminate all Bosnian Muslims if they could have gotten away with it, as manifested by their subsequent mass extermination of at least 7,000 Bosnian Muslim men and boys at Srebrenica in July of 1995.

But in 1993 it was not necessary for me to argue to the World Court that Yugoslavia intended to exterminate all the Bosnian Muslims. Rather, I argued to the World Court that at that point in time the best estimate was that Yugoslavia had exterminated about 250,000 Bosnians out of the population of about 4 million Bosnians, including therein about 2.5 million Bosnian Muslims. Therefore, I argued to the World Court that these dead victims constituted a "substantial part" of the group and that the appropriate interpretation of the words "or in part" set forth in Article II of the Genocide Convention should mean a "substantial part."

The World Court emphatically agreed with me and rejected Rosenne's specious, reprehensible, and deplorable arguments. So on 8 April 1993 the International Court of Justice issued an Order for three provisional measures of protection on behalf of the Republic of Bosnia and Herzegovina against Yugoslavia that were overwhelmingly in favor of Bosnia to cease and desist from committing all acts of genocide against all the Bosnians, both directly and indirectly. This World Court Order for the indication of provisional measures of protection was the international equivalent of a U.S. domestic Temporary Restraining Order and Injunction combined. The same was true for the Second World Court Order with three additional provisional measures of protection that I won for the Republic of Bosnia and Herzegovina against Yugoslavia on 13 September 1993 on the basis of the 1948 Genocide Convention.

In its final Judgment on the merits in the Bosnia case that was issued in 2007, the World Court definitively agreed with me once and for all time that in order to constitute genocide, a state must only intend to destroy a "substantial part" of the group "as such":

198. In terms of that question of law, the Court refers to three matters relevant to the determination of "part" of the "group" for the purposes of Article II. In the first place, the intent must be to destroy at least a substantial part of the particular group. That is demanded by the very nature of the crime of genocide: since the object and purpose of

the Convention as a whole is to prevent the intentional destruction of groups, the part targeted must be significant enough to have an impact on the group as a whole. That requirement of substantiality is supported by consistent rulings of the ICTY and the International Criminal Tribunal for Rwanda (ICTR) and by the Commentary of the ILC to its Articles in the draft Code of Crimes against the Peace and Security of mankind (e.g. Krstić, IT-98-33-A, Appeals Chamber Judgment, 19 April 2004, paras. 8-11 and the cases of Kayishema, Byilishema, and Semanza there referred to; and Yearbook of the International Law Commission, 1996, Vol. II, Part Two, p. 45, para. 8 of the Commentary to Article 17).

In other words, in order to find Sri Lanka guilty of genocide against the Tamils, it is not required to prove that Sri Lanka has the intention to exterminate all Tamils. Rather, all that is necessary is to establish that Sri Lanka intended to destroy a "substantial part" of the Tamils living on Sri Lanka.

Furthermore, in paragraphs 293 and 294 of its 26 February 2007 Bosnian Judgment, the World Court found that you did not even need 250,000 exterminated Bosnians in order to constitute genocide, let alone six million exterminated Jews. Rather, even the seven thousand exterminated Bosnian Muslim men and boys at Srebrenica were enough to constitute genocide. According to the World Court, these victims constituted about one-fifth of the Srebrenica community. Certainly since the World Court ruled in its 2007 Judgment that the extermination of 7000 Bosnians at Srebrenica constituted "genocide," then a fortiori Sri Lanka's extermination of 50,000 Tamils in Vanni two years later in 2009 also constituted genocide.

Historically the only way a people who have been subjected to genocide like the Tamils on Sri Lanka have been able to protect themselves from further extermination has been the creation of an independent state of their own. Indeed as the entire world witnessed during the first six months of 2009, Sri Lanka wantonly, openly, shamelessly, and gratuitously exterminated over 50,000 Tamils in Vanni. Yet not one state in the entire world rose to protect them or defend them or help them as required by Article I of the 1948 Genocide Convention. Hence the need for the Tamils on Sri Lanka to create their own independent state in order to protect themselves from further extermination and total annihilation by Sri Lanka.

International law and practice establish that an independent state of their own is the only effective protection as well as the only appropriate reparation for a people who have been the victims of genocide. Bosnia's Statehood was the only thing that prevented the Bosnians from going the same way the Jews did in 1939. The creation of the Independent State of Tamil Eelam will be the only thing preventing the Tamils on Sri Lanka from going the way of history. Create Tamil Eelam!

No amnesty for war criminals, says UN's Navi Pillay

[TamilNet, Sunday, 08 January 2012, 04:01 GMT]

Granting amnesty to perpetrators of war crimes and human rights abuses under Yemen's presidential power transition deal would be against international law, the United Nations human rights chief said on Friday, undermining the peace agreement, Reuters reported. The implications of this to pending litigation of sitting and ex-Presidents in courts around the world are significant according to legal sources in Washington. Professor Francis Boyle commented that while the UN pronouncements were directed towards Yemen, for bringing the culpable Sri Lanka leaders to justice for crimes committed during the Mu'l'livaaykkaal massacre, continued action outside Sri Lanka by Tamil expatriates was crucial.

Professor Boyle in a note sent to TamilNet said: "The GOSL [Government of Sri Lanka] are so brazen in their genocidal criminality that they are not even going to bother giving themselves "amnesty." They will continue to tough it out and figure they can get away with it forever. So far every government in the world including and especially India has let them do so, as well as the United Nations Organization. It is up to us People to turn the situation around and hold the GOSL accountable. 50,000 massacred Tamils in Vanni demand no less of our Common Humanity!"

Noting that Pillay has previously blamed Yemeni government forces for using live ammunition against unarmed protesters and has said President Ali Abdullah Saleh should not get amnesty in a deal to persuade him to leave power, Reuters summarized Navi Pillay's statement as follows:

"I have been closely following the events in Yemen, particularly the very contentious debate about an amnesty law to be presented to Parliament shortly."

"International law and the U.N. policy are clear on the matter: amnesties are not permissible if they prevent the prosecution of individuals who may be criminally responsible for international crimes including war crimes, crimes against humanity, genocide, and gross violations of human rights."

"Based on information we have gathered, there is reason to believe that some of these crimes were committed in Yemen during the period for which an amnesty is under consideration. Such an amnesty would be in violation of Yemen's international human rights obligations."

Saudi Arabia has supported Saleh by donating diesel and crude oil and the United States, which long backed Saleh as a pillar of its "counter-terrorism" strategy, helped craft the power transition deal giving him immunity from prosecution, Reuters report said.

Boyle: US should publicly accuse Colombo of committing war crimes

[TamilNet, Monday, 30 January 2012, 00:40 GMT]

Pointing to the recent investigative reports in media outlets noting US may possess crucial supporting material to incriminating evidence from senior military commanders of Colombo committing warcrimes, to exposures on Wikileaks of Colombo-based US Ambassadors' reported knowledge of high level Sri Lanka officials' complicity to war crimes, and to incriminating reports from the UN and NGOs on alleged war-crimes, Professor Boyle of University of Illinois, College of Law, said, in similar circumstances Secretary of State Eagleburger accused Radovan Karadzic of committing war-crimes during the Bosnian genocide, and the Obama administration can, and should, do the same thing to political and military leaders in Colombo.

Acting U.S. Secretary of State Larry Eagleburger publicly condemns Karadzic

In a note sent to TamilNet, Professor Boyle said, "Under similar circumstances during the Bosnian genocide, U.S. Secretary of State Lawrence Eagleburger under President Bush Sr. publicly accused Bosnian Serb President Radovan Karadzic of committing war crimes and crimes against humanity, on the basis of evidence compiled by the US Government, though he did not go so far as to accuse Karadzic of genocide because of the political implications.

"But it seems to me that Secretary of State Clinton or at least Assistant Secretary of State for Human Rights Mike Posner can and should do the same here. If the Bush Sr. administration did the right thing for the Bosnians, then certainly and a fortiori the Obama administration can and should do the right thing for the Tamils."

In addition to the evidence that has been emerging recently, Prof. Boyle said earlier, "United States Defense Department will have all the evidence necessary to indict Sri Lanka officials who were responsible for the 2009 May massacre. Expatriate Tamils have to keep working until they find a way to have this information accessible to UN prosecutors."

Boyle: Appointing alleged war criminals to UN posts a violation of UN Charter

[TamilNet, Wednesday, 08 February 2012, 05:30 GMT]

While Ban Ki-moon's spokesman Martin Nesirky insisted that Ban is powerless to stop the proposed appointment of alleged war criminal Shavendra Silva to an UN adviser position, Professor Boyle, an expert in international law, said, "U.N. Secretary-General has a Charter obligation to determine that the terms of article 101(3) have been satisfied before he appoints someone to the Staff irrespective of any alleged recommendation by the General Assembly," and therefore, "Ban to appoint a presumptive war criminal to his Staff would be ultra vires his powers under the terms of article 101(3) and thus a violation of the Charter itself."

Text of the legal note Professor Boyle sent to TamilNet follows:

The United Nations Charter establishes Six Independent Organs: The Security Council, the General Assembly, the Economic and Social Council, the Trusteeship Council , the Secretariat, and the International Court of Justice. The U.N. Charter was deliberately drafted so that no one Organ had the right to order around any other Organ. Chapter XV of the Charter sets forth the independent powers and responsibilities of The Secretariat. According to article 97 thereof, the Secretary-General is the chief administrative officer of the United Nations Organization.

Article 101 of the Charter provides: "The staff shall be appointed by the Secretary-General under regulations established by the General Assembly."

However, these General Assembly regulations cannot trump the terms of the Charter itself. In this regard, article 101(3) clearly states: "The paramount consideration in the employment of the staff and in the determination of the conditions of service shall be the necessity of securing the highest standards of efficiency, competence, and integrity."

The U.N. Secretary-General has a Charter obligation to determine that the terms of article 101(3) have been satisfied before he appoints someone to the Staff irrespective of any alleged recommendation by the General Assembly. Certainly the U.N. Secretary-General has a Charter obligation to reject a presumptive war criminal for appointment to the Staff on the grounds of his prima facie absence of "integrity."

Indeed, for the U.N. Secretary General to appoint a presumptive war criminal to his Staff would be ultra vires his powers under the terms of article 101(3) and thus a violation of the Charter itself.

For these reasons, the U.N. Secretary General must reject both Silva and Kohona for any U.N. Staff Appointment.

Inner City Press reported that even many member states describe the appointments as a travesty or a "new low," and say they are pushing Sri Lanka to pull Silva back, even if only to replace him with Permanent Representative Palitha Kohona, who also played a role in the White Flag killing of prospective surrenderees, along with Ban's chief of staff Vijay Nambiar.

Professor Francis A. Boyle taught United Nations Law in the College of Harvard University during the 1976-1977 Academic Year, and later at the University of Illinois College of Law in Champaign. See his *Foundations of World Order* (Duke University Press: 1999).

Boyle warns Tamil diaspora against "Stall and Delay" diplomacy at UNHRC

[TamilNet, Tuesday, 13 March 2012, 23:55 GMT]

Noting the U.S. ambassador to UNHRC Eileen Donahoe's statement that the resolution forwarded by the U.S. has been toned down from an earlier version that sought a government action plan on accountability and reconciliation by June, to now calling for the U.N. Human Rights Commissioner to report to the Council a year from now on the steps Sri Lanka has taken," Professor Boyle, an expert in international law and a keen observer of Sri Lanka politics, said the U.S. Government is going along with the Government of Sri Lanka (GoSL) strategy to run the clock out on the Tamils, just as the Israelis are doing to the Palestinians with USA support. The Tamil diaspora and supporters like us should not fall into this trap, but instead come up with a entirely new strategy."

"I served as Legal Adviser to the Palestinian Delegation to the Middle East Peace Negotiations starting in the Fall of 1991. Since that time, Israel's strategy has always been to STALL AND DELAY while they destroy the Palestinians.

"The entire world is going along with that strategy. GoSL is doing the same thing to the Tamils here. And the entire world is going along with it. We are being treated like the Palestinians. We need to come up with an entirely new strategy.

"If we proceed down this path there will never be GoSL accountability for anything. GoSL will drag it all out until the Tamils are dead. Stall for time until the clock runs out like at a basketball game or a football game when your side is ahead. GoSL is trying to run out the clock on us," Boyle said in a note sent to TamilNet.

Boyle compares Syria action, dismisses UNHRC resolution as a "fraud"

[TamilNet, Friday, 06 April 2012, 23:53 GMT]

Dismissing the US sponsored United Nations Human Rights Council Resolution as "a fraud," Professor Francis Boyle, an expert in international law, said, "if the US were serious about Government of Sri Lanka (GoSL) genocide, crimes against humanity and war crimes against the Tamils, US would have done something like it did to Syria this week." The U.S. State Department established a Clearinghouse on Syria and provided $1.25m to assist to "collect, collate, analyze, and securely store evidence, documentation, and other information concerning human rights abuses and violations, while protecting witnesses and sources."

While the conduct of the Syrian Government is similar to that of the Rajapakse Government in its crimes committed against the Tamils, the number of people affected in Syria is an order of magnitude less than that in Sri Lanka.

Boyle pointed out that until U.S. takes action similar to that it has taken against Syria in helping the Tamils to "collect, collate, analyze, and securely store evidence" that will enable the victims to "develop case dossiers that could support prosecutions in Syrian, hybrid, or international courts," diaspora should not be optimistic about U.S.'s intentions.

Full text of the announcement on Syria by the State Department follows:

Recognizing that perpetrators of gross violations of human rights in Syria must be held to account, and that the Syrian people will lead the way, the United States will work with international partners to establish a Syria Accountability Clearinghouse that will support Syrian and international efforts to promote accountability. By providing a forum for coordination, the Clearinghouse will advance efforts to assist and train the Syrian people and partner organizations to collect, collate, analyze, and securely store evidence, documentation, and other information concerning human rights abuses and violations, while protecting witnesses and sources. The record that is compiled could be used for a broad range of transitional justice and reconciliation processes, including truth-seeking, memorialisation, and prosecutions. These efforts will also help develop trial-ready dossiers against individuals responsible for violations of international or domestic criminal law. The Clearinghouse will be guided by a Steering Committee of representatives of the Syrian people, cooperating states, and regional organizations.

Projects that could be coordinated via the Syria Accountability Clearinghouse would aim to:

• Train and mentor Syrian investigators/lawyers, human rights actors, and other NGOs/independent actors to collect information about the full range of human rights abuses and violations.

• Establish a secure storage facility, including a database, for collected information.

• Establish protection and security best practices and procedures and seek assistance from states to implement them.

• Establish a "Prosecutors' Unit" to collect and analyze available evidence and develop case dossiers that could support prosecutions in Syrian, hybrid, or international courts.

There may also be ways for the Clearinghouse to complement the efforts of the Office of the High Commissioner for Human Rights, which is facilitating safe and secure storage of information and evidence collected by the Commission of Inquiry.

The Syria Accountability Clearinghouse will maintain secure virtual linkages with affiliated groups and organizations around the world, including in Syria. The United States will provide an initial $1.25 million to support the Clearinghouse and related accountability efforts, and ask other partner nations and organizations to provide additional funding and support for these accountability efforts. While the US sponsored resolution's thrust was in the implementation of the recommendations of the LLRC, the recent "factual supplement" on Sri Lanka's war released by the US Office of Global Criminal Justice headed by Ambassador Stephen Rapp, pointed out the serious defects of the LLRC in addressing the International Humanitarian, and Human Rights Law violations.

Veteran Tamil activist and humanist reaches 88 in exile

[TamilNet, Monday, 23 April 2012, 20:06 GMT]

Solomon Arulanandam David (S.A. David), popularly known as Gandhiyam David, who presided the Gandhian movement which spread simple agriculture, self-sustenance, and importance to early education as a way of life in the deprived villages of Tamil Eelam for nearly a decade from 1972, reaches 88-years Tuesday as he spends his older years among his friends in Chennai. TamilNet extends its wishes to Mr David as it recognizes his unique and selfless contribution to Northeast Tamils and the hill-country Tamils displaced by Sinhala intimidation, riots and pogroms in the 1970s and 80s. David was assisted by another humanist of the 70s, the late Dr Rajasundaram. Rajasundaram was killed in the Welikade prison massacre in 1983, whereas his friend, David, escaped, re-incarcerated in Batticaloa jail to escape again in the famous Batticaloa jail break.

David's contribution in the history of the struggle of Eezham Tamils is that at the inception of the armed struggle he had conceived the importance of a grassroots civil movement to accompany it.

S.A. David at 88

Threatened by the popularity of the spreading Tamil cultural consolidation and self-reliance in the most underdeveloped areas of the Northeast, and the opportunities presented to fleeing hill-country Tamils to begin life anew in the Northeast, Colombo framed charges against Mr

David and Dr Rajasundaram under the Prevention of Terrorism Act (PTA) and jailed both, according to reports.

Dr Rajasunderam was killed in the Welikade Prison massacre of June 1983. Mr David escaped Welikade massacre, but was later taken to Batticaloa prison. Tamil prisoners decided to break out of the prison, and in the successful jail break, twenty prisoners escaped first, and Mr David was taken by a supporter through the jungles to Poonakari from where he found his way to Rameswaram by boat.

David has been living in exile in Anna Nagar in Chennai. He has been critical of how the Tamil refugees, who fled violence and repression in Sri Lanka, are being treated in India being denied of freedom of movement and right to citizenship.

Talking to TamilNet from his Anna Nagar Residence, Mr David said, "I appeal to the expatriate Tamils to continue the struggle in the Gandhian way to impose the moral responsibility on the leading Governments of the West to facilitate the birth of Tamil Eelam. There is no question in my mind that Tamils have the right to live freely in their own homeland.

"Studying Thirukkural is a must for the future generations of Eezham Tamils," Mr David said, reflecting his solid grounding on the Gandhian principles that motivated his work with the Tamil people in Vanni in the 1970s.

Mr. David added, "I salute Professor Francis Boyle's contributions to our struggle, and when the time is appropriate I am certain that he will help our people to fight the legal battle in the International Court of Justice (ICJ), and in the International Criminal Court (ICC), if the Security Council accepts to take our case."

Excerpts from Mr David's biography follows:

In 1972, I came back to Sri Lanka to devote myself heart and soul to alleviate the suffering of my people, the Tamils. After intense study by reading and personal observation of many systems around the world in Europe, America, Israel, Africa and Far East I chose the Gandhian model as most suited to the genius and traditions of the soul of my people and proceeded to systematically bring my people to the Gandhian way of life.

Together with Dr. Rajasunderam of Vavuniya, a tireless energetic worker, in five years we had built up a sound network of District Centers throughout the traditional homelands of the Tamils in the island of Sri Lanka, in Jaffna, Kilinochchi, Mannar, Mullaitivu, Vavuniya, Trincomalee and Batticaloa. At the time of our arrest, 450 pre-schools with an average of thirty students each were providing daily milk and triposha and Kindergarten teaching facilities to village children.

Twelve model one-acre farms in Vavuniya, Trincomalee and Batticaloa were showing the villagers the simplest safest and quickest way to economic, social and cultural revival. Mobile clinics equipped with basic preventive and curative medicine were making regular rounds to outlying villages. A training center was preparing thirty to forty young women, every three months, for Gandhian work in their own villages. In addition, Gandhian with other social service organizations was assisting 5000 refugee families from Tea Estates to settle down to safe life among the traditional Tamil villages.

The quality and quantity of Gandhian work impressed Foreign Aid Organizations and Tamils living overseas so much that we were receiving and operating on an yearly budget of Rs. 5,000,000/-.

All the time we were aware that the Sinhala Government was keeping its watchful eye over us. In April 1983 the Government took the decisive step to arrest me and Dr. Rajasundaram.

The charges on which we were arrested as told in the indictment given to us on 22 July 1983, three and a half months after the arrest and solitary confinement, torture of body and mind were:

o Meeting Uma Maheswaran and not informing the police
o Meeting Santhathiar and not informing the police
o Assisting Uma and Santhathiar to escape to India

We could be sentenced to fifteen to twenty years of imprisonment on these charges.

I have experienced partial freedom and enjoyed it. I wanted total freedom for myself and my people. Instead, I was caught up in total bondage. It was hell. Now I realize total freedom would be heaven indeed.

The following is a response from Professor Francis A. Boyle, the author of *The Tamil Genocide by Sri Lanka*, to Mr S.A. David:

Dear Friend:
Thank you very much for your kind and gracious tribute to me. It is most greatly appreciated coming from someone who has worked so hard and suffered so much for the Tamils in Sri Lanka. I do look forward to meeting with you personally the next time I lecture in Chennai. And I hope you have a wonderful 88th Birthday Celebration. STOLAT!
Professor Francis A. Boyle

Exiled in Chennai, Mr David has been following the progress of, and writing about, the struggles of the Tamil refugees in different countries.

"Yearning for the homeland," a book on S. A. David in Tamil by Nanjil Natarasan is expected to be released at an event on the 29th in Anna Nagar felicitating Mr David's 88th birthday. The book is available with Kaanthalakam, Sasirekha, Chennai (tamilnool@tamilnool.com).

Mr Maravanpulavu K. Sachithananthan, continuing in his activities for the Tamil cause, was associated with Mr David during the Gandhian period. He currently provides moral support to Mr David.

Mr David's last wish, his friend Sachithananthan said, is that his body is buried in the Vanni area when Tamil Eelam becomes a reality.

ICC a fraud, only goes after Africa's tin-pot dictators, says Boyle

[TamilNet, Sunday, 03 June 2012, 00:09 GMT]

Commenting on the recent sentencing of Charles Taylor by the UN's Special Court for Sierra Leone (SC-SL) for 50 years and the ruling by the UN's International Criminal Tribunal for Rwanda (ICTR) giving life imprisonment to Rwanda's Nzabonimana, Professor Boyle, an expert in International Law, who teaches at the University of Illinois College of Law, told TamilNet, that UN's "International Criminal Court (ICC) has become a joke and a fraud. I supported it originally. But no more. It has no credibility whatsoever. It [ICC] just goes after tin-pot dictators in Africa while real war criminals such as Bush...get off scot-free... I am keeping Rajapakses et al on my list of things to do," Boyle said.

Tamil circles, while not disagreeing with this harsh assessment of the U.N., say that the sheer weight of Sri Lanka's brutality amounting to genocide will ultimately force the UN to take action against the ruling Rajapakse family and Sri Lanka, if the diaspora and the rights organizations are successful in keeping the memory of the Mu'l'livaaykkaal massacre alive.

- SC-SL Decision on Charles Taylor
  <http://www.tamilnet.com/img/publish/2012/06/SC-SL-Taylor_Decision.pdf>

Charles Taylor, former President of Liberia

Judge Lussick, an Australian-born Samoan, and two other judges calling the crimes committed by Charles Taylor, the former president of Liberia, in the neighbouring country of Sierra Leone as "some of the most heinous and brutal crimes recorded in human history," sentenced the 64-year old Taylor that will exceed his life span.

Abetting mass murder, rape and amputation is a truly extraordinary crime deserving an extraordinary punishment, and the court took the position that Mr. Taylor's status as a head of state at the time of the offences was an aggravating factor; a public trust had been betrayed, said Canada's *Globe and Mail*.

"Any head of state or government should take pause before authorizing aid to armed factions in civil wars which may turn out to be viciously barbarous. Presidents and prime ministers should long remember Charles Taylor," the paper warned.

- ICTR Decision on Nzabonimana
<http://www.tamilnet.com/img/publish/2012/06/ICTR-Nzaboni
mana_Judgement_120531-Summary.pdf>

Callixte Nzabonimana, former Rwandan youth minister

Meanwhile, within a week after the Taylor judgement, the International Criminal Tribunal for Rwanda (ICTR) found former Rwandan youth minister Callixte Nzabonimana guilty of playing a key role in the genocide, conspiracy, incitement and extermination of nearly 800,000 minority Tutsis and politically moderate Hutus in 100 days between April and June 1994.

A meeting held in the town of Murambi, in the central Gitarama province led to "an agreement" between Nzabonimana and other ministers "to encourage the killing of Tutsis... with the specific intent to destroy, in whole or in part, the Tutsi population as such in Gitarama prefecture," the AFP said referring to the court's verdict.

UN culpable under "complicity clause," says Professor Boyle

[TamilNet, Sunday, 18 November 2012, 22:22 GMT]

Dismissing the "recommendations" of the Petrie report as "UN double talk" similar to the language used by the UN to excuse UN's complicity in the Srebrenica massacre, Professor Boyle, an expert in International Law, said that the Petrie report, however, provides legal evidence to establish UN's culpability on the element of "complicity" to war crimes and genocide, as defined in the Article 3(e) of 1948 Genocide Convention. Further, Boyle said, contrary to the claims in the Petrie report, the UN Secretary General (UNSG) has independent powers, and need not adhere to the dictates of the Security Council.

Noting the reasoning in Para-18, that "without clear Security Council support, the UN felt it could not play a lead role and made no attempt to implement a comprehensive strategy," Boyle said, "the UNSG has independent powers under Chapter 15 and Article 99 of the Charter. The SG is not an agent of the Security Council. Rather the Secretariat is one of 6 Independent Organs of the UNO. This is just a cop-out by Ban Ki-moon (BKM). He had the authority to act and he should have acted and he refused to act. Either the Americans pressured him or else he did not care," Boyle said. "Once again in my book *The Tamil Genocide by Sri Lanka* I made the case for complicity in genocide by BKM. I stand by those conclusions," Boyle added.

- Report of the Secretary-General's Internal Review Panel on United Nations action in Sri Lanka
  <http://www.tamilnet.com/img/publish/2012/11/The_Internal_Review_Panel_report_on_Sri_Lanka.pdf>

In Para-33, the Petri report criticizes the UN on lack of meeting on Sri Lanka: "Throughout the final stages of the conflict, Member States did not hold a single formal meeting on Sri Lanka, whether at the Security Council, the Human Rights Council or the General Assembly."

- Convention on the Prevention and Punishment of the Crime of Genocide
  <http://www.tamilnet.com/img/publish/2012/01/CPPCG.pdf>

Boyle comments: "UNSG had the power to convene an Emergency Meeting of the Security Council, but refused. BKM had the legal authority and the responsibility to act and he failed and refused to do that. That is the essence of complicity in crimes, including genocide.

"Realistically one cannot expect UN humanitarian and unarmed officials on the ground to risk their lives if they do not want to, which is different from the UN peacekeeping force at Srebrenica. But BKM should have been doing all he could have under his independent powers under Article 19 and Chapter 15 of the Charter to stop the Vanni Genocide. He did not. He should have. That makes him an accomplice," Boyle said.

Comments on other salient paragraphs in the Petrie report that caught Professor Boyle's attention, follow:

- Para-22: Notice UN DPA admitting that they "would be complicit if they did not act on it." In other words, mens rea. Criminal intent
- Para-25: UN briefed on Tiger atrocities but not GOSL atrocities. a whitewash, more complicity.
- Para-26: More whitewashing of GOSL crimes. UN aiding and abetting GOSL crimes, including genocide.
- Para-28/29: More whitewashing and covering up of GOSL crimes by UN.
- Para-50: Boyle dismisses as "Nonsense." These UN officials knew exactly what they were not doing and why they were not doing it. These are highly competent and intelligent people. Obviously, the UNSG did not give the order and the resources to get the job done. People were deliberately stalling and delaying. This was malfeasance, not negligence, by the UN and SG.
- Para-52/53: UN deliberately understated GOSL atrocities so as to avoid international cries of war crimes, crimes against humanity and genocide that would have produced international pressure on the UN Security Council to act. More BKM/UN complicity with GOSL crimes if not worse.
- Para-54: Reflects mercenary motive of the UN.
- Para-55: Why did UN refuse to assist and protect surrendered LTTE. They were out of combat under Geneva Convention Article 3 and were entitled to all the protections in there at a minimum.
- Para-61: Yes, no one kept a written record because they did not want to incriminate themselves in writing.
- Para-63: A sick joke and a demented fraud that the Special Adviser on Genocide would not speak out. That was his job. He deliberately failed and refused to perform it and thus became an accomplice himself.
- Para-69: UNSG BKM should have gone to the UN General Assembly. Boyle cites the example of Second UN Secretary General Hammarskjold, who Boyle said would have gone to the General Assembly as he did during his leadership.
- Para-71: BKM should have convened an emergency meeting of the Security Council under article 99.
- Para-70: Notice UN already had the Channel 4 information and refused to do anything with it.

- Para-73: Another instance of whitewash of malfeasance and complicity by BKM.
- Para-76: This was a case of UN malfeasance and complicity, not negligence and nonfeasance or misfeasance.

Referring to Para-77, where the report states, "the Security Council was deeply ambivalent about even placing on its agenda a situation that was not already the subject of a UN peacekeeping or political mandate; while at the same time no other UN Member State mechanism had the prerogative to provide the political response needed, leaving Sri Lanka in a vacuum of inaction," Boyle points out "basically UN is admitting that they did what the Permanent 5 on the Security Council wanted them to do, which was nothing."

Systemic disappearances qualify as crimes against humanity in ICC, says Boyle

[TamilNet, Wednesday, 26 December 2012, 22:46 GMT]

The enforced disappearances of human beings that are widespread and systematic, such as the abductions of Tamils in the North East including the midnight abduction of 28-year-old Mrs Soundararajan Sivamalar in Uduvil, Jaffna, on Christmas eve by Sri Lanka's Terrorism Division, are a Crime against Humanity under the Rome Statute for the International Criminal Court (ICC), Professor Boyle of the University of Illinois College of Law said. "So if Gotobhaya travels to an ICC Member State, it might be possible to get him prosecuted in the visiting country under its domestic implementing legislation for the Rome Statute," Boyle said.

Spokesperson for Tamils Against Genocide (TAG), a US-based activist group said, "While we are fighting to overturn the protection given to the primary genocidaire, Mahinda Rajapakse, by the United States Department of State under the extra-legal and discretionary application of the doctrine of Head of State Immunity, we will not have a similar issue with sibling Gotabhaya Rajakapakse, when he travels to a ICC signatory state," TAG said.

Boyle added, "under the ICC Rome Statute, it is a requirement that member states enact domestic implementing legislation making ICC Rome Statute Crimes domestic crimes as well. Hence it might be possible to prosecute Gotobaya under these domestic ICC Crimes even if the ICC does not have jurisdiction.

"This is how the objectors scared President Bush out of traveling to Switzerland by demanding his prosecution if he showed up there under their domestic implementing legislation for the ICC even though the USA is not a party to the Rome Statute," Boyle added.

- ICC-Australia's Implementing Legislation
  http://www.tamilnet.com/img/publish/2012/12/ICCAustralia.pdf

Most of Europe now has domestic implementing legislation for the ICC. International Criminal Court Act No. 41, 2002 facilitates compliance by Australia with obligations under the Rome Statute of the International Criminal Court, and for related purposes.

Systematic rape of Tamils violates Genocide Convention, says Prof. Boyle

[TamilNet, Wednesday, 27 February 2013, 00:51 GMT]

Professor Boyle, an expert in International Law and who represented nearly 40,000 raped Women of Bosnia and argued their case for genocide before the International Court of Justice (ICJ) in The Hague, commenting on the Human Rights Watch (HRW) report, "Sri Lanka: Rape of Tamil detainees," said, "[c]learly, this continuing Campaign of widespread and systematic rape by the Government of Sri Lanka against the Tamils violates Article II(b) of the 1948 Genocide Convention, to which Sri Lanka is a contracting party."

The relevant part of article II states:
"In the present Convention, genocide means any of the following acts committed with intent to destroy, in whole or in part, a national, ethnical, racial or religious group as such:

...

(b) Causing serious bodily or mental harm to members of the group;...."

According to Article I of the Genocide Convention, all of the Contracting Parties thereto (which includes most of the civilized word) "undertake to prevent and to punish" these acts of genocide against the Tamils by the GOSL, Professor Boyle said, and asked, "Where is the United Nations Security Council? Its Permanent Members? The United States, Britain, France, Europe and India? The U.N. Human Rights Council?

"The United Nations Secretary General? And his Special Advisor on the Prevention of Genocide?

"They are all derelict in their duties under the Genocide Convention and the jus cogens customary international law obligations "to prevent and to punish" the ongoing GOSL genocide against the Tamils. They have all become Accessories After The Fact to the GOSL genocide against the Tamils in violation of Article III(e) of the Genocide Convention that criminalizes their "(e) Complicity in genocide," Professor Boyle said.

As the Lawyer for the Republic of Bosnia and Herzegovina during Yugoslavia's War of Extermination against the Bosnians, Professor Boyle represented raped Women of Bosnia, and won two World Court Orders of Provisional Measures of Protection overwhelmingly on their behalf on 8 April 1993 and 13 September 1993 against Yugoslavia to cease and desist from committing all acts of genocide against them and against all the other Bosnians on the basis of the 1948 Genocide Convention. Details can be found in Professor Boyle's book *The Bosnian People Charge Genocide!*(1996), (available on Amazon.com).

Adopting draft resolution will violate Genocide Convention, says Boyle

[TamilNet, Thursday, 21 March 2013, 00:01 GMT]

Commenting on the draft resolution being circulated by the United States at the the Geneva sessions of the UNHRC, Francis Boyle, Professor at the School of Law, University of Illinois and an expert in international law said that UNHRC and its member states, by adopting the draft resolution (3rd draft) will be abetting the on-going systematic structural genocide in violation of the 1948 Genocide Convention. The vote on Sri Lanka resolution is likely to take place as early as Thursday, according to sources in Geneva.

Full text of Prof. Boyle's comment follows:

By means of adopting this draft Resolution, the U.N. Human Rights Council and its Member States will thereby further whitewash and "bluewash" and facilitate and aid and abet the ongoing campaign of genocide by the GoSL against the Tamils in violation of the 1948 Genocide Convention and in particular but not limited to their article 1 obligation "to prevent and to punish" genocide as well as their article 3(e) obligation that prohibits and criminalizes "complicity in genocide."

The US-sponsored draft resolution "calls" the Sri Lankan government to conduct an "independent and credible" investigation into allegations of human rights violations. The draft resolution has not ceded to demands of human rights bodies for an independent international investigation, as being called by the UN High Commissioner for Human Rights Navaneetham Pillay.

* * *

Also last year, in March 2012, Professor Boyle had warned the Tamil diaspora and supporters like him against falling into the trap being created by the US Government.

"I served as Legal Adviser to the Palestinian Delegation to the Middle East Peace Negotiations starting in the Fall of 1991. Since that time, Israel's strategy has always been to STALL AND DELAY while they destroy the Palestinians."

"The entire world is going along with that strategy. GoSL is doing the same thing to the Tamils here. And the entire world is going along with it. We are being treated like the Palestinians. We need to come up with an entirely new strategy."

"If we proceed down this path there will never be GoSL account-ability for anything. GoSL will drag it all out until the Tamils are dead. Stall for time until the clock runs out like at a basketball game or a football game when your side is ahead. GoSL is trying to run out the clock on us," Boyle had said in a note sent to TamilNet.

* * *

Amidst lack of strategy by the Tamil diaspora activists, the stu-dents of Jaffna University, by their peaceful protests which were brutally attacked by the SL military in November 2012, effectively exposed how the 'LLRC' was being implemented by the Sri Lankan State on the ground.

Now, the students in Tamil Nadu have come forward with a strat-egy to arrest the situation. Their strategy is peoples struggle to checkmate the realities in the region. By continuing to hold mass demonstrations and hunger strikes, protesting the resolution, they have exposed the ultimate culprits to not only the Tamil public across the world, but also to the Es-tablishment-centric Tamil politicians in the island and political activists in the diaspora.

Genocidal double talk by India, US—Prof. Boyle

[TamilNet, Friday, 22 March 2013, 01:46 GMT]

Professor Francis A. Boyle, an expert in international law, called the statements made by the U.S. Secretary of State, John Kerry, and by India's ambassador to the U.N., Dilip Sinha, after the adoption of the US resolution on Sri Lanka in the Geneva sessions of the UNHCR, as "genocidal double-talk," pointing out the "blatant hypocrisy" in praising a resolution that looked at Colombo to implement the recommendation of its local "truth" commission. While rights groups and Tamils demanded an "international" investigation into the killings in Mu'l'l'vaaykkaal, leaked U.S. State Department memos had earlier revealed US officials acknowledging the futility of local investigations when culpability for the war-crimes pointed at Sri Lanka's President Rajapakse and his siblings.

""The end of the conflict in Sri Lanka provided a unique opportunity to pursue a lasting political settlement, acceptable to all communities in Sri Lanka, including the Tamils," said India's ambassador, Dilip Sinha. "We urge Sri Lanka to take forward measures to ensure accountability. We expect these measures to be to the satisfaction of the international community," Sinha was quoted as saying.[1]

A press statement released by Kerry said:

Today's vote in the UN Human Rights Council encourages the Government of Sri Lanka to continue on the path toward lasting peace and prosperity following decades of civil war and instability. This resolution, which builds on a similar 2012 resolution, reaffirmed that Sri Lanka must take meaningful action on reconciliation and accountability in order to move forward. The United States, together with international partners, calls upon the Government of Sri Lanka to fulfill its public commitments to its own people on these longstanding issues.

While some important progress has been made, there is much work still to be done. We look to the Government of Sri Lanka to implement the recommendations of the Lessons Learnt and Reconciliation Commission (LLRC) and to reverse recent negative developments on rule of law and human rights. The United States stands ready to assist with this vital work. I look forward to continuing our engagement with the Government of Sri Lanka and strengthening our friendship with the Sri Lankan people.[2]

Meanwhile, reports from New York said that the U.N. has established a commission to investigate human rights violations in North Korea, saying some of them may amount to "crimes against humanity." The U.N. Human Rights Council unanimously passed a resolution Thursday to create the commission, which will probe "systematic, widespread and grave" rights violations in North Korea. The resolution also condemns alleged torture and labor camps for political prisoners in North Korea.

"The North Koreans get a Commission and the Tamils get a scrap of paper," Boyle said.

Also, noting the "double-standards" in the announcement by United Nations Secretary-General Ban Ki-moon regarding an investigation into the possible use of chemical weapons in Syria, and the US statement supporting this investigation, Boyle said, "an immediate UN Investigation for the Syrians. Next to nothing for the Tamils."

[1] http://www.npr.org/templates/story/story.php?storyId=174951313
[2] http://www.state.gov/secretary/remarks/2013/03/206486.htm

New US Secretary of State responsible for Geneva injustice: Boyle

[TamilNet, Sunday, 24 March 2013, 15:15 GMT]

The New US Secretary of State John Kerry, who assumed office on 1 Feb 2013, was the Chairman of the Committee on Foreign Relations in 2009 that brought out a report advising the USA to help Sri Lanka's military without insisting on political solutions. Finding a clear link between the 2009 Kerry Report and Kerry's State Department, US Professor of Law, Francis A Boyle said, "The callous and callow Kerry Report came right after the GOSL genocidal massacre of about 100,000 Tamils in Vanni, recommending that the United States government abandon all principles and instead aid and abet the continued GOSL repression and persecution of the Tamils. That is precisely the policy we now see in operation with Kerry as U.S. Secretary of State. This latest UNHRC Resolution sponsored by Kerry's State Department and acting pursuant to his Instructions proves it. Kerry should be fired," said Boyle.

The U.S. Secretary of State, John Kerry's recent press statement which characterized the UNHRC Sri Lanka resolution as encouraging "the Government of Sri Lanka to continue on the path toward lasting peace and prosperity following decades of civil war and instability," and which expressed U.S.'s readiness "to continue engagement" with Colombo, and sidestepped accountability for the war-crimes committed by Sri Lanka, has alarmed Tamil activists, and raised the specter of a resumption of a passive US policy based on the 2009-Kerry report. This report was assailed by rights groups as "incredibly shoddy, ill-informed piece of work that grossly overstates the strategic importance of Sri Lanka to the U.S. and woefully understates the degree of abuses carried out by Colombo."

The December 2009 Report, "Sri Lanka: Recharting U.S. Strategy after the War," released by the Committee on Foreign Relations of which John Kerry was the Chairman, recommended, inter alia:

- Recharting U.S. strategy after the war
  http://www.tamilnet.com/img/publish/2009/12/FRCtamil report.pdf

US should focus on economy and security of the island instead of humanitarian considerations, IDPs and civil society; should also invest in Sinhalese parts of the country instead of just focusing on North and East; should resume training of Sri Lankan military officials to ensure human rights in future operations as well as to build critical relationships and implied that US should not emphasize on political reform as a condition to assistance, bringing rift in US- Sri Lanka relations making the latter to align with countries of alternative model of development.

Diaspora circles commented after the release of the Kerry report that while pre-2006 US policy gave verbal precedence to political solution over military solution, and later provided support to a military solution, has now isolated the Tamil national struggle as a non-entity in U.S.'s geopolitical considerations.

Rights group slammed the contents of 2009 Kerry report. "Maybe the people who wrote the report don't know anything about Sri Lanka or maybe they're of the school that says that everything on the planet is strategic," said Brad Adams, Asia Director for Human Rights Watch. "The huge human-rights and humanitarian problems that continue there are not small; they're central to any principled diplomatic engagement with Sri Lanka at this point. So [the notion] that we are in a competition with China, which I think is driving this, is misplaced," Adams further said.

In this context, the Secretary of State Kerry's statement on the UNHCR resolution[1] has dismayed Tamil diaspora circles over the possible ominous policy evolution in a downward direction as regards Tamils' future welfare, and on the possible adverse impact to the Tamil struggle seeking justice, accountability, and assertion of political and fundamental rights.

---

[1] http://www.state.gov/secretary/remarks/2013/03/206486.htm

Ambassador Blake cannot reverse Tamil genocide: Prof. Boyle

[TamilNet, Wednesday, 27 March 2013, 00:43 GMT]

Responding to the statements made during the U.S. Assistant Secretary of State for South Asia, Robert Blake's, interview with the BBC, where Blake appears to characterize the "GOSL's mass extermination of over 100,000 Tamils in Vanni in 2009" as nothing more than "some of the negative trends that have occurred with respect to rule of law and human rights in Sri Lanka," that needs to be "reversed," Professor Francis A. Boyle, an expert in international law, said, while Blake cannot reverse the genocide, the "start of "revers{ing}" them is to establish an International Investigative Commission in order to prosecute them." Blake also denies in the interview that he [and the international community] had any knowledge of the magnitude of the casualties during the final months of the war.

Ambassador Blake makes the following statement to the BBC:

My message is what Secretary Kerry said in his statement yesterday which is that while some important progress has been made, much work still needs to be done. We look to the government of Sri Lanka to implement the LLRC recommendations and reverse some of the negative trends that have occurred with respect to rule of law and human rights in Sri Lanka. And the United States stands ready to assist.

Professor Boyle responds: "So notice that Blake is simply parroting the Kerry Statement, which in turn is based upon the Kerry Report that I have already commented upon before for TamilNet[1] and thus will not repeat here.

"But according to Blake/Kerry the GOSL's mass extermination of over 100,000 Tamils in Vanni in 2009 is nothing more than " some of the negative trends that have occurred with respect to rule of law and human rights in Sri Lanka."

"In other words, as far as the United States government is concerned, the GOSL genocide, crimes against humanity and war crimes against the Tamils are just " some of the negative trends that have occurred with respect to the rule of law and human rights in Sri Lanka" that should be "reverse{d}." But how does the GOSL or the United States "reverse" genocide, war crimes, crimes against humanity and 100,000 exterminated Tamils? The start of "revers{ing}" them is to establish an International Investigative Commission in order to prosecute them!

"Article I of the 1948 Genocide Convention clearly requires contracting parties such as the United States and Sri Lanka "to prevent and to punish" the GOSL genocide against the Tamils. Obviously the United States maliciously failed and refused "to prevent" the GOSL genocide against 100,000+ Tamils in 2009 in egregious violation of its obligation to do so under Article I of the Genocide Convention.

"Today the very least the United States can now do is "to punish" the GOSL genocide against 100,000+ Tamils in Vanni in 2009 as also required by Genocide Convention Article I.

"Have Blake and Kerry maliciously failed and refused to read the Genocide Convention?" Boyle asked.

---

[1] http://www.tamilnet.com/art.html?catid=13&artid=36163

Joke and a fraud: Boyle slams Kerry's New Year message

[TamilNet, Friday, 12 April 2013, 11:46 GMT]

Noting the new U.S. Secretary of State, John Kerry's New Year Statement that included, "[t]he New Year brings with it a new opportunity for all Sri Lankans to join together in the spirit of peace and reconciliation," Professor Boyle, an expert in international law and a keen watcher of the treacherous conduct of the international community in watching the genocide of Tamils unfold in Sri Lanka, said, "Kerry [is] lumping the Tamils in with the genocidal Sinhala. It would be like Kerry congratulating the German Jews together with the German Nazis on the German New Year."

Full statement of Prof. Boyle sent to TamilNet follows:

Boy, this is a real Joke and a Fraud. Kerry lumping the Tamils in with the genocidal Sinhala. It would be like Kerry congratulating the German Jews together with the German Nazis on the German New Year.

Then Kerry asking the German Jews "to join together in the spirit of peace and reconciliation" with the German Nazis. And then Kerry in the name of President Obama asking the German Jews to "work" with the German Nazis in order "to make progress on reconciliation and accountability four years after the end of the" Holocaust "which divided your country."

According to Kerry there should be "new beginnings and fresh promise" between the German Jews and the German Nazis.

Kerry has a law degree from Boston College Law School. Obviously, they never taught the Nuremberg Charter, the Nuremberg Judgment and the Nuremberg Principles there.

The following is the full New Year message released in a press statement from Secretary Kerry's office:

Senator John Kerry
I congratulate Sri Lankans around the world as you celebrate Sinhala and Tamil New Year, and offer my warmest wishes for happy holiday and prosperous New Year.

Every year this celebration brings the hope of new beginnings and fresh promise. The New

Year brings with it a new opportunity for all Sri Lankans to join together in the spirit of peace and reconciliation.

On behalf of President Obama and the American people, I am eager to support the Sri Lankan people in this journey as you work to make progress on reconciliation and accountability four years after the end of the conflict which divided your country.

The United States stands ready to partner with Sri Lanka and all Sri Lankans as you deal with these important issues.

Earlier, Prof Boyle concluded that there was a clear link between the 2009 Kerry Report and Kerry's State Department, and said, "The callous and callow Kerry Report came right after the GOSL genocidal massacre of about 100,000 Tamils in Vanni, recommending that the United States government abandon all principles and instead aid and abet the continued GOSL repression and persecution of the Tamils. That is precisely the policy we now see in operation with Kerry as U.S. Secretary of State. This latest UNHRC Resolution sponsored by Kerry's State Department and acting pursuant to his Instructions proves it. Kerry should be fired," said Boyle.

Let Prince do the dirty work at CHOGM: Boyle

[TamilNet, Thursday, 09 May 2013, 00:29 GMT]

While Colombo media advanced the theory that Queen Elizabeth's age was factor in her skipping the Commonwealth Heads of Government Meeting [CHOGM] in Colombo, and the British media opined that the Queen was slowly scaling down her royal responsibilities and transferring duties to Prince Charles, Professor Francis Boyle who teaches law at College of Law, University of Illinois, surmised that the reason for Her Majesty the Queen skipping Colombo was, as a constitutional monarch, the Queen was not willing to be seen with genocidal Rajapakses. "Let [Prince] Charles do the dirty work. He is not head of anything. So his being there [in Colombo] will not insult anyone or anything but himself," Prof. Boyle said in a note sent to TamilNet.

"My guess is that the Queen decided to have nothing to do with the genocidal Rajapakses. Good for her! Constitutionally, she is the Head of State not only for the United Kingdom but also for the Commonwealth Countries themselves," Professor Boyle said.

Meanwhile a commentary in Canada's *The Star* debunked some academic pundits' dismissal of Stephen Harper's likely boycott of the international meeting in Sri Lanka as nothing more than political pandering, and added that Harper's critics are making a cynical mistake.

The paper argued that "there's a solid case behind the Harper government's view that boycotting the Commonwealth meeting is required to convey principled condemnation of what's happening to human rights and democracy in Sri Lanka. It is disputable, of course, whether a boycott is indeed the best tactic here.... But apart from the tactical question, it is clear that there exist significant principles and relevant facts worth acting. (Indeed, Amnesty International Canada is supporting a complete boycott of the Commonwealth meeting in Sri Lanka by all Canadian officials, not just the prime minister.)

Professor Boyle further added his criticism of the United Nations which "announced Tuesday that it had appointed a retired Australian judge, Michael Kirby, to lead a panel charged with investigating human rights abuses and possible crimes against humanity in North Korea 'with a view to ensuring full accountability,'" (*NYT*, Wednesday[1]) asking why the UN has not carried out a similar international investigation into Sri Lanka's war-crimes.

---

[1] http://www.nytimes.com/2013/05/08/world/asia/obama-backs-policy-of-south-koreas-president-on-north.html?pagewanted=all&_r=0

International Criminal Law Developments

[Interview, *International Law Journal of London*, Thursday, June 26, 2013]

Parasaran Rangarajan [PR]: Good afternoon everybody the date is July (June) 26th, 2013 and we are with Professor Francis Boyle, international professor and lawyer at the University of Illinois. My name is Parasaran Rangarajan and I am the editor in chief for the International Law Journal of London. We will be spending some time with him today going over the exciting developments in the world of international law and relations as well as go over some of Dr. Boyle's career accomplishments. How are you doing today professor?

Francis Boyle [FB]: Well, thank you very much for having me on and my best to your audience but its June 26th. July 26th I will be on vacation. Go ahead.

PR: So first off, I would like to touch on your most recent work with the Transitional Government of Tamil Eelam (TGTE). As former counsel to Bosnia and Herzegovina, you represented Muslim genocide victims at the International Court of Justice. In what ways are the circumstances similar to Rajapakse's genocide of Tamils in Sri Lanka? Why was Rajapaske not held accountable at the International Courts?

FB: Right, well I just sent you the paper I recently delivered at the TGTE conference on May 18th going through all this in great detail. You are certainly free to publish that paper in your forthcoming journal and also on your webpage. You certainly have my permission with the copyright on there, go right ahead so I'm not going to go through all that here. As for Rajapakse's not being held accountable so far, the major obstacle we have is Sri Lanka is not a party to the Statute for the International Criminal Court (ICC). You know that's not the end of the matter at all. I'm still working on it trying to figure out how to do this. The 112 states, I think, that are now party to the Rome Statute are all obligated to have domestic implementing legislation for the Rome Statute. So we might be able to hold the Rajakapskes to account under their respective domestic implementing legislation, in the Rome Statute states themselves. For example, the U.S. government is not a party to the Rome Statute either, but Bush was going to go to Switzerland which is a party and has domestic implementing legislation.A Swiss parliamentarian had found out about my complaint against Bush and the rest of them lodged with the ICC and publicly demanded Bush be prosecuted in the event Bush entered Switzerland. This got back to Bush and he decided not to travel to Switzerland. But if he had traveled to Switzerland, dossiers had already been prepared to try to get him arrested and prosecuted. So the Rajapakses face the same type of situation and we'll stay on top of it. What can I say? You have to understand the atrocities they inflicted here were so enormous that it's going to take time for justice to be done. It might even take a generation until they're old men. But I think they will be held accountable as is happening now for example with the Argentine dictators and torturers thanks to the Mothers of the Plaza de Mayo who are now the Grandmothers of the Plaza de Mayo. But they have insisted justice be done for the dirty war in Argentina in the early 1970's and justice is now being done. So yes, international justice is slow but I believe it will happen. We have a large number of lawyers on it, not just the TGTE but other Tamil groups I work with. We'll move forward but we need more lawyers that's for sure to do this work.

PR: Yeah because I think many people feel that there has been a double standard as we have seen with Gaddafi's war crimes and now they're persecuting Assad in Syria so that's why that question that came up.

FB: Of course there is a double standard. But I was able to get Milosevic prosecuted at the International Criminal Tribunal for the Former Yugoslavia for every crime in the ICTY Statute including two counts of genocide, one count for genocide in general and other count for Srebrenica and it took me 8 years to do that work. I first went after Milosevic in 1993 and he died on trial at The Hague in 2006 at the close of the prosecution evidence against him. So yeah, what can I say? These things take time, they take lawyers, and take resources. There's no silver bullet here. People have to understand that.

PR: Right, right and as a Tamil myself I appreciate much of the work you are doing here and I wanted to convey that. Do you think a UN referendum is possible after September's provincial elections and do you think it will lead to international recognition of a separate Tamil state? If so, how long do you think this process will take?

FB: That's a much harder question. I also sent you my paper that I gave at the TGTE conference on the right of Tamils to self-determination and their own state. You are free to publish that both in your journal and on your website despite the copyright. I hereby waive that so fix that if you want. That's going to take a longer time. The TGTE has set the process in motion with the adoption of the Tamil Freedom Charter. So in terms of time frame, I was the legal advisor to then Chairman Yasser Arafat of the Palestine Liberation Organization (PLO). The Palestinian Declaration of Independence, I started that in 1987 and finally on November 29th, 2012 the UN General Assembly recognized Palestine as a UN Observer State. So 1987 to 2012 that took 25 years of work, hard work. The TGTE has just started the process now. I'm hoping I will be around 25 years from now. I try to stay in shape and take good care of myself. But that's why we need more lawyers, doctors, and news media experts and everyone to pitch in here to do this type of work. I think it can be done. If we're using the Palestinians as a precedent here and one precedent that has worked that I have worked with from the get-go. It was my idea in 1987 and it took 25 years. Today the state of Palestine is de jure recognized by about 133 other states, now recognized as a state by UN General Assembly, full state membership in UNESCO, and Palestine has the votes to be admitted to the United Nations Organization as a state itself. The only thing preventing that is the threat of a veto and pressure by the Obama administration. But I already figured out a way for Palestinians to get around that invoking the "Uniting for Peace Resolution" (UNGA Resolution 377). So, we'll see what they have to do. I don't know, it's their right to self-determination, not mine. Just as it is the Tamils' right to self-determination, not mine. I'm just a lawyer

PR: Well we definitely appreciate the work that you are doing and considering that Israel is a supporter of the Sri Lankan state who recently had several human rights resolutions passed against it, can you envision any cooperation between the PLO and TGTE to hold the genocidal states accountable?

FB: I haven't seen any cooperation yet, that doesn't mean anything negative one way or the other. The Palestinians have been up against a wall since 1948 dealing with this problem. The Tamils have been up against a wall since 1948 dealing with this problem. In both cases, it was the British who created this problem. And they've been off and on their own pretty much abandoned and betrayed by everyone. Now, I've worked with both groups, the Palestinians the early 1980's, Tamils I didn't get involved since late 1990's. So we'll have to see how this develops. So right now both groups are working on their own in their own constituencies and things of that nature.

PR: So like you said you were the legal advisor to the PLO Chairman Yasser Arafat in the late 1980's and have been working with Palestinians since then. I spoke to the UK Foreign Office recently who said they would have recognized a Palestinian state if they had provided assurances that they would not go to the ICC. Do you think this trade off would have been worth it? If not, what can we expect at the ICC and International Court of Justice (ICJ) as we move forward?

FB: It's just a cop-out by the UK government, they can always come up with some excuse why they're not going to recognize the State of Palestine. In fact, Palestine already went to the ICC pursuant to my advice after Operation Cast Lead by Israel. I recommended to Palestinian President Abbas that they accept the Rome Statute for the ICC under Article 12 (3) which he did do. Eventually the first ICC prosecutor Moreno Ocampo, copped out and punted, and rejected their acceptance. So Palestine's already gone, they might go back, I really can't say. But remember the British created this problem in the first place. So they're simply going to tell you whatever lie they can to be against the Palestinians and support Israel and the Zionists. The entire British government is run by Zionists so what else do you expect them to say? They're not going to help the Palestinians. They never have. The British created the problem in the first place. Nothing has changed. It's that simple. You can quote me on that.

PR: It will be interesting to see how that plays out if they do go to the ICC definitely.

FB: Well it's on the agenda. Like I said Palestine has already gone once. Bensouda the new prosecutor has recommended they return. So we'll see. The documents are there, and we'll see what President Abbas decides to do. It's his call. The PLO Executive Committee serves as the provisional government for the State of Palestine. President Abbas is not a dictator over there. He is accountable to the PLO Executive Committee that serves as the provisional government for the State of Palestine. He is their President. So they can go back anytime they want to. But you know it's a very difficult situation for them to be in. You have to understand, legally there are no obstacles. Palestine already went once, they can go back. And I want to condemn in the strongest terms possible Moreno Ocampo. He is a completely shameless ICC prosecutor. I'm not expressing any opinion on Bensouda, she just started the job, so ok let's see what happens. But Moreno Ocampo is completely shameless and unprincipled and turned the ICC into nothing more than the white man's court where all he did was go after tin-pot dictators in Africa. Bush and his henchmen escaped accountability. Tony Blair, his henchman, escaped accountability, and Israel escaped any accountability under Ocampo's watch. So he's worthless but I heard he's going to go work for FIFA or something. Well fine let him go play soccer or football as they call it in Europe. He's completely worthless, spineless, and unprincipled on that and you can quote me on that too.

PR: Thank you very much, we understood you were a War Crimes Prosecutor in Malaysia which convicted former President Bush and Prime Minister Blair of crimes against humanity. Could you tell us a little bit about those charges? What legal effects do these convictions hold and are they binding in terms of arrests if they were to enter Malaysia?

FB: Well there were two sets of proceedings. The first a year and a half ago was against Bush and Blair for crimes against peace over Iraq. They were found guilty unanimously. The second was against Bush, Cheney, Rumsfield, Rice, and some of their lawyers for torture and war crimes. They were also found guilty. So we are making efforts to get the convictions enforced in every state in the world where these individuals show up. It's just like any enforcement of any criminal judgment, no different. I drew up a démarche and if we have any word that any of these individuals are going to show up in a foreign country, we send a démarche to the foreign country. We request that pursuant to our convictions, they be arrested and investigations opened and they be prosecuted under the relevant standards of international law recognized in these foreign states. So that's where we stand today. We'll keep at it. There's a whole secretariat there in Malaysia administering this process and we're monitoring where these individuals travel and we'll keep at it. Again, you have to understand these people have enormous power, there's the British Empire behind Blair and the American Empire behind Bush and the rest of them. And again it might take what happened with the Argentina junta, a generation for them to be held accountable. But I can see this can happen. But we're going to need lawyers, resources, and things of that nature. So it's not going to happen tomorrow but it will happen in time. You have to look at this in a historical perspective.

PR: Do you feel that there have been any breaches of international law or war crimes being committed in the latest conflict in Syria by fueling the conflict and arming terrorists in which thousands of innocent citizens are being killed?

FB: Yes, I discussed this in my new book just came out, *Destroying Libya and World Order* that you can get at Amazon.com. Chapters 5-6 and the conclusion segway into Syria. Clearly what the United States, Britain, France, Saudi Arabia, Qatar, Turkey, and now Libya are now doing in Syria by arming, equipping, supplying, and directing these fundamentalist terrorist groups is illegal. It was condemned by the International Court of Justice in the Nicaragua case in 1986 so that precedent is there. All you have to do is go back and read the Nicaragua case and change the name from Nicaragua to Syria and indeed, I point this out in the relevant passages in my book. You can get a copy of my book and see it there and post it on the web page if you want to. So it's all in there right.

PR: In 2006 the Islamic Republic of Iran requested you to represent them at the International Court of Justice in lawsuits against Western and European nations in order to deem the UN sanctions against them as illegal. Under what basis are those sanctions illegal and why didn't the lawsuits move forward as requested?

FB: Well I want to make it clear, Iran never asked me to represent them. Rather the Iranian lawyers asked me to submit a proposal to them on how to sue at the International Court of Justice the United States and other states that were threatening to attack them over this bogus nuclear issue and also imposing economic sanctions on them. So I did submit a memorandum on this to Iran's lawyers. It's quite extensive and then answered the follow-up questions I received from them. There it stands as of today, I haven't heard back from them for a year from their lawyers so I really don't know. There was just an election, there's going to be a change in government. Who knows what they're going to do? Apparently there's a new President, you know he might very well first try negotiations and that's great. I've advised several governments over the years and governments generally prefer diplomacy to litigation which is fine. So let's see what Iran decides to do with their new government. I would certainly hope that President Obama would negotiate in good faith with the new government of Iran. I can't say I'm overly optimistic because up to this point in time and despite President Obama's Cairo speech, we have not seen good faith negotiations by the United States with the government of Iran. It could happen and I hope it would happen and that litigation could be avoided. But if not, perhaps certainly the new government will decide to authorize these lawsuits. I also want to make it clear, Iran has outstanding international lawyers of their own who would be fully capable of doing these lawsuits without me. But if they want me to be involved, I would happy to be involved. Again this is for them to do, they already have my memorandum on how to do it.

PR: There have been many allegations by many African nations that the ICC has unfairly targeted African nations for war crimes. What do you make of this allegation and do you think that creating an International Court Chamber at the African Court of Justice will help alleviate some of these claims?

FB: I think these claims are correct. Under Moreno Ocampo, the ICC became the white man's court. All he did was go after Black tin-pot dictators in Africa. He avoided the wholesale murderers and killers in the United States, Britain, and Israel. And I think that's correct. Indeed I know that the African states are considering pulling out of the ICC. I think that would be a good idea. They should all pull out because it's clear that the ICC is nothing more than a tool set up by the white racist European colonial states together with Japan which is also a racist state to go after them. And I think the idea of them setting up their own court is an excellent idea and just boot the ICC out of Africa. "He who pays the piper calls the tune." And at the ICC, if you look at the contributions, it's basically Europe, Korea, and Japan. We know all of Europe is racist and Japan is racist for sure. So I think as far as Africa is concerned, the ICC is hopeless, that's perfectly clear. They need to set up their own tribunal and try their own people.

PR: In conclusion, do you have any remarks or messages for those aspiring to be international lawyers such as you out there?

FB: Man, there's an enormous amount of work out here which needs to be done. So much that I spend full time, 6-7 days a week working on the different things I work on and we need more lawyers. There's no question about it to give advice, counsel, representation, and everything else that's going on. We have to have more lawyers. There just aren't enough out there to bring peace and justice to the world. So keep on with your studies, study international law, human rights law, certainly the constitutional law of whatever state you plan to practice in. Get your license to practice law, and then move out and do it!

Can Power, silent on Sri Lanka genocide, redeem herself in UN, asks Boyle

[TamilNet, Saturday, 20 July 2013, 00:50 GMT]

The Director of Multilateral Affairs and Human Rights of the U.S. National Security Council, Samantha Power, who has been nominated for U.S. ambassador to the United Nations, has been attending a Senate hearing on the nomination this week where she has been forcefully advocating action to stop "the grotesque atrocities being carried out by the Assad regime," Washington media reported. Professor Boyle, pointing out Power's conspicuous silence during the killing of Tamil civilians reaching genocidal proportions by the Sri Lanka military, said that Power now has a chance to "redeem" herself by establishing an International Criminal Tribunal for Sri Lanka, as did her predecessor Madeline Albright on the former Yugoslavia.

Professor Boyle said, "[Samantha] Power stood by and watched 150,000 Tamils be exterminated by the GOSL and did nothing to stop it that I am aware of.

"Despite the fact that Article I of the Genocide Convention clearly required that the United States government and all of its officials "undertake to prevent and to punish" genocide, Power did not "prevent" the GOSL genocide against the Tamils," Boyle said, adding, "But now she has the opportunity to redeem herself, the Obama administration and the United States government by acting "to punish" the GOSL genocide against the Tamils.

"Her predecessor Madeleine Albright as US Ambassador to the United Nations almost single-handedly established the International Criminal Tribunal for the Former Yugoslavia for the punishment of all the Serbian genocidaires against the Bosnians, including Milosevic, Karadzic, and Mladic, inter alia. Power has the right, the power and the obligation to do the same against the GOSL genocidaires, especially the Rajapakses.

"We must all demand and settle for nothing less from her than what Madeleine Albright did for the Bosnians: Bring all the GOSL genocidaires to Justice," Professor Boyle said.

Ms. Power won a Pulitzer for "A Problem from Hell: America and the Age of Genocide," her book about America's response to genocide. In the book she argues that American foreign policy in this area has failed; we promised "never again" after the Holocaust but willfully ignored genocides in Cambodia, Iraq, Bosnia, and Rwanda, she had earlier said, before she was invited to join the Obama's first campaign.

Professor Francis A. Boyle is the author of *The Tamil Genocide by Sri Lanka* (Clarity Press: 2010)," and *The Bosnian People Charge Genocide!* (Aletheia Press: 1996).

UN Sri Lanka tribunal will avoid ICC jurisdictional issues, says Boyle

[TamilNet, Tuesday, 23 July 2013, 00:43 GMT]

The United Nations General Assembly (GA) must immediately establish an International Criminal Tribunal for Sri Lanka (ICTSL) as a "subsidiary organ" under U.N. Charter Article 22, and organized along the lines of the International Criminal Tribunal for Yugoslavia (ICTY), which was established by the Security Council, said Professor Francis Boyle, an expert in International Law, while commenting on the appointment of Samantha Power as the U.S. Ambassador to the United Nations, and advocating that Ms. Power should follow the leadership of Madeline Albright who spearheaded the setting up of the ICTY. This will avoid the jurisdictional hurdles in the ICC taking up criminal matters related to a non-signatory state, Boyle added.

The purpose of the ICTSL would be to investigate and prosecute Sri Lanka war crimes, crimes against humanity and genocide against the Eelam Tamils—-just as the ICTY did for the victims of international crimes committed by Serbia and the Milosevic Regime throughout the Balkans, Professor Boyle said.

According to Boyle, the establishment of ICTSL would provide some small degree of justice to the victims of Sri Lanka's war crimes, crimes against humanity and genocide against the Tamil People in North-East--just as the ICTY has done in the Balkans. Furthermore, the establishment of ICTSL by the U.N. General Assembly would serve as a deterrent effect upon Sri Lanka's polical leaders such as Sri Lanka's President Mahinda Rajapakse, his sibling and Defense Secretary, Gothabaya Rajapakse, another brother and minister for Development, Basil Rajapakse, Military Commander Sarath Fonseka and other top generals that they will be prosecuted for their further infliction of international crimes upon the Tamils from the NorthEast of Sri Lanka, Professor Boyle said.

Tamil political activists agreed that without such a deterrent, Sri Lanka will likely continue the cultural genocide including forced colonization, grabbing land from Tamil civilians, and militarization of day-to-day life and engaging the military in civilian affairs.

"For the U.N. General Assembly to establish ICTSL could stop the further development of this momentum towards a regional if not global catastrophe," Boyle added.

"People need to understand that Power could push for an International Criminal Tribunal for Sri Lanka on the basis of UN Charter article 22 to be set up by the UN General Assembly, thus avoiding the jurisdictional problems with the International Criminal Court since Sri Lanka is not a party and it appears that China would veto any referral by the Security Council to the ICC," Boyle further said.

"The UN General Assembly could take the Statute for the International Criminal Tribunal for Yugoslavia and transform it into the Statute for the International Criminal Tribunal for Sri Lanka," Professor Boyle said.

Francis A. Boyle is a graduate of the University of Chicago and Harvard Law School. He has advised numerous international bodies in the areas of human rights, war crimes, genocide, nuclear policy, and bio-warfare. He received a PhD in political science from Harvard University.

Administer justice to GoSL genocidaires on basis of Truth, says Boyle

[TamilNet, Saturday, 27 July 2013, 18:51 GMT]

Commenting on Prime Minister Dr Manmohan Singh's statement that India has "long advocated the creation of an environment in Sri Lanka in which all communities, particularly the Sri Lankan Tamils, are masters of their own destiny within the framework of a united Sri Lanka," Professor Boyle, an expert in International law, said that this was not an appropriate remedy to deal with genocidaires, adding, "It would be like asking the Jews to engage in a Truth and Reconciliation Process with the Nazis. The very idea is absurd and insulting upon its face alone." India's Prime Minister was responding to Chief Minister Jayalalithaa statement urging the Center to ensure that the process of democratic decentralization, integral to the survival of the Tamils in Sri Lanka, should lead to the Tamils realizing their legitimate aspirations.

Professor Boyle said, "Most experts in the fields of international human rights law and international criminal law believe that a Truth and Reconciliation Process is not the appropriate remedy to deal with genocidaires and their victims.

"It would be like asking the Jews to engage in a Truth and Reconciliation Process with the Nazis. The very idea is absurd and insulting upon its face alone," Boyle said.

Prof Boyle added, "Rather, the international community set up the Nuremberg Charter, Judgment, and Principles as well as the Genocide Convention to deal with the Nazi extermination of the Jews.

"That is why I have proposed that the United Nations General Assembly establish The International Criminal Tribunal for Sri Lanka as a "subsidiary organ" under U.N. Charter Article 22 that would be modeled upon the Statute for the International Criminal Tribunal for Yugoslavia.

"Justice must be administered to the GOSL genocidaires on the basis of Truth. Therefore, we must have a Truth and Justice Process with respect to the GOSL genocidaires," Boyle said.

"Perfidious Albion cannot change its spots"

[TamilNet, Tuesday, 05 November 2013, 03:12 GMT]

Asserting that the Commonwealth is simply a reincarnation of the British Empire and the British Imperial system, Professor Boyle, an expert in international law, remarked that placing the alleged genocidaire Mahinda Rajapakse as the Commonwealth Chairperson-in-office for the next two years, "will expose the Commonwealth as a Sick Joke." Professor Boyle found Prince of Wales and British Prime Minister David Cameron's attendance to CHOGM despicable and drew similarity to the American Founding Father Thomas Paine's characterization of the British as "Perfidious Albion cannot change its spots," after the massacres of American soldiers at Lexington by the British Hessian mercenaries.

In a note sent to TamilNet commenting on the Commonwealth Heads of Government Meeting (CHOGM) in Colombo, Professor Boyle said: "The Commonwealth has never been anything more than the reincarnation of the British Empire and the British Imperial System. Rajapakse as its Head for two years will expose the Commonwealth as a Sick Joke and a Demented Fraud to the entire World. Good riddance! Ditto for Prince Charlie!

"To paraphrase one of America's greatest Founding Fathers Tom Paine in his classic pamphlet Common Sense written right after what he correctly called the massacres of American citizen-soldier Minutemen at Lexington and Concord by British professional Hessian mercenaries: Who founded the British Monarchy? It was that Norman Bastard and his Gang of Bandits, William dubbed the Conqueror. Perfidious Albion cannot change its spots," Boyle added in his comment.

This will be the first time in 40 years that Queen Elizabeth II will not be present at the CHOGM.

The Prime Minister of Canada, Stephen Harper, stated that he would not attend the meeting as a protest of Sri Lanka's failure to improve its human rights record, as he said he would at the previous CHOGM.

Harper further elaborated that Canada may cease its contributions to the funding of the Commonwealth should no action be taken by the organization against Sri Lanka.

Senator Hugh Segal, Canada's envoy to the Commonwealth, exclaimed that the Commonwealth Secretariat was acting "as a 'shill'" for Sri Lanka's government.

In October 2013, the legislature of the Indian state of Tamil Nadu passed a unanimous resolution demanding that the Indian government completely boycott the meeting and also sought the temporary suspension of Sri Lanka from the Commonwealth until Sri Lanka takes steps to grant Tamils all the same rights that the Sinhalese have.

In Malaysia, Lim Guan Eng, Chief Minister of the state of Penang, and the Secretary General of the Democratic Action Party called on the Malaysian government to boycott the summit as a protest against what the two claimed was human rights violations committed by the Sri Lankan government against Tamils.

The New Zealand Green Party also placed similar calls for a boycott.

Tamils should guard against being misled by IC, says Boyle

[TamilNet, Monday, 23 December 2013, 19:45 GMT]

"Based upon my first-hand personal experiences working with the Palestinians at their peace negotiations and the Bosnians at their peace negotiations, the Tamils cannot trust the United States, the United Kingdom, the United Nations, the European Union and its Member States to do the right thing for them. The Tamils can only trust in themselves," responded Professor Francis Boyle on Monday, when TamilNet asked him what would be his advice to the Tamil diaspora in engaging with the 'International Community.' TamilNet posed the question to Professor Boyle following his recent interview on Bosnian 'peace' negotiations to the Institute for Research of Genocide, Canada.

[Full text of Prof Boyle's interview to the Institute for Research of Genocide is at <http://instituteforgenocide.org/?p=6988>]

When asked whether ethnicity or nationalism, or socio-economic problems was the main issue of the conflict, Boyle said, "it was outright genocide by Yugoslavia and Milosevic against the Bosnians. They proclaimed independence as was requested by the European Union. The EU put out guidelines and said to Bosnia and Croatia that they needed to have elections. They had elections and they voted for independence and they were hit with genocide and aggression," Boyle told the Canadian organization on Genocide research.

On the behavior of the British representative at the peace negotiations for Bosnia, Boyle said, "I dealt personally with David Owen. He is a typical British, imperialist, establishment, racist individual who believed Muslims were an inferior race of people. We were just supposed to do what he told us to do. I made it clear that that was not going to happen on my watch."

"Europe just did not want a Muslim state in Europe. It was that simple. It went back to the crusades."

[...]

This has to do with anti-Muslim prejudice in Europe going back to the Crusades, at least. At that time, before 9/11 2001, we really didn't have that in the United States. We didn't have experience with the Crusades and all the rest of that. But eventually, Clinton would go along with a carve-up too," Boyle said.

On the conduct of US representative in the talks, Boyle said, "Cyrus Vance was running the show. That was clear. He was the de facto representative of the US Government. Everyone knew that. Even though he technically represented the United Nations, everyone knew that Vance was there speaking pretty much on behalf of the US Government. He had been former Secretary of State. That's the way people looked at Vance, that he had the backing of the US Government behind him. Of course Vance never said that, to the best of my knowledge, but that is the way people looked at Vance."

Compelling need to correct UN's mortal sins against Tamils, says Boyle

[TamilNet, Monday, 20 January 2014, 00:05 GMT]

Commenting on the Genocide Discussion held at the United Nations on the 15th January, where the Deputy Secretary-General Jan Eliasson discussed strategies to heed to early warning of mass atrocities, Professor Boyle, an expert in International Law, said, "[w]hat is needed now is for the United Nations to establish an outside Independent Commission of Investigation of distinguished experts along the lines of the Rwanda Commission with a mandate to investigate the entirety of GOSL atrocities against the Tamils. Only then might the United Nations atone for its Mortal Sins against the Tamils." The U.N., which withheld information on Sri Lanka's killings, and refused to take up Sri Lanka in the Security Council during the Mu'l'livaaykkaal killings, continued to avoid mentioning Sri Lanka, even while it touted "Rights Up Front" doctrine modeled after Sri Lanka massacres.

Prof. Boyle's comment sent to TamilNet follows:

"The United Nations and its Secretary General Ban Ki-moon did not lift one finger to prevent and to stop the ongoing genocide against the Tamils by Sri Lanka in Vanni in 1999. Since the United Nations and SG Ban Ki-moon had an obligation to do so, that renders them all "complicit" in the GOSL genocide against the Tamils in violation of Genocide Convention article 3(e) that prohibits and criminalizes "complicity in genocide."

"I have documented these matters in my book *The Tamil Genocide by Sri Lanka* (Clarity Press: 2010) and in the subsequent comments I have written for Tamilnet. So I will not bother to repeat any of that analysis here.

"What is needed now is for the United Nations to establish an outside Independent Commission of Investigation of distinguished experts along the lines of the Rwanda Commission with a mandate to investigate the entirety of GOSL atrocities against the Tamils. Only then might the United Nations atone for its Mortal Sins against the Tamils. Otherwise, the entirety of the United Nations Organization shall always remain Guilty as Sin for what it did not do for the Tamils-- Just like Rwanda and Srebrenica," Prof. Boyle said.

- Rights Up Front, Sri Lanka Report
  http://www.tamilnet.com/img/publish/2014/01/sriban
  1rightsupfronticp.pdf

- UN: Petrie Report
http://www.tamilnet.com/img/publish/2014/01/
PetrieReport.pdf

While Deputy UNSG, Jan Eliasson, describes the "profound internal reflection" UN should take following the "systemic failure" in addressing the humanitarian situation in Sri Lanka, but what was conspicuously absent was the description of atrocities of genocidal proportions in Sri Lanka and the condemnation of the State the atrocities demand.

However, Eliasson without mentioning the word genocide says, that what happened in Sri Lanka was close to what happened in Rwanda 15 years earlier.

Innercity Press which covered the UN action during the Mu'l'livaaykkaal massacres[1] points to the hollow rhetoric of the UN officials, and asserts, "[e]ven while admitting "systemic failure," this underplays the degree to which the UN was complicit in what happened: it pulled out of Kilinochchi, an envoy was sent who was perceived [John Holmes or Nambiar] to just want the LTTE Tamil Tigers wiped out, so much that a ceasefire was never even called for," ICP said.

---

[1] http://www.innercitypress.com/sriban1internal101113.html

USA softer than UK in wooing genocidal Colombo: Boyle

[TamilNet, Monday, 03 February 2014, 10:14 GMT]

"Everyone must redouble their pressure on the Obama administration directly at the White House and the Cameron government directly at No. 10 Downing Street in order to get that international commission of investigation at the UNHCR in March. With elections coming up in India, everyone must redouble their pressure on the Tamil Nadu government to get them to pressure the Indian government to support that international commission of investigation at the UNHRC in March. The one hope we have is that the GOSL continues to be so obstinate, stubborn, pig-headed and genocidal that they will do nothing," said Professor Boyle, an expert in International law and a keen observer of Sri Lanka's genocidal politics said in a comment sent to TamilNet.

The UNHRC should authorize an international commission of investigation of GoSL war crimes, crimes against humanity and genocide against Eelam Tamils, he further said.

Following U.S. Assistant Secretary for South and Central Asia, Nisha Desai Biswal's visit to the island, where Biswal noted the "desire within the Sri Lankan people to resolve the issues of the war and to move forward and to bring sustainable peace and prosperity for all Sri Lankans, and we want to work with Sri Lanka as it moves down that path," Professor Boyle commented that "[t]he one hope we have is that the GOSL [The Government of Sri Lanka] continues to be so obstinate, stubborn, pig-headed and genocidal that they will do nothing," expressing confidence that, soon, the International Community will be left with no alternative except to conduct an Independent International Investigations into the war-crimes and crime of genocide in Sri Lanka.

During the visit Nisha Biswal and Ambassador Sison flew to Jaffna and also met with members of civil society, the Bishop and visited the historic Nalloor Temple.

Full text of Prof. Boyle's comment on the visit of Biswal to Sri Lanka follows:

> "It appears that Biswal is trying to nudge the GOSL into making it seem to be doing more on its fake accountability and reconciliation process so as to avoid the UNHRC adopting a resolution in March that would authorize an international commission of investigation of GOSL war crimes, crimes against humanity and genocide against Eelam Tamils.

"Notice that one of the reporters correctly pointed out that she [Biswal] is taking a much softer line than Cameron and she basically admits it. Not a good sign at all.

"Remember that U.S. Secretary of State Kerry—Biswal's Boss—when he was in the U.S. Senate as Chair of its Foreign Relations Committee issued that horrendous and abominable report arguing that the U.S. must promote its strategic interests with the GOSL against China despite its massive human rights violations against the Tamils.

"I have already commented on that for TamilNet. Clearly, Biswal is carrying out Kerry's pro-GOSL policy. Kerry is more concerned about keeping the genocidal GOSL happy so that he can further pursue his "pivot" against China than he is with promoting the basic human rights of the Eelam Tamils.

"Everyone must redouble their pressure on the Obama administration directly at the White House and the Cameron government directly at No. 10 Downing Street in order to get that international commission of investigation at the UNHCR in March. With elections coming up in India, everyone must redouble their pressure on the Tamil Nadu government to get them to pressure the Indian government to support that international commission of investigation at the UNHRC in March. The one hope we have is that the GOSL continues to be so obstinate, stubborn, pig-headed and genocidal that they will do nothing."

* * *

Transcript from the US Embassy in Colombo of the press conference with Assistant Secretary Nisha Biswal, follows:

AMBASSADOR SISON: I am so pleased to be with you all this evening in order to introduce you to our new Assistant Secretary for South and Central Asia, Nisha Biswal.

The Assistant Secretary was sworn in in December, less than two months ago by our U.S. Secretary of State John Kerry in December and she has made scheduling the trip to Sri Lanka a real priority on her schedule, given the importance of the U.S. relationship with Sri Lanka and with the Sri Lankan people.

Assistant Secretary Biswal arrived yesterday morning. We have had a very busy Friday and Saturday with her. Yesterday we met with the Minister of External Affairs; the Minister of Economic Development; the Minister of Justice; and the Secretary of Defense as well as with members of civil society, representative of the UNP and the TNA including the Chief Minister of Northern Province.

This morning we had an early start and we flew up to Jaffna, met with members of civil society, the Bishop and the Governor. We also had the delightful opportunity today to take the Assistant Secretary on a tour of two beautiful and historic temples, Nallur Temple in Jaffna this morning, and Gangaramaya Temple here in Colombo this afternoon, to show the Assistant Secretary a little of the history, culture, and diversity of this beautiful country.

So we are delighted to have this opportunity to introduce you to Assistant Secretary Biswal. Nisha, welcome.

ASSISTANT SECRETARY BISWAL: Again, thank you everyone for joining us late this afternoon. I'm very pleased to be returning to Sri Lanka after many years, this time as Assistant Secretary.

Over the last two days I have had frank discussions with the government, with opposition, and with civil society representatives in Colombo and in Jaffna. It has been terrific to meet so many Sri Lankans who care so deeply about their country.

The United States and Sri Lanka have a longstanding partnership dating back to this country's independence. This friendship is based on our people's shared democratic values and strong economic and cultural ties.

The late Senator Edward Kennedy said it very well when he said, "Our relationship is not just government to government, but it is people to people, citizen to citizen and friend to friend." It is in that spirit that I am here.

In meetings this week with senior officials as well as with senior UNP and TNA leaders and a diverse range of civil society leaders I reiterated our longstanding desire to see further progress for all people of Sri Lanka. The meetings were productive, collaborative, but also addressed a range of serious challenges.

We reiterated our commitment to Sri Lanka but we conveyed our concerns to senior government officials about the insufficient progress in addressing justice, reconciliation and accountability.

The United States has always supported a Sri Lankan process to resolve the issues emanating from the conflict. But as I have noted earlier, the patience of the international community is wearing thin over the pace of progress, including with the implementation of the recommendations of the LLRC.

We are concerned about the worsening situation with respect to human rights including continued attacks against religious minorities as well as the weakening of the rule of law and an increase in level of corruption and impunity. All of these factors lead to undermine the proud tradition of democracy in Sri Lanka.

Furthermore, let me state that we are aware that in the past individuals who have met with foreign officials have been met in turn with intimidating visits and threatening phone calls. I would say that we view this very seriously and find it completely unacceptable.

I conveyed to senior officials that the United States is motivated here out of a vision for an inclusive, peaceful, prosperous and unified Sri Lanka. It is this vision, this inclusive vision which also motivates the United States to sponsor a third resolution in the United Nations Human Rights Council, calling on Sri Lanka to do more to promote reconciliation, democratic governance, justice and accountability at the UN Human Rights Council in March. While it's too soon to say what the text will say, let me underscore that it will be carried out in the spirit of friendship with the Sri Lankan people.

As true partners and friends the United States stands ready to support Sri Lanka as it continues to move forward to establish a just and lasting peace.

In 2013 the U.S. embassy in Colombo donated $2.1 million worth of a forensics laboratory and training to the Sri Lankan government and we are prepared to offer additional technical assistance and support to ensure that credible, transparent, independent and verifiable investigations can take place.

As we see Asia taking on a leading role in the global economy, we don't want to see a Sri Lanka that is left behind, but without justice and reconciliation, without accountability, there can be no sustained peace and equitable prosperity for the people of Sri Lanka. Respect for human rights, promoting transparent and democratic governance are essential to flourish in this global economy.

Unfortunately, continued deterioration in these areas is already beginning to take its toll on Sri Lanka's democratic traditions and institutions. The United States believes in the spirit of the Sri Lankan people and stands with you as you advocate for peace, prosperity, and a brighter future for all of your citizens.

With that, I'm prepared to take your questions. Thank you.

QUESTION: I am Zacki Jabbar from the Island Newspaper.

There is a lot of terminology here. Would you specifically move a resolution on war crimes or is it more seeking resolution on asking for war crimes to be probed?

ASSISTANT SECRETARY BISWAL: Like I said, it's too early to determine what the text of the resolution will be exactly, but what we have called for in the prior two resolutions has been for a process, a Sri Lankan led process, to address issues of justice, reconciliation and accountability and for Sri Lanka to implement the recommendations of the LLRC.

QUESTION: I am Shehan Baranage from Derana TV Colombo
You stated that U.S. was anyway insisting on a local process; a Sri Lankan process to investigate the war crimes or whatever. Will this be continued even in the third resolution? Right now the world is thinking there could be an international investigation or whatever. But however, will U.S. back that

kind of investigation or would U.S. still insist for a Sri Lankan investigation to proceed?

ASSISTANT SECRETARY BISWAL: I think it's too early to say. I will say that while our strong preference has always been for a Sri Lankan process to unfold, I have also very clearly noted that lack of progress in Sri Lanka has led to a great deal of frustration and skepticism in my government and in the international community. And as I have said, patience is wearing thin. So I cannot tell you at this point what will be in that resolution. Our hope has always been that this would be a Sri Lankan process.

QUESTION: I am Prasad from National television

You mentioned about the aim of this resolution is to strengthen the reconciliation process in Sri Lanka. But don't you think that this will create more divisions in Sri Lankan society because some Sri Lankans feel that it's engineered by some separatists and Diaspora groups. There are a lot of feelings in Sri Lanka. So don't you think that your aim will achieve, true reconciliation will be achieved with this?

ASSISTANT SECRETARY BISWAL: The divisions have existed long before the resolutions. And five years, almost five years after the end of the conflict meaningful steps at reconciliation have yet to be taken. It has been the desire of many to provide space for the Sri Lankan people to come together, to heal the wounds of war. But when that space is not used productively and aggressively to pursue peace and to pursue reconciliation, to pursue justice and accountability, then it draws the concern of the international community and that is where we find ourselves.

QUESTION: I am Shihar from Reuters.

Madam, from your meetings with the Northern people, the Bishop and other civil society; what's your view on the progress of reconciliation in the North? And why they need, I mean some people they themselves say they want an international inquiry on certain things. In your view why they need such kind of thing? Are they basically not confident of the government process? Why?

ASSISTANT SECRETARY BISWAL: Well I would say that there has not been sufficient actions taken by the government to address issues of justice and accountability. We heard from many people about people who are still unaccounted for, whose whereabouts and fate is unknown to their family members. We heard about individuals and organizations that continue to feel threatened and intimidated. And when such a climate persists five years after the end of conflict, then I think that there is some cause for those individuals to feel that an international process is needed.

QUESTION: I am Stefani Lageras from MTV/MBC

The question I have today is what is the basis in which the U.S. is planning on tabling a resolution in March? Given the fact that UNHRC Chief Navi Pillay is yet to give a written report on progress made on Sri Lanka. She has given an oral statement but a written report is yet to be issued. So what is the basis on which the U.S. is planning on tabling a resolution?

ASSISTANT SECRETARY BISWAL: We look forward to the written report of the UN High Commissioner for Human Rights and we are very concerned about the findings presented in her oral report which corroborates our own understanding based on the many conversations we have had with many individuals and organizations in this country and organizations, human rights organizations around the world who have also been following with great concern the developments in this country.

So it is because we have had clear expectations delineated in prior years about our hopes and expectations for implementation of the recommendations of the LLRC and the lack of progress against those recommendations that we feel that we must go before the Human Rights Council once again and seek a resolution to underscore our mounting concern.

QUESTION: You mentioned -- I'm Shaheen from News 1st by the way.

You mentioned that patience is running thin amongst all international countries. Well, Sri Lankan government representatives have over and over again pointed out that they need more time. Have you taken this into consideration?

ASSISTANT SECRETARY BISWAL: The process of reconciliation is a long one and no one expects that it would be completed overnight, but it must be begun in earnest and substantial and credible steps must be undertaken to create the climate that allows people to feel that there is an earnest attempt at reconciliation.

And while there have been some significant steps that we have acknowledged and applauded when they have occurred, those have been too few and far in between. And the culture of deterioration of human rights gives us great concern when churches and mosques are burned down, when people feel that they cannot practice their faith freely and without fear, then I believe the urgency that has gripped the international community is justified.

QUESTION: I'm P.K. Balachandran from New Indian Express.

I'd like to know why this time you have not gone to India which plays a big role in the UNHRC, and whether you plan to consult India before you decide on a resolution.

Second question is, whether at any point of time it is possible that economic sanctions might be applied against Sri Lanka?

ASSISTANT SECRETARY BISWAL: Certainly we are talking to and working closely with colleagues across the international community including the Indian government with whom we talk on a regular basis about bilateral and regional issues, both in Washington and in New Delhi. I will be going to Geneva as I leave Sri Lanka and I will seek an opportunity to meet with the Indian High Commissioner while I'm there.

QUESTION: How about economic sanctions?

ASSISTANT SECRETARY BISWAL: We are not at this point discussing sanctions. We are still very much committed to seeing progress on these issues. We believe that there is a desire within the Sri Lankan people to resolve the issues of the war and to move forward and to bring sustainable peace and prosperity for all Sri Lankans, and we want to work with Sri Lanka as it moves down that path.

QUESTION: Amal Jayasinghe from France Press.

Sometime in November the British Prime Minister was in Colombo, he was saying that if there is no progress by March he will use Britain's position in the UN to press for an international investigation. You seem to be taking a much softer line. Is that a fair reading?

ASSISTANT SECRETARY BISWAL: Well, I have noted that our very strong desire has always been to see a Sri Lankan process unfold, but I have also been very clear that we are frustrated with the pace within Sri Lanka and we are concerned that rather than seeing the same progress that we are seeing deterioration in the human rights climate in this country. We will have to see what the way forward is but it is my strong desire, it is the strong desire of my government to see a Sri Lankan process unfold.

QUESTION: I'm Ranga Jayasuriya from Ceylon Today

You said you are not at a point to discuss the economic sanctions. Are you at a point right now to discuss international war crime investigation on Sri Lanka?

ASSISTANT SECRETARY BISWAL: As I have noted, we have been strongly urging for a Sri Lankan process to investigate the final days of the war. We understand growing concern, frustration and skepticism amongst many in my country and many in the international community that has led to increasing calls for international investigations and international processes. I'll leave it there.

QUESTION: Ma'am, in your opening statement you made several references to the Sri Lankan people, underscoring sort of friendship and lots of taking on board of what the Sri Lankan people feel.

In the five years since the end of the war in several elections, the Sri Lankan people in terms of the majority seems to have put their weight behind the current regime. Is the U.S. government taking note of that fact? As much as there is frustration and urgency among the international community about its lack of progress, the Sri Lankan people seem to still be happy with the way things are going. How much is that a factor that the U.S. has taken on board in terms of contemplating this resolution against Sri Lanka?

ASSISTANT SECRETARY BISWAL: I think that there is a need for dialogue and there is a need for leadership. And there is a need for the media to be able to convey in clear terms perspectives of all sides. I will note there is decreasing space for media to be able to provide those perspectives and that will certainly influence, therefore, the climate in the country. I would hope that that can be reversed.

I just want to say thank you again, and I look forward to being able to return many times in my tenure. Thank you.

UN resolution neither prevents nor punishes GoSL genocide, says Boyle

[TamilNet, Wednesday, 26 March 2014, 03:18 GMT]

While noting that ""investigation" by the UNHCR is better than nothing—with all due and sincere respect for the UNHCR," Professor Boyle, an expert in international law, said, dissemination of that "investigation" will be subject to the control of the UN Human Rights Council for political reasons and the dissemination of that UNHCR "investigation" will be dragged out for as long as possible by the Human Rights Council, thus enabling the GOSL to continue its campaign of ongoing genocide against the Tamils despite the requirement of article 1 of the Genocide Convention that every UN Human Rights Council state member is obligated both "to prevent and to punish" the GOSL genocide against the Tamils," Boyle said.
Pointing to the following text in the UN resolution

> ...requests the High Commissioner to ... b) to undertake a comprehensive independent investigation into alleged serious violations and abuses of human rights and related crimes by both parties in Sri Lanka, during the period covered by the Lessons Learnt and Reconciliation Commission, and establish the facts and circumstances of such alleged violations and of the crimes perpetrated with a view to avoiding impunity and ensuring accountability, with input assistance from relevant experts and special procedures...

Professor Boyle, in a note sent to TamilNet, said:

> "After five years we are still not going to get an outside, independent commission of inquiry into GOSL atrocities committed during the genocidal massacre at Vanni against the Tamils. Instead of that we are going to get an "independent investigation" by the UN High Commissioner for Human Rights.

> "Notice the verbal chicanery involved here that reduces an "independent commission" to an "independent investigation" by the UNHCR, which are not the same thing. One would expect any "investigation" by the UNHCR to be "independent, " so the language is redundant.

> "I guess the Americans figure they can placate us with this obfuscatory language. Obviously, an "investigation" by the UNHCR is better than nothing—with all due and sincere respect for the UNHCR.

> "Meanwhile the dissemination of that "investigation" will be subject to the control of the UN Human Rights Council for political reasons and the dissemination of that UNHCR "investigation" will be dragged out for as

long as possible by the Human Rights Council, thus enabling the GOSL to continue its campaign of ongoing genocide against the Tamils despite the requirement of article 1 of the Genocide Convention that every UN Human Rights Council state member is obligated both "to prevent and to punish" the GOSL genocide against the Tamils.

"This third draft American resolution neither "prevents" nor "punishes" GOSL genocide against the Tamils. It is simply part of a Stall And Delay Strategy by U.S. Secretary of State John Kerry going back to his infamous Report in support of the GOSL against the Tamils when he was Chair of the U.S. Senate Foreign Relations Committee that I have already previously commented upon and will not repeat here again but can be found in the archives."

Reforms will not happen, genocide will continue, warns Prof. Boyle

[TamilNet, Friday, 18 September 2015, 00:21 GMT]

Asserting that war crimes and crimes against humanity "on discriminatory grounds" can constitute genocide, Professor Boyle, an expert in International Law and who teaches at the University of Illinois, commenting on the Office of the High Commissioner of Human Rights overview report on Sri Lanka made public Wednesday, said, that "a Truth and Reconciliation Process does not work within the context of genocide," and that instead of a hybrid court recommended by the OISL there is a "need for an International Criminal Tribunal for Sri Lanka or else referral by the United Nations Security Council to the International Criminal Court." Boyle also warned that reforms by GOSL will not happen and that "[t]he Sinhala genocide against the Tamils will simply and predictably continue."

- A/HRC/30/CRP.2 OISL Report
  http://www.tamilnet.com/img/publish/2015/09/A_HRC_30_CRP_2.pdf

- A/HRC/30/61 OHCHR Report
  http://www.tamilnet.com/img/publish/2015/09/A_HRC_30_61_ENG.pdf

The OISL report is divided into two parts, which are interlinked, an overarching report on promoting reconciliation (19 pages) and an accompanying detailed report (268 pages).

Detailed comment from Professor Boyle on the OISL overview report follow:

Par. 24: "... war crimes... and/or crimes against humanity. In some of these cases, the alleged acts were apparently committed on discriminatory grounds." In other words, genocide—though he does not use the word. But war crimes and crimes against humanity "on discriminatory grounds" can constitute genocide.

Par. 55: "....were treated as suspects and detained because of their Tamil ethnicity....may amount to the crime against humanity of persecution..." AND GENOCIDE.

Par. 59: Chandrika in charge of Office of National Unity and Reconciliation. A sick joke and a demented fraud! I think we could make the argument that she is a genocidaire herself. So this is "national unity and reconciliation" in the Sinhala Grave for the Tamils.

Pars. 80 & 81: A Truth and Reconciliation Process does not work within the context of genocide. They tried it in Bosnia and it got nowhere and failed. The same will happen here.

Par. 80: "...examine the entire period of conflict and insurgencies dating back to at least the 1970s..." Right. That is how long the Sinhala and their Government have been inflicting genocide against the Tamils.

Par. 84: "Without far-reaching institutional and legal reform {which is not going to happen}, there can be no guarantee of non-recurrence." Right! The Sinhala genocide against the Tamils will simply and predictably continue. Hence the need of the Tamils for their own State—Tamil Eelam!

Par. 88: In the cases of Bosnia and Rwanda where genocide occurred, there were established International Criminal Tribunals and Investigations and Prosecutors-- not hybrid courts and investigations and prosecutions involving nationals of the genocidal state and of the genocidal nationality: The International Criminal Tribunal for the Former Yugoslavia (ICTY) and the International Criminal Tribunal for Rwanda (ICTR). The same principles of international criminal law apply here. Hence the need for an International Criminal Tribunal for Sri Lanka or else referral by the United Nations Security to the International Criminal Court. If a Permanent Member of the Security Council vetoes a reference to the International Criminal Court, then the United Nations General Assembly can establish an International Criminal Tribunal for Sri Lanka (ICTSL) as a "subsidiary organ" pursuant to its powers under Article 22 of the United Nations Charter.

Chequered Swiss history of supporting Sri Lanka's crimes

[TamilNet, Sunday, 20 September 2015, 22:02 GMT]

Switzerland, besides U.S., U.K, and India, has played a key role in providing diplomatic sanctuary for Sri Lanka in international fora against censure for alleged criminal conduct against Tamils. The most strident display was when the Swiss sponsored a UN resolution calling "upon the Government of Sri Lanka to investigate and prosecute itself for war crimes and crimes against humanity," as the State killed tens of thousands of Tamil civilians in the final phases of 2009 war. This paved the way for the international community to whitewash a possible genocide. This practice continues to this day as Swiss Federal Department of Foreign Affairs (FDFA) and Swiss Peace [NGO] participate this week in a meeting organized by an NGO outfit to soften the Tamil call for international investigations on Sri Lanka genocide.

* Swiss Resolution on Sri Lanka
  http://www.tamilnet.com/img/publish/2009/05/SecondResolution_01.pdf

The 2009 Switzerland sponsored resolution to the U.N. Human Rights Council, prompted Professor Boyle, an expert in International Law and Professor at the University of Illinois College of Law, to comment[1] that Swiss action would be the same "as if the U.N. had invited the Nazi government to investigate and prosecute itself for genocide, crimes against humanity and war crimes against the Jews instead of supporting the Nuremberg Charter and Tribunal."

Boyle added, "[t]he glaring hypocrisy and blatant sophistry of the Swiss Resolution is heightened by the fact that Switzerland is the Depositary for the Four Geneva Conventions of 1949 and their Two Additional Protocols of 1977 and therefore bears a special obligation under international law to promote, guarantee and ensure their effective enforcement rather than their negation and nullification, which this Swiss Resolution will do. Obviously, Switzerland knows exactly what it is doing. The same is true for the 25 other state Co-Sponsors of the Swiss Resolution."

The enormity of Sri Lanka crimes bordering on genocide which have been documented in the UN OISL report, has established that the hurriedly passed Swiss resolution in 2009 was ill-conceived. The report also vindicates Prof. Boyle's characterization of the diplomatic blunder by the then Swiss Government and its UN diplomats. [The OISL report was authored by Marti Ahtisaari, former President of Finland, Dame Sylvia Cartwright, former High Court Judge of New Zealand and Asma Jehangir, former President of the Human Rights Commission of Pakistan.]

Further, Switzerland stands accused of its stand to support 'Sri Lanka' when the possibility of grave criminality was clear during the war.

In addition, the SL State has provided ample testimony during the past six years of its inability and/or unwillingness to prosecute perpetrators of dastardly crimes against the Tamil people during the war. Swiss and other sponsors continue to allow more space and time to genocidal Sri Lanka to avoid reaping the legal consequences of possible culpability. Swiss decision makers cannot be unaware of the following factors that point to SL conduct during the war and during the six years following the war:

• Culpability to most serious crimes are likely to be traced to command responsibility of high-level current and former Sri Lanka' officials, including the now deposed President Rajapakse, his sibling, Gotabhaya Rajapakse, and former military commanders including Retd. Maj.Gen. Sarath Fonseka. US Ambassador Patricia Butenis observed last January that no regime investigates "its own troops or senior officials for war crimes." She then added, in a devastating aside, that in the island "responsibility for many of the alleged crimes rests with the country's senior civilian and military leadership, including President Rajapakse and his brothers."

• Several commissions, including IIEGP and others, appointed to "investigate crimes" have clearly shown that the State used commissions as an instrument to buy time. Commissions with international participation had the same destiny; the internal eminent persons either quit, or the State disbanded the commissions prematurely.

• Throwing monkey wrench in the works: State scheming of additional delay and watering down of the seriousness of the "international court" for war-crimes by saying local complaints of graft will also be investigated by the court.

On the matter of asylum seekers and refugees, Switzerland with predictable self-interest, appears to support the view that 'Sri Lankan' rights record has improved vis-a-vis Tamils.

Of the nearly 50,000 Tamils living in Switzerland, nearly 3,000 are asylum seekers, and more than 1800 have been given temporary status by July 2013. However, Switzerland continued to deport Tamils who are refused refugee status even when there were reports of arrests of returnees. In Sept 2013 Swiss refugee authorities temporarily suspended deportations prompting Human rights groups to launch a petition calling for an end – not just a temporary suspension—to deportations to 'Sri Lanka.' The Rights groups also called on the Swiss authorities to break off negotiations on a formal repatriation accord with 'Sri Lanka.' The talks were started in 2009.

Tamil circles commented that the issue being tackled by the OISL report only about the conduct of the warring parties during the war. The Sinhala politicians, including the vocal majority of the intelligentsia, are resorting to inject extraenous issues including Sinhala accusations of graft with a view to sabotage the finely focused criminal investigations of war-crimes. However, it appears to be a formidable task, reading the strong language of Zeid report, not withstanding perhaps further assistance, if any, from the Swiss diplomats among others.

[1]http://www.tamilnet.com/art.html?catid=13&artid=29456

Resolution sponsors, voters, UNHRC become accessories to SL genocide: Boyle

[TamilNet, Friday, 02 October 2015, 20:49 GMT]

Accusing that the sponsor states of the UNHRC resolution on Sri Lanka, the States that voted for the Resolution, and the UN Human Rights Council itself have "all become Accessories After The Fact to Sri Lanka's Genocide, Crimes against Humanity and War Crimes against the Eelam Tamils," Professor Francis Boyle, an expert in international law and a professor at the College of Law, University of Illinois, said that the "Resolution calls for nothing more than the Genocidal Sri Lanka to set up a Domestic "Judicial" Mechanism dressed up with a transparent fig-leaf of international participation in order to cover-up and do damage control and damage limitation for the GOSL Genocide against the Eelam Tamils," adding that "[h]istory teaches that this GOSL Domestic Mechanism will fail," and "Genocide against Eelam Tamils will recur."

Full text of Professor Boyle's comment given to TamilNet follows:

I am not going to comment upon and refute all the lies, propaganda, disinformation and half-truths set forth in this Resolution. You can read my book *The Tamil Genocide by Sri Lanka* (Clarity Press: 2010) for my legal, political, and historical background analyses here. But in a nutshell the State Sponsors of this Resolution, those States that voted in favor of this Resolution, and the UN Human Rights Council itself have thereby all become Accessories After The Fact to Sri Lanka's Genocide, Crimes against Humanity and War Crimes against the Eelam Tamils.

Pursuant thereto, Operative Paragraph 6 of the Resolution calls for nothing more than the Genocidal Sri Lanka to set up a Domestic "Judicial" Mechanism dressed up with a transparent fig-leaf of international participation in order to cover-up and do damage control and damage limitation for the GOSL Genocide against the Eelam Tamils.

Domestic Mechanisms do not work and cannot work within the context of genocide, crimes against humanity and massive war crimes: The Nazis against the Jews; the Serbs against the Bosnians; the Hutus against the Tutsis. All required International Criminal Tribunals to bring Justice to the Victims. The Tamil Genocide by Sri Lanka likewise requires an International Criminal Tribunal to bring Justice to the Eelam Tamils.

History teaches that this GOSL Domestic Mechanism will fail. And for the reasons set forth by the High Commissioner for Human Rights in his Report, the GOSL Genocide against the Eelam Tamils will 'recur.'

I call upon all Tamils everywhere in the world not to be deceived by this Human Rights Chicanery perpetrated upon the Eelam Tamils by the self-styled UN Human Rights Council.

These are all International Crimes for which there is Universal Jurisdiction by any State in the World to prosecute the Sinhala perpetrators.

Indeed, every State in the World has an international legal obligation to prosecute the Sinhala genocidaires and war criminals should they set foot upon their respective territories. Many of them have been identified by Name in the Report by the High Commissioner.

And under international criminal law, there is no Statute of Limitations for their commission of genocide, crimes against humanity and war crimes against the Eelam Tamils.

Therefore, we must track them down and prosecute them all anywhere we find them in the world for the rest of their lives.

Just like the Jewish People are still doing today against the Nazis seventy years after the end of World War II. Legally, these Sinhala genocidaires and war criminals are just like Pirates—The Enemies of all Humankind!

Tamil Nadu, Global Tamils should be organized in addressing US-UN failure: Boyle

[TamilNet, Saturday, 10 October 2015, 22:40 GMT]

Professor Francis Boyle, an expert in international law, who teaches at University of Illinois, in an interview given to the 3CR radio broadcast in Melbourne Saturday in the "Tamil manifest" program said that he sees the millions of Tamils in Tamil Nadu, its Chief Minister Jayalalitha, a unified Tamil diaspora and the young generation of Tamils as the propelling agents to force the changes necessary to bring justice to the victims of Tamil genocide by taking the Sinhala genocidaires to Court. The horrendous nature of genocide needs an international tribunal to dispense justice, and the United Nations and the U.S have failed in their obligations, Boyle said. Geopolitical compulsions have pulverized U.S. foreign policy to collude with the genocidaires, Boyle told TamilNet.

Tamils in Tamil Nadu should exert pressure on New Delhi to take the case to the International Court of Justice (ICJ), Professor Boyle said adding that "if the 50 million Tamils living in Tamil Nadu can get Prime Minister Modi to do this, I will be happy to file the charges myself; draft the papers and file the charges. But we will need Prime Minister Modi, and unfortunately he seems to be supporting the process recommended by the Human Rights Council."

Full text of the interview is published below with permission from 3CR:

3CR: What's your opinion about the report tabled by the UNHRC on Sri Lanka?

Boyle: I thought the report was pretty good, except that the High Commissioner refused to use the word genocide, even though if you go through the report carefully it's clear he could have reached a conclusion of genocide but he refused. I also believe his predecessor Navi Pillay also refused to use the word genocide while the Vanni massacre was going on.

The other two UN reports, the UN experts report and the UN internal report [Petri Report], they also refused to use the word genocide. The reason is because if they used it, it raised the question as to why the United Nations did not act immediately and effectively to stop it. Other than that I thought it was a good report and we could certainly use it to press war crime charges and charges of crimes against humanity against the entire Sinhala leadership who the High Commissioner most conveniently mentioned by name. As for genocide charges we'll have to do more work on that because they didn't really pull together the types of evidence that we need to prove that in Court. I think we can do that.

3CR: What do you think of the resolution put forward by the USA?

- A/HRC/30/L.29: Promoting reconciliation, accountability and human rights in Sri Lanka
  http://www.tamilnet.com/img/publish/2015/10/A_HRC_30L29.pdf

Boyle: It's a total disgrace. It really is. And indeed yesterday the State Department put out a press statement claiming credit for and boasting about it and they were proud of it. It is a shocking, shameless resolution including praising the Sinhala military forces for their honorable service committing genocide against about 146,000 Tamils. But as I said in my other comments basically rendering themselves accessories after the fact to the Sinhala genocide, war crimes, and crimes against humanity against Eelam Tamils. And if you read the Genocide Convention to which US is a party, it clearly prohibits and criminalizes complicity in Genocide, and that's what we are seeing here.

U.S. State Department Press release:

"Sri Lanka: The U.S.-led resolution, which Sri Lanka co-sponsored, highlights the Sri Lankan government's efforts to advance respect for human rights and strengthen good governance since January 2015, encourages the reform of domestic laws to facilitate accountability for past crimes related to the Sri Lankan civil war, affirms the importance of the participation of foreign judges and prosecutors in domestic accountability mechanisms, and requests further reporting by the Office of the High Commissioner for Human Rights (OHCHR)."

3CR: Let's focus on the genocide question. The reason they refuse to even use the word genocide is clearly as you said, they have to take further steps. Then how cases like this is brought up at the International Court of Justice (ICJ). How does that work?

Boyle: We have tried consistently since the beginning of the crisis in Jan 2009 to get India to raise this issue at the ICJ for us. As you know even under the Gandhi Government they wouldn't do it because they were complicit in the GoSL [Government of Sri Lanka] genocide against Tamils, and now under Prime Minister Modi, BJP, so far he has not done it. I think it is going to take the leadership in Tamil Nadu under Chief Minister Jayalalitha to pressure Prime Minister Modi to do something here. I am here in the U.S. But I was there in Chennai after the massacre in June 2009, less than a month after the massacre. It was a national trauma over there; I spoke and I had a morning meeting with the members of the Tamil Nadu Bar Association discussing about steps that could be taken in India. Unfortunately I don't think there was much follow up.

3CR: So it has to be a state that should bring that accusation against another country? Would that be correct?

Boyle: That's correct. Right now the most likely candidate is India. Certainly if the 50 million Tamils living in Tamil Nadu can get Prime Minister Modi to do this, I will be happy to file the charges myself; draft the papers and file the charges. But we will need Prime Minister Modi, and unfortunately he seems to be supporting the process recommended by the Human Rights Council.

3CR: I wonder if you could draw out some points on this report. They have recommended a hybrid system, internal investigation, but the external international judicial process can be drawn in. There are two views on that. One the report says Sri Lanka can request international intervention. But local government in Sri Lanka and it's supporters are vehement in the point that we would determine who and when we invite into this process

Boyle: If you read the resolution itself, and what it actually approves was a purely domestic mechanism. As a matter of fact yesterday in the press release the State Department said, that it was a domestic mechanism. That is like asking Hitler and the Nazis to prosecute their own people for what they did to the Jews. Of course it's not going to happen. So we are dealing now with a domestic mechanism. History has taught that when you have genocide you must have an international mechanism, the Nazi genocide against the Jews, the Yugoslav genocide against the Bosnians. I was the lawyer for the Bosnians at the World Court and argued their case for genocide and won two Orders of provisional measures of protection on their behalf against Yugoslavia to cease and desist from committing all acts of genocide. Also there is the International Criminal Tribunal against Yugoslavia to prosecute genocide, war crimes and crimes against humanity. And the third case we have is Rwanda, that too was genocide, and that called for the International Criminal Tribunal for Rwanda.

The three known instances of genocide, certainly since the Second World War, have all required international mechanisms. But what we have here is nothing more than a domestic mechanism even bragged about by the US State Department that sponsored this resolution. It is a domestic mechanism with a fig-leaf of some degree of international participation as determined by the Government of Sri Lanka. It is going to be nothing more than a copping-out, damage control, damage limitation and it's not going to work.

3CR: One of my biggest concerns is that especially NGOs like Amnesty and HRW have accepted the report as a step in the right direction. What do you think of that type of support from credible organizations.

Boyle: As I said the report isn't that bad. The problem is the resolution which to some extent undercuts and denies the significance of the report. I was on the Board of Directors of Amnesty International USA for four years, and dealt with Amnesty at the highest levels. They are in the pockets of US, Britain, Israel, and they tow the party line of the major Western powers. Since we have seen that US and Britain have come out in favor of this resolution, this domestic mechanism, it does not surprise me at all that the NGOs have simply towed their party line. It is regretful, but that's pretty much how these NGOs work.

3CR: Can you tell us a little about the political side of things, where you have got China, Russia, Cuba, and US supporting the report and even the resolution. The political line up is massive against the Tamils of Sri Lanka. What do Tamils have to do to untangle this?

Boyle: We need to put together a comprehensive program here first to get the Government in Tamil Nadu working actively on our behalf internationally, that's where the real power is, and then second to get the Tamil diaspora around the world every one united together on a common front on a common program; that's the task that is facing us now. We have US, China, two major powers working in cahoots with the Sinhala Government. When Secretary of State Kerry was Chairman of Foreign Relations Committee he put out a completely horrendous report which I commented on in my book *The Tamil Genocide by Sri Lanka*, saying for strategic reasons US has decided to align with Sri Lanka, and that is exactly what they [US] have done.

We have a tough job ahead of us. We have 50 million Tamils in Tamil Nadu who have to get organized, and all the Tamils in the diaspora. You have to understand that the Human Rights atrocity here was enormous. I accept the figure given by the Bishop in Jaffna of about 146 thousand people. When you have figures that high in such a short period of time, it is going to take time, organization and resources to bring justice to bear on these Sinhala leaders, because now it's clear that the UN itself is not going to do it. So it's really up to us to do it.

3CR: Recently I read a news item that large number of Tamils were out on the streets protesting against the Resolution in Tamil Nadu and thousands were arrested. The problem is the relationship between the Central and State Governments. The Center completely controls the foreign affairs department.

Boyle: Let me interject here. We are in a better situation now with Prime Minister Modi than what we were with Gandhi. And Prime Minister Modi says he is a devout Hindu. What did the Sinhala Buddhists do here but wipe out 146 thousand Tamils from January through May. I don't have a precise breakdown of how many of them were Hindus and how many were Christians, but I suspect the vast majority of them were Hindus. Where is the Prime Minister Modi here? We need to bring this out that Tamil Hindus were exterminated and we expect Prime Minister Modi to do something on our behalf. So I think we are in a better situation here under Prime Minister Modi and we have to produce a change in New Delhi.

3CR: Can a provisional Government bring accusations of Genocide against a state?

Boyle: Unfortunately we don't really have a provisional government at this time. As you know the LTTE had set up a de facto state with a de facto government in Tamil Eelam but it was completely destroyed in May 2009, so we are dealing now with reorganizing something. I provide advice and counsel to Tamil organizations that ask my help, I try not to exclude one or any organization. We have an enormous task ahead of us.

3CR: The question of the LTTE is constantly brought up by many of the forces around this issue. For me it seems like blaming the victims and their actions for defending themselves in whichever way possible against the perpetrators, and yet there is a constant attempt to balance the LTTE activities against the Sinhala right-wing government or genocidal government. I like to hear your comments on this type of argument.

Boyle: Look, the LTTE is dead. It is eliminated. It's history. I think rather than arguing about the past, we should focus on the future. That would be the best advice I would give to Tamil organizations. Let's not argue about the LTTE, people can have different opinions, but with all due respect, that does not get us anywhere.

Let me give you one other piece of advice. I have worked on the Tamil issue since 1996. I have met many Tamils all over the world. Tamils are highly educated and highly professional wherever you go. But the issue is this. It seems to me most Tamils are doctors, engineers, professors. We need more young Tamils to become lawyers. That's what we need, and we need Tamil parents to tell their children that even though Law may not be a high prestigious profession as a doctor, engineer, scientists, for the good of the Tamil people we need young Tamils now to go to law school and get trained in International Law, Human Rights and things of that nature, and start to work to the benefit of the Tamil People. So we need Tamil parents to tell their children, go to law school and help our People, please!

Diaspora should mount independent legal campaign: Prof. Boyle

[TamilNet, Sunday, 08 November 2015, 23:18 GMT]

Pointing out that the United Nation's actions on Sri Lanka are unlikely to lead to establishing criminality for the Mu'l'livaaykkaal massacre on the State, Professor Francis Boyle, an expert in international law and who teaches at the College of Law, University of Illinois, advocates that the Tamil diaspora should organize a comprehensive legal campaign to bring charges in the International Court of Justice (ICJ), and in parallel, bring criminal and/or civil charges against Sri Lanka's genocidaires in the courts of the democracies of the West using domestic legal mechanisms underpinned by universal jurisdiction. Boyle asserted that genocide, crimes against humanity and war-crimes are international crimes that have no statute of limitations, and Rajapakses can be subjected to legal actions for the rest of their lives like the Jewish people's hunt for the Nazis.

Professor Boyle in an interview given to a rights group based in Toronto, further explained his history of observations in Sri Lanka and compared the 2009 Mu'l'livaaykkaal killings to the Bosnian and Rwandan genocides. He also added that the latest UN report, while avoiding to mention "genocide," mentions names of the possible perpetrators of war-crimes which will be useful in future independent legal actions outside Sri Lanka.

Boyle maintained that the estimate of the number of Tamil civilians killed by the Sri Lankan state should be maintained as 146,000, a figure compiled by Catholic bishops who were present during the killings and who maintained records. Prof. Boyle added that the figures mentioned in the three UN reports of 40 to 70,000 were significantly underestimated.

Boyle said that the numbers killed in the final stages of the war while providing a sufficient basis to establish the two legal elements of genocide, the mental element ["intent to destroy in whole or in part of a group"] and the physical element [one or more of five possible acts, which includes "killing members of the group"], it will be useful to go back to 1948 to expose the clear pattern on intent. He noted that UN Zeid's report goes back to 1983 pogrom against Tamils.

When asked for comments on Prof. Boyle's advice, the spokesperson for Tamils Against Genocide [TAG], an US-based activist group that seeks legal redress for war-affected Tamils, said, "We fully agree with Prof. Boyle. Diaspora Tamils should exercise their legal option if the Tamils in the NorthEast are ever to get justice or legal redress.

"It's unfortunate that the leading Tamil party on the ground, the TNA, is admonishing the Tamils not to press for State criminality on genocide, arguing the available evidence is not sufficient. This is an untenable legal position for the following reasons: (a) the last phase of the war was a war-without-witness, and evidence of the mass atrocities are buried in the killing fields of Vanni. Only an independent investigation with modern forensic tools will expose the evidence and the extent of criminality, (b) seeking a charge of genocide will not foreclose reaching a verdict on other less culpable charges. Further, in criminal cases prosecutors routinely use this strategy, and (c) a large number of Tamils, including lawyers, and many other international activists believe that the crime in Mu'l'livaaykkaal was "genocide." One can argue that zealous advocacy for the victims by agile and competent lawyers in this case is to seek the highest level of culpability, "genocide."

"TAG believes that TNA may have a hidden motive to assist Sri Lanka (and the West) in whitewashing the genocidal crimes, and that Tamils should challenge the TNA, and mount a serious legal campaign charging Sri Lanka for the crime of genocide," TAG spokes person added.

Professor Boyle had earlier warned that the "Truth and Reconciliation process" as outlined in the Office of the High Commissioner of Human Rights overview report on Sri Lanka, "does not work within the context of genocide," and that instead of a hybrid court recommended by the OISL there is a "need for an International Criminal Tribunal for Sri Lanka or else referral by the United Nations Security Council to the International Criminal Court." Boyle also warned that reforms by GOSL will not happen and that "[t]he Sinhala genocide against the Tamils will simply and predictably continue."

Samantha Power rehabilitates genocidal Sri Lanka: Boyle

[TamilNet, Monday, 23 November 2015, 20:41 GMT]

"Power's visit is just a public relations exercise designed to rehabilitate the genocidal GOSL government. In other words, Power has become an Accessory After The Fact to the GOSL genocide against the Eelam Tamils. Power has now become part of the GOSL's "Problem from Hell," said Professor Boyle, an expert in International Law and who teaches at the College of Law, University of Illinois, after following the events of Ms. Samantha Power's visit to Sri Lanka this weekend. Criticizing Ms. Power for avoiding questions on genocide, Boyle said, Power was guilty of unwittingly exhibiting racial bias in asking Tamil journalists whether they trusted Colombo, while she never would have asked the white-skinned Bosnian Muslims if they trusted the genocidal maniacs running the Government of Republika Srpska.

Full text of Professor Boyle's comment follows:

Power knows from her direct and personal experience on Bosnia that it is still extremely dangerous for Bosnian Muslims living in Srebrenica at risk to their own lives. She would never have asked any Bosnian Muslim journalists living in Srebrenica if they trusted the genocidal maniacs running the Government of Republika Srbska, who are now in charge of Srebrenica thanks to Richard Holbrooke's Dayton Agreement whose 20th Anniversary she just opportunistically praised.

"She would have never put Bosnian Muslims on the spot in that way and insulted their intelligence in the process. Why did Power do this to Tamil Journalists in Jaffna living under the control of the GOSL genocidal maniacs? Does Power believe that dark skinned Tamils are dumber than white skinned Bosnians? Obviously, white skinned Bosnian Victims of Genocide mean a lot more to Power than dark skinned Tamil Victims of Genocide.

Power is a disgrace to the Irish who themselves are Victims of British Genocide. See my book *United Ireland, Human Rights, and International Law* (Clarity Press: 2012).

* * *

While Ms. Power tweeted on Sunday that she had agreed on demilitarization with Northern Sinhala Governor Palihakkara (Met with Gov Palihakkara in North #SriLanka. Agreed development, demilitarization in Jaffna cannot wait.), the official read-out[1] only said Power has expressed "support for expanding efforts to restore normalcy to former conflict areas."

Another tweet from her on Sunday said: "Urged Jaffna Chief Minister Wigneswaran to help reinforce #SriLanka precious moment for reconciliation/rebuilding."

On Monday she was tweeting: "Honored to meet Pres .@MaithripalaS, who has committed to reconciliation, democ reform, justice. Good start so far," and "#SriLanka Opposition Leader Sampanthan: passionate voice for Tamil rights, getting results by bldng nat'l consensus."

Ms. Power was telling the NPC Chief Minister that Colombo had de-proscribed some diaspora groups, Colombo has to deal with pressure from Sinhala groups in the South, and that Sri Lanka is generally slow in implementing changes. [In fact, the Colombo regime has just reinforced the so-called ban on Tamil diaspora groups and activists, while avoiding some of the groups in the new Gazette notification.]

A spokesperson for Tamils Against Genocide (TAG), a US-based activist organization providing legal help to Tamil war-victims, said: "In her Pulitzer prize-winning book *A Problem from Hell*, Power was severely critical of US foreign policy arguing that '[n]o US president has ever made genocide prevention a priority,' the US political system is ruthlessly effective in consistently not intervening in the face of genocide, and 'that is why genocide rages on.' It is sad to see that Power herself has become the target of her own accusation, by first failing to convince the US administration to intervene, and subsequently promoting a policy of whitewashing Sri Lanka's genocide."

Ms Power was a former Balkan war correspondent, a foreign policy columnist at *Time* magazine and was a Professor at Harvard University before being invited to hold positions of power in the National Security domain by the Obama administration.

---

[1] http://usun.state.gov/remarks/7001

Boyle denounces Power's notion of "trust deficit"

[TamilNet, Wednesday, 02 December 2015, 22:55 GMT]

Commenting on US Ambassador to the UN Samantha Power's statement in an interview to the Sri Lanka's *Sunday Observer* that "[t]he entire country [Sri Lanka] needs to feel that there is positive and concrete action being taken to move forward...The government has commenced a journey and it must deliver the peace dividend to the people by calling for truth, justice and an end to impunity," Professor Boyle, an expert in International Law, said "Power knows full well that what she is saying here is total baloney and double-talk...It is ridiculous and preposterous for Power to talk about a 'trust deficit' between the GOSL and the Eelam Tamils—between the Genocidaires and their Victims."

Professor Boyle was troubled by the following response of Power in the *Sunday Observer* interview[1]:

Sunday Observer. During the meetings with the government leaders, what specific did the US call for?

US Ambassador to UN, Samantha Power:
The United States has repeatedly called for robust mechanisms and speedy actions to bridge the trust deficit that exists in the North. The entire country needs to feel that there is positive and concrete action being taken to move forward. There is a lot of international goodwill for the island, due to the recent political changes. The government has commenced a journey and it must deliver the peace dividend to the people by calling for truth, justice and an end to impunity.

Boyle said that "[i]t is ridiculous and preposterous for Power to talk about a "trust deficit" between between the GOSL and the Eelam Tamils—between the Genocidaires and their Victims. I do not recall Power ever talking about a "trust deficit" between Yugoslavia and the Bosnians—between those Genocidaires and their Victims."

Full text of Boyle's comment sent to TamilNet follows:

"In July of 2005 both Power and I separately attended the Tenth

Anniversary of the Genocidal Massacre at Srebrenica in Bosnia and Herzegovina. I was there in my capacity as the Attorney for the Mothers of Srebrenica and Podrinja. After the Memorial Service at the Potocari Memorial and Graveyard located on the Killing Fields of Srebrenica itself, we both spoke at a Conference at the Holiday Inn Hotel in Sarajevo. Power knows full well that what she is saying here is total baloney and double-talk.

"When it came to the Serbian atrocities against the Bosnians, the United States sponsored at the United Nations Security Council the establishment of the International Criminal Tribunal for the Former Yugoslavia—not some type of domestic mechanism under the control of the Serbian Genocidaires. At the time, I was the Attorney of Record for the Republic of Bosnia and Herzegovina before the International Court of Justice, and arguing their case for genocide against Yugoslavia.

"By comparison, with respect to the genocidal massacre of Tamils in Vanni in 2009 by the Government of Sri Lanka, the United States worked in cooperation with the GOSL Genocidaires to establish a so-called domestic mechanism whereby the GOSL will be able to cover-up their international crimes. There is no way the GOSL will or can deliver a "peace dividend" to the Eelam Tamils. This is because the GOSL has already inflicted upon the Eelam Tamils the proverbial "peace of the grave."

"It is ridiculous and preposterous for Power to talk about a "trust deficit" between the GOSL and the Eelam Tamils—between the Genocidaires and their Victims. I do not recall Power ever talking about a "trust deficit" between Yugoslavia and the Bosnians—between those Genocidaires and their Victims. Based upon her direct and personal experience in Bosnia, Power knows better. She was also behind me at Harvard Law School. As a self-styled human rights lawyer, Power has now knowingly become an Accessory After The Fact to the GOSL genocide, war crimes and crimes against humanity perpetrated upon the Eelam Tamils," Boyle said.

From 1993 to 1996, when Power's and Prof. Boyle's paths crossed in Sarajevo, Power worked as a journalist, covering the Yugoslav Wars for *U.S. News & World Report,* the *Boston Globe, The Economist,* and *The New Republic.* When she returned to the United States, she attended Harvard Law School, receiving her J.D. in 1999.

[1] http://www.sundayobserver.lk/2015/11/29/fea11.asp

Systematic enforced disappearances an international crime, says Boyle

[TamilNet, Monday, 14 December 2015, 23:21 GMT]

Noting the re-emerging threat of white van abductions and enforced disappearances in the historic homeland, the NorthEast, of Eezham Tamils, Professor Francis Boyle, an expert in international law, said that systematic enforced disappearances is a crime against humanity under the Rome Statute, and in Sri Lanka this criminality of the Government of Sri Lanka is "an indicium of genocide against the Eelam Tamils." Boyle noted, as evidence of his concern, the recent incident in Jaffna where Colombo's military intelligence operatives threatened the editors of a local newspaper that they would have to face the "white van" if the paper failed to retract a published story on missing persons.

"When the enforced disappearances of human beings become either widespread or systematic, they become a Crime against Humanity under the Rome Statute for the International Criminal Court. In the case of Sri Lanka, its enforced disappearances of Eelam Tamils is both widespread and systematic and thus constitutes a Crime against Humanity.

"It also constitutes ongoing international criminal activity by the GOSL unless and until the victims have been accounted for. Furthermore, this GOSL Crime against Humanity is an indicium of threatened and ongoing genocide against the Eelam Tamils," Boyle said in his comment to TamilNet.

A three-member delegation of the United Nations Working Group on Enforced or Involuntary Disappearances (WGEID), visited Sri Lanka last month to investigate disappearances of civilians during the country's three-decade civil war. It found that successive governments systematically employed military and paramilitary forces to abduct, torture and ultimately disappear civilians, political opponents and journalists—irrespective of the ethnicity of the target, World Socialist said in its website.

"WGEID's first visit in October 1991 investigated and ultimately confirmed reports that state forces had engaged in enforced disappearances...The vast majority of enforced disappearances were never effectively investigated or prosecuted," Amnesty said in its coverage ahead of the visit by the UN staff.

- TAG Report: Blueprint on Sri Lanka's White Van operations
  http://www.tamilnet.com/img/publish/2012/07/WhiteVanv7-15.pdf

Tamils Against Genocide (TAG), a US-based rights group that seeks legal redress to war-affected Tamils, published in 2012 an operational blueprint of Sri Lanka's White Van abductions, and the complicity of State Institutions.

The blueprint was based on affidavits from surviving abductees, a video deposition from an ex-member of Liberation Tigers who was spared execution at the last moment, information revealed from recent capture of white van abductors in the South, and other circumstantial evidence including open death threats issued by Sri Lanka's Defense Secretary, Gotabhaya Rajapakse.

TAG concluded that the white van phenomenon is not a random occurrence of isolated events, but a systemic well-organized criminal enterprise carried out by independently operating cells consisting of criminal gangs and military personnel and activated by directives from high level State officials.

Aided by UN, US, genocide continues under Sirisena, says Boyle

[TamilNet, Friday, 08 January 2016, 02:02 GMT]

Noting recent rights groups reports that Tamils continue to face torture and gang rapes a year after President Maithripala Sirisena came to power in Sri Lanka promising reform, Professor Boyle, an expert in international law, who teaches at the University of Illinois College of Law, said that it is obvious that the "Sinhala Genocide against the Eelam Tamils continues apace under Sirisena," and that the GoSL, the U.S. Government and the UNHRC "perpetrated ... a fraud upon the Eelam Tamils by calling for the establishment of nothing more than a so-called "domestic mechanism" by the GOSL Genocidaires that will give them the legal cover and fig-leaf to continue their campaign of outright genocide against the Eelam Tamils."

Full text of the comment Prof. Boyle sent to TamilNet follows:

"I have not yet had the time to read this Report itself that just came out. But it is obvious from this Synopsis that the Sinhala Genocide against the Eelam Tamils continues apace under Sirisena.

"The World should have expected nothing else from the Genocidaire Sirisena.

"It is also obvious that the GOSL, the United States government and the UN Human Rights Council perpetrated a sick joke and a demented fraud upon the Eelam Tamils by calling for the establishment of nothing more than a so-called "domestic mechanism" by the GOSL Genocidaires that will give them the legal cover and fig-leaf to continue their campaign of outright genocide against the Eelam Tamils.

"Any international expert that gets involved in this so-called "domestic mechanism" will thereby become an accomplice to the GOSL genocide against the Eelam Tamils in violation of Genocide Convention Article III (e) that criminalizes: "Complicity in genocide." All Tamils around the world should note their names. He who pays the piper calls the tune," Boyle commented.

- ITJP Sri Lanka: January 2016 report on survivors of torture and sexual violence in 2015
  http://www.tamilnet.com/img/publish/2016/01/STOP_report_3_v5.1-2.pdf

South Africa-based group The International Truth and Justice Project (ITJP) and UK-based group Freedom From Torture (FFT) said this week that Tamils have undergone arbitrary detention, torture, and gang rape by Sri Lanka military.

The ITJP said a "well-organized machine" continued to torture and repress Tamils and it was not merely a case of a few "rotten apples."

Further, recent reports from Jaffna, alleged complicity of Colombo in destroying evidence and the remaining traces of a newly discovered makeshift torture chamber inside the recently released lands in Valikaamam North in Jaffna at a locality known as Pazhai-Veemankaamam.

Tamil journalists had filmed the locality earlier this week. After the video evidence was published, the Sri Lanka Defense Ministry in Colombo instructed its military at Palaali to remove the traces of the torture chamber, according to an earlier report filed in TamilNet.[1]

---

[1] http://www.tamilnet.com/art.html?catid=13&artid=38076

Colombo makes mockery of UN endorsed domestic mechanism—Boyle

[TamilNet, Thursday, 14 January 2016, 23:52 GMT]

Noting Sri Lanka Cabinet spokesperson Rajitha Senaratne's statements that there was no deadline to complete the accountability process on the war, that his Government is in talks with the United Nations with regards to the accountability process, and that the process will be a domestic process and not a "hybrid process" as proposed by the UN High Commissioner for Human Rights, Professor Boyle, an expert in International Law, and who teaches at University of Illinois, College of Law, said that by these words "GOSL has publicly stated that it will continue its Crimes against Humanity against the Eelam Tamils. This makes an absolute and total mockery of the so-called "domestic mechanism" that was endorsed by the UN Human Rights Council."

Full text of Prof. Boyle's comment to TamilNet follows:

"When the Enforced Disappearances (EDs) of human beings is either widespread or systematic, it becomes a Crime Against Humanity in violation of the Rome Statute for the International Criminal Court and customary international criminal law.

"In the case of the GOSL genocide against the Eelam Tamils, EDs are both widespread and systematic and therefore Crimes against Humanity too. EDs are also ongoing criminal offenses in violation of international criminal law until the fates of the disappeared persons are accounted for.

"So by means of this statement that there is "no deadline" on the accountability process for the EDd persons, the GOSL has defiantly indicated to the entire world that it will continue its ongoing international criminal activity of enforced disappearances of human beings against the Eelam Tamils, which are Crimes against Humanity.

"In other words, the GOSL has publicly stated that it will continue its Crimes against Humanity against the Eelam Tamils. This makes an absolute and total mockery of the so-called "domestic mechanism" that was endorsed by the UN Human Rights Council.

"Any international expert who participates in the genocidal GOSL's "domestic mechanism" will be aiding and abetting the GOSL's EDs Crimes against Humanity against the Eelam Tamils.

"Every Tamil in the world must take note of these so-called international experts who get involved in the genocidal GOSL's "domestic mechanism," Professor Boyle said.

Switzerland misleads, terminology counts: Prof Boyle

[TamilNet, Thursday, 21 January 2016, 09:25 GMT]

"The Swiss have no credibility whatsoever when it comes to Tamil Eelam and the Eelam Tamils. Under the circumstances of ongoing GOSL genocide, 'terminology' means everything if we want to survive," responded Professor Francis Boyle to the current Switzerland involved 'deliberations' that have taken place in Jaffna earlier this week. "At the end of the day, the Swiss will sell us out to the GOSL once again," Professor Boyle, who is an expert in International Law and who teaches at the University of Illinois College of Law, warned Eezham Tamils. He also noted the Swiss history of supporting Sri Lanka's crimes, especially pointing out that the Swiss sponsored a UN resolution which "congratulated" Sri Lanka as the State killed tens of thousands of Tamil civilians in the final phases of 2009 war.

Professor Boyle's comment on the Swiss statement follows:

Professor Francis Boyle

"The Eelam Tamils must not listen to the Swiss. They have already abandoned and betrayed us to the Fate of Genocide at the bloody hands of the GOSL. They are doing so again.

"The Swiss have no credibility whatsoever when it comes to Tamil Eelam and the Eelam Tamils. Under the circumstances of ongoing GOSL genocide, "terminology" means everything if we want to survive.

"To the best of my knowledge, the Swiss have not used the word "genocide" to condemn what the GOSL has done to the Eelam Tamils. The Swiss are good for nothing! At the end of the day, the Swiss will sell us out to the GOSL once again," Professor Boyle wrote.

* * *

Meanwhile, commenting on 'terminology', there is no justification for the international community fearing and yielding in to the genocidal State in Colombo, said Tamil activists for alternative politics in the island.

'Cultural identity' is fundamental for any meaningful development is what the culture and development theory coming from the West itself, says.

Without identity in nation, land and the exercise of power, cultural identity is not possible. Psychological equality of nations could come only through equality in terminology.

The terminology 'vertical' itself, promoted by Professor Eva Maria Belser, is another way of imposing unitary State and is not doing justice to the parallel context of nations in the island, the activists further said.

* * *

- Swiss Resolution on Sri Lanka
  http://www.tamilnet.com/img/publish/2009/05/
  SecondResolution_01.pdf

The 2009 Switzerland sponsored resolution to the U.N. Human Rights Council, had earlier prompted Professor Boyle to comment that Swiss action would be the same "as if the U.N. had invited the Nazi government to investigate and prosecute itself for genocide, crimes against humanity and war crimes against the Jews instead of supporting the Nuremberg Charter and Tribunal."

Boyle was irked earlier by the action of the Swiss on the resolution to add, "[t]he glaring hypocrisy and blatant sophistry of the Swiss Resolution is heightened by the fact that Switzerland is the Depositary for the Four Geneva Conventions of 1949 and their Two Additional Protocols of 1977 and therefore bears special obligation under international law to promote, guarantee and ensure their effective enforcement rather than their negation and nullification, which this Swiss Resolution will do. Obviously, Switzerland knows exactly what it is doing. The same is true for the 25 other state Co-Sponsors of the Swiss Resolution."

The Swiss government and allied NGOs have demonstrated their willingness to support the international community to whitewash a possible genocide. This practice continues to this day as in September 2015 the Swiss Federal Department of Foreign Affairs (FDFA) and Swiss Peace [NGO] participated in a meeting organized by an NGO outfit to soften the Tamil call for international investigations on Sri Lanka genocide.

Also, on the matter of asylum seekers and refugees, Switzerland with predictable self-interest, had appeared to support the view that 'Sri Lankan' rights record has improved vis-a-vis Tamils.

Refusal to use "genocide" indicates male fides—Boyle

[TamilNet, Monday, 25 January 2016, 18:11 GMT]

Tamils need an "acid test" in order to dispose of all the international charlatans and hucksters now coming your way. If they will not use the word "genocide," then they are doing GOSL's genocidal dirty work for it against the Eelam Tamils," said Professor Francis A. Boyle, and expert in international law who teaches at the University of Illinois, College of Law. A keen observer of the Tamil conflict for the past several years, Prof Boyle said he has been watching with alarming interest the involvement of several countries in the West including the US, UK and many members of the European Union in resolving the conflict, but ultimately ending up whitewashing Sri Lanka's international crimes, and displaying an illogical hesitancy in admitting that the Tamils constitute a nation.

The full text of additional comments sent to TamilNet follows:

Professor Francis A. Boyle, University of Illinois

"We need some acid test to determine the good faith of all these foreigners who say they want to help us like the Swiss and the Norwegians and the Americans and the British and the Europeans and the United Nations Officials, etc.

"I submit that acid test of their bona fides must be: Have you used the word 'genocide' to condemn what the GOSL has done to the Eelam Tamils? If not these foreigners are worthless. In fact, they are more dangerous than useless.

"Terminology counts for everything for a People being subjected to ongoing genocide like the Eelam Tamils by the GOSL," Boyle wrote.

"Obviously, we are not going to have the time or the resources to investigate all these foreigners going over there offering to "help" the Eelam Tamils now. But if they refuse to use the word "genocide," then their "advice" and "services" should be rejected. A simple one-word Acid Test: "genocide." Pass or Fail.

"Jews don't take seriously anyone who denies the Nazi Holocaust against the Jews. Tamils should not take seriously anyone who denies the GOSL Holocaust against the Tamils," Boyle added.

Prof. Boyle is convinced that the alleged crimes by the State of Sri Lanka on Tamils fall within the definition of the crime of genocide, and have said in several fora that he would be ready to represent the Tamils in the International Court of Justice (World Court) when a member nation is ready to file a case against Sri Lanka.

UN should refer Sri Lanka to ICC, or setup criminal tribunal, says Boyle

[TamilNet, Friday, 29 January 2016, 02:20 GMT]

Condemning Sri Lanka's President's rejection of any international involvement in investigating alleged war crimes committed during Sri Lanka's civil war, Professor Francis Boyle, an expert in International Law and who teaches at the University of Illinois College of Law, said "Sri Lanka's President Sirisena himself has now driven the proverbial stake through the heart of the genocidal Vampire of a GOSL domestic mechanism dressed up with the fig-leaf of meaningless international participation," and added, "[i]f the reference of the GOSL to the International Criminal Court by the U.N. Security Council is still stymied by a threatened veto...the UN must establish an International Criminal Tribunal for Sri Lanka as a "subsidiary organ" under U.N. Charter article 22."

Full text of Prof. Boyle's comment follows:

"Sri Lanka's President Sirisena himself has now driven the proverbial stake through the heart of the genocidal Vampire of a GOSL domestic mechanism dressed up with the fig-leaf of meaningless international participation that was recommended by the bogus United Nations Human Rights Council at the behest of the pro-GOSL United States government.

"A President is Head of State. A President has Extraordinary and Plenipotentiary Powers to act in the name of the State and definitively bind that State as a matter of international law. What a President says goes for good. Under basic principles of international law, when a President rejects something that is it. There is nothing more to argue about.

"The so-called domestic mechanism with the window-dressing of international participation is now Dead as a Doornail thanks to President Sirisena himself.

"So the situation is now like the World expecting the Nazis to investigate and prosecute themselves for their crimes against the Jews, including genocide, crimes against humanity and war crimes. Instead the World set up the Nuremberg Tribunal for that purpose.

"If the reference of the GOSL to the International Criminal Court by the U.N. Security Council is still stymied by a threatened veto by one or more of its Permanent Members acting in cahoots with the GOSL (i.e., United States, Britain, France, Russia, China), which seems likely, then the United Nations General Assembly must establish an International Criminal Tribunal for Sri Lanka as a "subsidiary organ" under U.N. Charter article 22," Professor Boyle said.

Boyle condemns U.S. endorsement of Sri Lanka on Independence Day

[TamilNet, Saturday, 06 February 2016, 01:50 GMT]

Professor Francis Boyle, an expert in International Law and who teaches at the University of Illinois College of Law, condemned as "revolting and disgusting" Under Secretary for Management Organization of American States, Patrick F. Kennedy's congratulatory remarks and endorsement of Sri Lanka on Thursday the 4th of February, Sri Lanka's Independence Day. Responding to Secretary Kennedy's statement that "plenteous in prosperity" and "in wisdom and strength renewed" as very apt portrayal of Sri Lanka's destiny, Boyle said "Yes, the Genocidal GOSL's "destiny" is to exterminate the Eelam Tamils and to steal all of Tamil Eelam. And the United States government is going to help the Genocidal GOSL to continue to do so."

Full text of Boyle's comment sent to TamilNet follows:

I can understand that for political and diplomatic reasons the United States would congratulate the Genocidal Sri Lanka on its National Day because it so congratulates all States and Governments with which it has diplomatic relations. But these gushing words of Endorsement by Kennedy on behalf of the United States Government are truly revolting and disgusting. As an American Citizen I condemn them in the strongest terms possible. Kennedy does not speak for me.

> "And like Sri Lankans of today, Americans are still striving to address some of the very challenging problems that have long bedeviled us."

Yes well with all of our faults, we Americans have not inflicted genocide, war crimes and crimes against humanity against 136, 000 of our own Citizens. Upon the Indians we did over a century ago, but they were not our own Citizens—not to justify America's Genocide against the Indians, which I also condemn.

> "We also have many of the same core values,…."

Does that include America inflicting genocide, war crimes and crimes against humanity against our own Citizens?

> "…and the accomplishments of the Sri Lankan people and

their government over the past year have made all of us
rightly proud.."

Does that mean that the United States government is "rightly proud"
of the ongoing genocide and crimes against humanity that the GOSL is
today inflicting upon the Eelam Tamils?

"You have ... co-sponsored, with the United States, a
strong resolution at the UN Human Rights Council on
human rights in Sri Lanka..."

As I have repeatedly pointed out on Tamilnet this UN Human Rights
Council Resolution is a sick joke and a demented fraud that perverts everything Human Rights is supposed to stand for and has now been publicly
repudiated by the President of Sri Lanka himself. How can Kennedy and
the State Department says this with a straight face?

"...returned 1,300 hectares of land to their rightful owners
in the Northern and Eastern provinces..."

I don't know if this claim is true. But it is a fact that the GOSL continues to steal more of Tamil Eelam every day and to inflict ethnic cleansing
upon the Eelam Tamils living there.

"....welcoming Sri Lanka as a Millennium Challenge
Corporation Threshold Partner..."

In other words, America will be giving the Genocidal GOSL a lot
more money to continue to facilitate its genocide, crimes against humanity,
and ethnic cleansing of the Eelam Tamils.

"...And the United States is committed to helping you, in
whatever way we can,..."

In other words, the United States government will continue to AID
AND ABET the GOSL Genocide, Crimes against Humanity, and Ethnic
Cleansing of the Eelam Tamils.

"The Sri Lankan government has more laudable ventures
underway..."

So does the United States government consider the Ongoing
GOSL Genocide, Crimes against Humanity, and Ethnic Cleansing against
the Eelam Tamils to be "laudable"?

"....The world is watching Sri Lanka. Your solutions, if successful, can become the blueprint for future generations, in distant nations,..."

Yes indeed. The GOSL Lesson here is that: Genocide Works! Always Again!

".... It describes a country that is "plenteous in prosperity..." and, "in wisdom and strength renewed." Those phrases may have been written in the last century, but they are, I strongly believe, a very apt portrayal of Sri Lanka's destiny in this century."

Yes, the Genocidal GOSL's "destiny" is to exterminate the Eelam Tamils and to steal all of Tamil Eelam. And the United States government is going to help the Genocidal GOSL to continue to do so.

US, UN bureaucracy behind Zeid's soft stand on Sri Lanka—Boyle

[TamilNet, Wednesday, 10 February 2016, 01:37 GMT]

Responding to Tamil activists accusation that "they witnessed a total lack of understanding on the part of UN Rights Chief Zeid Raad al-Hussein on the deep-rooted structural crimes taking place against Tamils in the East under the Mahaweli Minister and SL President Maithiripala Sirisena," Professor Boyle, an expert in international law, and who teaches at the University of Illinois College of Law, said, "Zeid is not an idiot. He knows full well that the GOSL has inflicted genocide on the Eelam Tamils that continues as of today. Zeid was sent there by the United States Government and the United Nations Bureaucracy to do damage control and damage limitation on behalf of the Genocidal GOSL Regime against the Eelam Tamils. He who pays the piper calls the tune."

Prof. Boyle, in a comment sent to TamilNet said:

"So Zeid knows and admits that the White Van Abductions against the Eelam Tamils continue—A Crime against Humanity.

"Zeid knows and admits that torture continues against the Eelam Tamils, which is an international crime, and when it is widespread and systematic becomes a Crime Against Humanity, which is the case here.

"And Zeid knows and admits that the GOSL "police" wantonly inflict violence and excessive force upon the Eelam Tamils, yet another Crime against Humanity.

"Zeid knows and admits that the GOSL continues to Rape Eelam Tamil Women, which is an international crime and in this case since it is widespread and systematic constitutes a Crime against Humanity. Etc.,etc., etc. throughout the rest of Zeid's Statement.

"When you add up all these atrocities that Zeid admits are still going on today, Zeid knows full well that the GOSL Genocide against the Eelam Tamils still continues as of today.

"Zeid is no idiot. He was sent there by the United States government and the United Nations Organization to do the dirty work of damage control and damage limitation on behalf of the Genocidal GOSL Regime against the Eelam Tamils.

"He who pays the piper calls the tune," Boyle said.

"Towards the end of his Statement Zeid blames "both sides." That is the functional equivalent of the United Nations blaming the Jews for the

Genocide and Holocaust that Hitler and the Nazis inflicted upon the Jews. Never again?

"No, according to Zeid and the United Nations Organization: Genocide Pays! Always again!

"Zeid and the United Nations are Accessories After The Fact to the GOSL Genocide against the Eelam Tamils, and Aiders And Abettors to the ongoing GOSL Genocide against the Eelam Tamils," Boyle said on Zeid's concluding statement on Sri Lanka visit.

* * *

Noting Sri Lanka analyst with the International Crisis Group (ICG) Alan Keenan's comment to IRIN website,[1]

> "There is a sense that the sheen is off the government, the sense that people are beginning to lose some trust in this process....Acting on some of the other recommendations in the report could be a way for Sirisena to burnish his fading reputation....the overarching goal of implementing such measures is to help "rebuild the integrity of the justice system,"

Professor Boyle said, "[n]otice that the so-called International Crisis Group is doing damage control and damage limitation for the Genocidal GOSL Regime against the Eelam Tamils.

"The Europeans are going to sell out the Eelam Tamils to the Genocidal GOSL Regime by restoring Sri Lanka access to their Generalized System of Preferences for hard cash soaked in the Blood of Tamils.

"And the Americans are going to do the same by giving the Genocidal GOSL Regime access to their Millennium Challenge Corporation.

"Tamil lives are worth nothing to the Europeans, the Americans, and the United Nations," said Boyle expressing his ire with the Western powers.

---

[1] http://www.irinnews.org/report/102417/sri-lanka-war-crimes-in-the-spotlight-as-un-rights-chief-visits

APPENDICES

Francis Boyle took the case of Bosnia to the International Court of Justice in The Hague in 1993, winning two Orders for provisional measures of protection against the rump Yugoslavia in favor of Bosnia and Herzegovina.

APPENDIX I

TRYING TO STOP AGGRESSIVE WAR AND GENOCIDE AGAINST THE PEOPLE AND THE REPUBLIC OF BOSNIA AND HERZEGOVINA

by

Francis A. Boyle

Professor of International Law

4 April 1997

There are numerous accounts of the aggression and genocide perpetrated by the rump Yugoslavia and its Bosnian Serb surrogates against the People and the Republic of Bosnia and Herzegovina that have been written by journalists, historians, ambassadors, political scientists, and others. This paper tries to tell the story of Bosnia from the perspective of international law. The aggression and genocide against Bosnia and the refusal of the international community to stop it will prove to be one of the pivotal events of the post World War II era. This paper will try to explain what happened, why it happened, and, most importantly, what was wrong with what happened.

It is hoped that this analysis will prove useful to the People of Bosnia and Herzegovina as they struggle to reconstruct their lives and their State. Hopefully, a record of what happened in the past will provide the Bosnian People with a guide for the direction of their future. Concerning the utility of this study for the rest of the world, as George Santayana has said: "Those who cannot remember the past are condemned to repeat it."

On March 19, 1993, this author was appointed General Agent with Extraordinary and Plenipotentiary Powers "to institute, conduct and defend against any and all legal proceedings" for the Republic of Bosnia and Herzegovina before the International Court of Justice by His Excellency President Alija Izetbegovic while attending the so-called Vance-Owen negotiations in New York. The very next day the author instituted legal proceedings on behalf of the Republic of Bosnia and Herzegovina before the International Court of Justice in The Hague against the rump Yugoslavia for violating the 1948 Genocide Convention. On April 8, 1993, the author won an Order for provisional measures of protection from the World Court against the rump Yugoslavia that was overwhelmingly in favor of Bosnia and Herzegovina.

Generally put, the World Court ordered the rump Yugoslavia immediately to cease and desist from committing all acts of genocide in the Republic of Bosnia and Herzegovina, whether directly or indirectly by means of its surrogate Bosnian Serb military, paramilitary, and irregular armed units:

52. For these reasons,
The COURT,
Indicates, pending its final decision in the proceedings instituted on 20 March 1993 by the Republic of Bosnia and Herzegovina against the Federal Republic of Yugoslavia (Serbia and Montenegro), the following provisional measures:

A.   (1) Unanimously,
The Government of the Federal Republic of Yugoslavia (Serbia and Montenegro) should immediately, in pursuance of its undertaking in the Convention on the Prevention and Punishment of the Crime of Genocide of 9 December 1948, take all measures within its power to prevent commission of the crime of genocide;

(2) By 13 votes to 1,
The Government of the Federal Republic of Yugoslavia (Serbia and Montenegro) should in particular ensure that any military, paramilitary or irregular armed units which may be directed or supported by it, as well as any organizations and persons which may be subject to its control, direction or influence, do not commit any acts of genocide, of conspiracy to commit genocide, of direct and public incitement to commit genocide, or of complicity in genocide, whether directed against the Muslim population of Bosnia and Herzegovina or against any other national, ethnical, racial or religious group;

IN FAVOUR: President Sir Robert Jennings; Vice-President Oda; Judges Ago, Schwebel, Bedjaoui, Ni, Evensen, Guillaume, Shahabuddeen, Aguilar Mawdsley, Weeramantry, Ranjeva, Ajibola;
AGAINST: Judge Tarassov;

B.   Unanimously,

The Government of the Federal Republic of Yugoslavia (Serbia and Montenegro) and the Government of the Republic of Bosnia and Herzegovina should not take any action and should ensure that no action is taken which may aggravate or extend the existing dispute over the prevention or punishment of the crime of genocide, or render it more difficult of solution.

In his Declaration attached to the World Court's Order of 8 April 1993, the late Judge Tarassov from Russia provided a most authoritative interpretation of Paragraph 52A(2) of the Court's Order:

> ...In my view, these passages of the Order are open to the interpretation that the Court believes that the Government of the Federal Republic of Yugoslavia is indeed involved in such genocidal acts, or at least that it may very well be so involved. Thus, on my view, these provisions are very close to a pre-judgment of the merits, despite the Court's recognition that, in an Order indicating provisional measures, it is not entitled to reach determinations of fact or law...

As I told the world's news media from the floor of the Great Courtroom of the Peace Palace in The Hague immediately after the close of the World Court's proceedings wherein this Order was handed down, I fully agreed with Judge Tarassov in the following sense: This Order was indeed a pre-judgment on the merits that genocide had been inflicted by the rump Yugoslavia against the People and the Republic of Bosnia and Herzegovina, both directly and indirectly by means of its surrogates in the Bosnian Serb military, paramilitary, and irregular armed units.

The unanimous ruling in Paragraph 52A(1) indicated that the World Court believed there was more than enough evidence to conclude that the rump Yugoslavia itself had inflicted genocide against the People and the Republic of Bosnia and Herzegovina. The 13 to 1 ruling in Paragraph 52A(2) indicated that the World Court believed there was more than enough evidence to conclude that the rump Yugoslavia was legally responsible for the atrocities inflicted by the Bosnian Serb military, paramilitary, and irregular armed forces against the People and the Republic of Bosnia and Herzegovina. The 13 to 1 ruling in Paragraph 52A(2) also indicated that the World Court believed that there was more than enough evidence to conclude that these surrogate Bosnian Serb military, paramilitary, and irregular armed forces had inflicted acts of genocide, conspiracy to commit genocide, direct and public incitement to commit genocide, and complicity in genocide, against the People and the Republic of Bosnia and Herzegovina.

As the Lawyer for the entire Republic of Bosnia and Herzegovina and for all of its People, I had expressly asked the World Court to protect all of the national, ethnical, racial and religious groups in Bosnia from acts of genocide perpetrated by the rump Yugoslavia and by its surrogate Bosnian Serb military, paramilitary, and irregular armed forces, which the World Court did do in Paragraph 52A(2) of this Order. Of course, the first and foremost victims of this genocide were the Bosnian Muslims, but also came those Bosnian Croats, those Bosnian Serbs and those Bosnian Jews who supported the Republic of Bosnia and Herzegovina. However, most of the evidence of genocide that I submitted to the World Court concerned acts of genocide against Bosnia's Muslim population, to which the Bosnian Parliament awarded the name "Bosniaks." So the World Court went out of its way to protect by name "the Muslim population of Bosnia and Herzegovina" from acts of genocide by the surrogate Bosnian Serb military, paramilitary, and irregular armed forces in Paragraph 52A(2) of this 8 April 1993 Order.

Only the late Judge Tarassov from Russia objected to this express protection of Bosnian Muslims by name in his separate Declaration: "The lack of balance in these provisions is the clearer in view of the way in which the Court has singled out one element of the population of Bosnia and Herzegovina." Once again, I agree with Judge Tarassov in the sense that the overwhelming weight of the evidence did indeed call for the World Court to protect the Bosnian Muslims from genocide expressly by name. This entire World Court Order of 8 April 1993 was so completely unbalanced against the rump Yugoslavia and its surrogate Bosnian Serb military, paramilitary, and irregular armed forces because the evidence of their genocide against the People and the Republic of Bosnia and Herzegovina and, in particular, against the Bosnian Muslims, was so overwhelming.

The unanimous World Court ruling in Paragraph 52B was also a victory for the People and the Republic of Bosnia and Herzegovina. I had expressly asked the World Court to impose this protective measure upon both Bosnia and the rump Yugoslavia, which the Court did indeed do. My calculation was that the rump Yugoslavia would definitely violate this measure, whereas Bosnia would obey it. I felt it would be difficult to imagine how the victim of genocide could aggravate or extend the dispute over genocide with the perpetrator of genocide, or render that dispute more difficult of solution.

By voluntarily asking for the imposition of this measure upon both Bosnia and the rump Yugoslavia, I intended to entangle the rump Yugoslavia into a full-scale breach and open defiance of the most comprehensive World Court Order that I could obtain. This is exactly what happened. The rump Yugoslavia paid absolutely no attention whatsoever to the entirety of this 8 April 1993 Order. Whereas, by comparison, Bosnia obeyed this self-imposed requirement of Paragraph 52B not to aggravate or extend the dispute over genocide, or render it more difficult of a solution.

By means of obtaining the measure set forth in Paragraph 52B, *inter alia*, I intended to prepare the groundwork for harsher Security Council sanctions against the rump Yugoslavia. I also hoped to pave the way for a then already anticipated second round of provisional measures at the World Court in which I intended to expand the basis of my original Application/ complaint against the rump Yugoslavia beyond the fixed parameters of the 1948 Genocide Convention. I needed to do that in order to break the genocidal arms embargo against Bosnia and also to stop the proposed racist carve-up of the Republic pursuant to the so-called Vance-Owen Plan, and then later, its successor, the genocidal Owen-Stoltenberg Plan.

By issuing this Order on 8 April 1993 the World Court necessarily and overwhelmingly rejected the bald-faced lies put forward by the rump Yugoslavia's Lawyer Shabtai Rosenne from Israel, that the bloodshed in Bosnia was the result of a civil war for which the rump Yugoslavia was in no way responsible. The World Court also overwhelmingly rejected Rosenne's argument that President Izetbegovic was not the lawful President of the Republic and therefore could not lawfully institute this lawsuit against the rump Yugoslavia and appoint me as Bosnia's Lawyer to argue this genocide case before the World Court. The World Court also overwhelmingly rejected Rosenne's request that provisional measures along the lines of those found in Paragraphs 52A(1) and (2) be imposed upon Bosnia because there was no evidence that the Government of the Republic of Bosnia and Herzegovina had committed genocide against anyone. Many of these so-called issues are still misrepresented by the rump Yugoslavia and its supporters around the world today despite the fact that they were decisively resolved by the World Court as long ago as 8 April 1993.

The World Court's Order of 8 April 1993 was an overwhelming and crushing defeat of the rump Yugoslavia by Bosnia on all counts save one: The World Court said nothing at all about the arms embargo, apparently because the Genocide Convention itself says nothing at all about the use of force to prevent genocide. Nevertheless, in this regard, the World Court did state quite clearly in Paragraph 45 of its 8 April 1993 Order that in accordance with the requirements of Article I of the Genocide Convention "...all parties to the Convention have thus undertaken 'to prevent and to punish' the crime of genocide..." The implication was quite clear that in the opinion of the World Court all 100+ states that were parties to the Genocide Convention had an absolute obligation "to prevent" the ongoing genocide against Bosnia. Therefore, although technically the World Court directed its 8 April 1993 Order against the rump Yugoslavia, the Court was telling every other state in the world community that each had an obligation "to prevent" the ongoing genocide against the People and the Republic of Bosnia and Herzegovina.

The World Court continued in Paragraph 45 with the following language: "...whereas in the view of the Court, in the circumstances brought to its attention and outlined above in which there is a *grave risk* of acts of genocide being committed..." (Emphasis added.) In other words, the World Court went as far as it could consistent with its Rules of Procedure toward definitively ruling that acts of genocide were actually being committed by the rump Yugoslavia and its surrogate Bosnian Serb armed forces against the People and the Republic of Bosnia and Herzegovina. At the time, this "grave risk of acts of genocide" language set forth in Paragraph 45 of the 8 April 1993 Order was as close as the World Court could go to rendering a pre-judgment on the merits of the dispute, as pointed out by the late Judge Tarassov in his Declaration.

Several hours after I had won this World Court Order for Bosnia, on 8 April 1993 the Clinton administration announced the imposition by NATO of a complete air interdiction zone above the Republic of Bosnia and Herzegovina whereby NATO jet fighters would shoot down any Serb jets, planes, and helicopters. The Serbs were no longer able to kill the Bosnians from the sky! Late that evening Hague time I was interviewed live by the BBC and asked to give my opinion on this so-called "no-fly zone" over Bosnia that was announced earlier in the day from Washington, D.C.: "...I certainly hope that the NATO pilots do not fly over Bosnia, watch the genocide, rape, murder, torture and killing go on, take pictures, send them back to NATO Headquarters, Washington, London and Paris, and then do nothing to stop it!" Yet, most tragically of all, that is exactly what happened until the Fall of 1995.

In accordance with its own terms, an original copy of this 8 April 1993 Order was transmitted "to the Secretary-General of the United Nations for transmission to the Security Council." In other words, the World Court officially informed the member states of the U.N. Security Council (1) that genocide was currently being inflicted by the rump Yugoslavia and its surrogate Bosnian Serb armed forces against the People and the Republic of Bosnia and Herzegovina; and also (2) that the member states of the Security Council had an absolute obligation under the Genocide Convention "to prevent" this ongoing genocide against Bosnia. According to Article 94(2) of the United Nations Charter, the Security Council is supposed to enforce such World Court Orders.

As I had anticipated, the rump Yugoslavia paid absolutely no attention whatsoever to the World Court's 8 April 1993 Order, and immediately proceeded to violate each and every one of its three provisional measures. But instead of punishing the rump Yugoslavia, the Security Council's Permanent Members—the United States, Britain, France, Russia, and China—decided to punish Bosnia, the victim, by imposing upon it the so-called Owen-Stoltenberg Plan as the successor to the Vance-Owen Plan, which had been rejected by the so-called Bosnian Serb Parliament. The Owen-Stoltenberg Plan would have carved-up the Republic of Bosnia and Herzegovina into three ethnically based mini-states, destroyed Bosnia's Statehood, and robbed Bosnia of its Membership in the United Nations Organization. Furthermore, in accordance with an internal study prepared by the United States Department of State, this proposed tripartite partition of Bosnia would have subjected approximately 1.5 to 2 million *more* Bosnians to "ethnic cleansing," which I had already argued to the World Court was a form of genocide.

Therefore, soon after my return from The Hague, the author set out to break the genocidal arms embargo against Bosnia and to stop this genocidal carve-up of the Republic of Bosnia and Herzegovina by drafting a Second Request for Provisional Measures of Protection to the International Court of Justice on behalf of Bosnia. Pursuant thereto, on July 26, 1993, the author spent the day at United Nations Headquarters in New York with

Ambassador Muhamed Sacirbey of the Republic of Bosnia and Herzegovina, publicly briefing large numbers of Ambassadors, as well as privately briefing the Non-Aligned member states of the Security Council and the then President of the Council Ambassador Diego Arias from Venezuela, about this Second Request to the International Court of Justice for an Interim Order of Protection on behalf of the Republic of Bosnia and Herzegovina. In that location and on that day, as Bosnia's Lawyer I publicly threatened to sue the Permanent Members of the Security Council over the arms embargo, with Ambassador Sacirbey sitting at my side. As I said at that time and place, the Security Council's arms embargo against the Republic of Bosnia and Herzegovina had aided and abetted genocide against the Bosnian People.

The five Permanent Members of the Security Council--United States, United Kingdom, Russia, France, China--bear special responsibility for aiding and abetting genocide against the People and the Republic of Bosnia and Herzegovina in violation of the 1948 Genocide Convention. I would have been happy to have sued the Permanent Members of the Security Council for Bosnia, and had offered to do so on more than one occasion to the Bosnian Presidency. The same condemnation can be applied as well to all those U.N. member states that had served on the Security Council from 1992 through 1995 and had routinely supported the continuation of this genocidal arms embargo against Bosnia.

That evening, the author flew to The Hague and filed this Second Request for Interim Protection at the World Court on 27 July 1993. The very next day, 28 July 1993, the author flew to Geneva in order to serve as the Legal Adviser to President Alija Izetbegovic, then Foreign Minister (later Prime Minister) Haris Silajdic,* and all of the Members of the collective Presidency of the Republic of Bosnia and Herzegovina during the so-called Owen-Stoltenberg negotiations. There I personally disrupted the Owen-Stoltenberg Plan to carve-up the Republic into three pieces, to destroy Bosnia's Statehood, and to rob Bosnia of its Membership in the United Nations Organization. In addition, President Izetbegovic had also instructed me to negotiate in good faith over the so-called "package" of proposed documents with David Owen and his lawyer Paul Szasz. The author served in that capacity until August 10, 1993, when the talks had broken down. The author then returned home in order to prepare for Bosnia's second oral argument before the World Court.

The author then argued the Second Request for provisional measures of protection for Bosnia and Herzegovina before the World Court on 25 and 26 August 1993. The author then won the Second Order of Provisional Protection on behalf of Bosnia from the World Court on 13 September 1993. Generally put, this second World Court Order demanded that the Court's first Order of 8 April 1993 "should be immediately and effectively implemented":

---

*Now Bosnian President.

61. For these reasons,
THE COURT
(1) By 13 votes to 2,
Reaffirms the provisional measure indicated in paragraph 52 A (1) of the Order made by the Court on 8 April 1993, which should be immediately and effectively implemented;

IN FAVOUR: President Sir Robert Jennings; Vice-President Oda; Judges Schwebel, Bedjaoui, Ni, Evensen, Guillaume, Shahabuddeen, Aguilar Mawdsley, Weeramantry, Ajibola, Herczegh; Judge ad hoc Lauterpacht;
AGAINST: Judge Tarassov; Judge ad hoc Kreca;

(2) By 13 votes to 2,
Reaffirms the provisional measure indicated in paragraph 52 A (2) of the Order made by the Court on 8 April 1993, which should be immediately and effectively implemented;

IN FAVOUR: President Sir Robert Jennings; Vice-President Oda; Judges Schwebel, Bedjaoui, Ni, Evensen, Guillaume, Shahabuddeen, Aguilar Mawdsley, Weeramantry, Ajibola, Herczegh; Judge ad hoc Lauterpacht;
AGAINST: Judge Tarassov; Judge ad hoc Kreca;

(3) By 14 votes to 1,
Reaffirms the provisional measure indicated in paragraph 52 B of the Order made by the Court on 8 April 1993, which should be immediately and effectively implemented.

IN FAVOUR: President Sir Robert Jennings; Vice-President Oda; Judges Schwebel, Bedjaoui, Ni, Evensen, Tarassov, Guillaume, Shahabuddeen, Aguilar Mawdsley, Weeramantry, Ajibola, Herczegh; Judge ad hoc Lauterpacht;
AGAINST: Judge ad hoc Kreca.

In his Dissenting Opinion attached to this second World Court Order of 13 September 1993, the late Judge Tarassov from Russia once again provided a most authoritative interpretation of its meaning and significance:

....

Given that requests for the indication of provisional measures have been submitted by both Parties in new proceedings and given the numerous communications on which those requests are based, regarding acts which allegedly relate to the crime of genocide and which have purportedly been committed in this inter-ethnic, civil conflict in Bosnia and Herzegovina by all ethnic groups against each other, the Court's decision to make an order ascribing the lion's share of responsibility for the prevention of acts of genocide in Bosnia and Herzegovina to Yugoslavia is a one-sided approach based on preconceived ideas, which borders on a pre-judgment of the merits of the case and implies an unequal treatment of the different ethnic groups in Bosnia and Herzegovina who have all suffered inexpressibly in this fratricidal war. I, as a judge, cannot support this approach. ...

....

...While the one-sided, unbalanced Order of the Court might not necessarily be 'an obstacle to a negotiated settlement,' it will obviously not facilitate its successful completion. ...

Once again, I fully agreed with the late Judge Tarassov's characterization of this second World Court Order of 13 September 1993 in the following sense:

It was indeed completely "one-sided" and "unbalanced" in favor of Bosnia and against the rump Yugoslavia and its surrogate Bosnian Serb armed forces. This second World Court Order clearly did ascribe "the lion's share of responsibility" for the atrocities in Bosnia to the rump Yugoslavia and its surrogate Bosnian Serb military, paramilitary, and irregular armed forces. This second Order clearly represented a "one-sided approach" by the World Court in favor of Bosnia against the rump Yugoslavia and its surrogate Bosnian Serb armed forces. Moreover, this second Order clearly accorded the Bosnian Muslims "unequal treatment" because of the Order's reaffirmation of their express protection by name. The World Court had indeed developed the "preconceived ideas" that the Bosnian Muslims were the primary victims of Serb genocide against the People and the Republic of Bosnia and Herzegovina precisely because of the overwhelming evidence I had submitted to that effect starting on 20 March 1993 when I originally filed the lawsuit. Finally, this second World Court Order of 13 September 1993 was even more of "a pre-judgment on the merits of the case" than was the first Order of 8 April 1993.

Immediately after the receipt of this second World Court Order, the Serb Ambassador sat down dejectedly in the Hall of the Peace Palace just outside the Great Courtroom and was asked by the world news media what he thought about the new Order: "It is even worse than the first one!" The world news media then asked me what I thought about his comment: "It is the first truthful statement they have ever made here at the World Court." You have to give the devil his due when he is telling the truth.

In order to render this second Order, the World Court once again necessarily and overwhelmingly rejected the bald-faced lies put forward by Rosenne and in addition now by three Serb lawyers who had joined him, that what was happening in Bosnia was a civil war for which the rump Yugoslavia bore no responsibility. Once again, the World Court overwhelmingly rejected Rosenne's argument that President Izetbegovic was not the legitimate President of the Republic of Bosnia and Herzegovina entitled to have me argue these proceedings before the World Court in his name and in the name of the Republic. Finally, the World Court once again overwhelmingly rejected the request by Rosenne to impose a proposed provisional measure against Bosnia along the lines of Paragraph 52A(1) of its 8 April 1993 Order because there was still no evidence that the Republic of Bosnia and Herzegovina had committed genocide against anyone.

This second World Court Order of 13 September 1993 was a crushing and overwhelming victory for Bosnia against the rump Yugoslavia on all counts but one: The World Court once again refused to say anything directly about the arms embargo, apparently because the Genocide Convention itself said nothing about the use of force to prevent genocide. Nevertheless, in Paragraph 50 of this second Order the World Court quoted verbatim Article I of the 1948 Genocide Convention and then expressly held: "...whereas all parties to the Convention have thus undertaken to prevent and to punish the crime of genocide;..." Once again, the World Court was telling all 100+ states parties to the Genocide Convention that each had an obligation "to prevent" the ongoing genocide in Bosnia, and this time by means of the "immediate and effective implementation" of its 8 April 1993 Order as called for by Paragraph 59 of this second Order, inter alia, which will be quoted in full below.

These preliminary conclusions become perfectly clear by means of a detailed examination of the next several paragraphs of this second World Court Order of 13 September 1993:

51. Whereas, as the Court recorded in its Order of 8 April 1993, the crime of genocide "shocks the conscience of mankind, results in great losses to humanity ... and is contrary to moral law and to the spirit and aims of the United Nations," in the words of General Assembly resolution 96 (1) of 11 December 1946 on "The Crime of Genocide";

52. Whereas, since the Order of 8 April 1993 was made, and despite that Order, and despite many resolutions of the Security Council of the United Nations, great suffering

and loss of life has been sustained by the population of Bosnia-Herzegovina in circumstances which shock the conscience of mankind and flagrantly conflict with moral law and the spirit and aims of the United Nations;...

In accordance with its own Rules of Procedure, during the two provisional measures phases of these proceedings the World Court could not technically render a final Judgment on the merits that the rump Yugoslavia and its surrogate Bosnian Serb armed forces had committed acts of "genocide" against the People and the Republic of Bosnia and Herzegovina expressly by use of that word. But in Paragraphs 51 and 52 of this second Order, the World Court did the next best thing:

The crime of "genocide" is a legal term of art that is based upon the existence of certain factual predicates as set forth in part by the General Assembly in Resolution 96(1) on "The Crime of Genocide." In Paragraphs 51 and 52 of this second Order the World Court found the existence of several facts necessary to constitute "The Crime of Genocide" in accordance with the General Assembly's Resolution even though the Court was prevented at this stage of the proceedings from ruling that "genocide" itself had actually been committed by the rump Yugoslavia by using that precise word. In other words, as far as the World Court was concerned, Bosnia had already won this lawsuit on the merits and had only to continue through the merits stage of the proceedings in order to obtain a pre-ordained final Judgment on the merits in Bosnia's favor against the rump Yugoslavia for genocide.

In Paragraph 51 of the second Order the World Court expressly referred to the crime of genocide as something that "shocks the conscience of mankind, results in great losses to humanity...and is contrary to moral law and to the spirit and aims of the United Nations," quoting from the U.N. General Assembly Resolution 96(1) on "The Crime of Genocide." Then in Paragraph 52 the World Court does expressly make the finding of fact that "...great suffering and loss of life has been sustained by the population of Bosnia-Herzegovina." This language is stronger than "great losses to humanity" found in the General Assembly's Resolution on "The Crime of Genocide" that the Court had quoted in the immediately preceding paragraph. In other words, the World Court rendered a formal finding of fact that the predicate to the crime of genocide—"great losses to humanity"—had been exceeded by the "great suffering and loss of life" sustained by the Bosnian People.

Paragraph 52 then continued: "...great suffering and loss of life has been sustained by the population of Bosnia-Herzegovina in circumstances which shock the conscience of mankind..." Notice that the World Court used the precise language taken directly from the General Assembly's Resolution on "The Crime of Genocide" that the Court had quoted in Paragraph 51, and employed that language with respect to the Bosnian People. In other words, the World Court found the existence of a second factual predicate of the international crime of genocide by the rump Yugoslavia against the People and the Republic of Bosnia and Herzegovina: "...shock the conscience of mankind..."

Finally, Paragraph 52 concludes: "...great suffering and loss of life has been sustained by the population of Bosnia-Herzegovina in circumstances which shock the conscience of mankind and flagrantly conflict with moral law and the spirit and aims of the United Nations..." By comparison, the General Assembly's Resolution on "The Crime of Genocide" quoted in Paragraph 51 only requires acts of genocide to be "contrary to moral law and to the spirit and aims of the United Nations." Notice that the World Court found that the circumstances in Bosnia "flagrantly conflict with moral law," which language is much stronger than the General Assembly's "contrary to moral law." Certainly, the word "conflict" is stronger than "contrary" even without the modifying adverb "flagrantly," which was not even required by the General Assembly's Resolution on "The Crime of Genocide." In other words, the World Court had found that a third factual predicate necessary to establish the crime of genocide had been far exceeded with respect to the People and the Republic of Bosnia and Herzegovina.

The conclusion is ineluctable that in Paragraphs 51 and 52 of this second World Court Order of 13 September 1993 the World Court found that several factual predicates necessary to constitute the crime of genocide had been committed by the rump Yugoslavia and its surrogate Bosnian Serb armed forces against the People and the Republic of Bosnia and Herzegovina, and that the Serb atrocities against the Bosnian People had by far exceeded the threshold level for genocide set forth by the General Assembly in its Resolution 96(1) on "The Crime of Genocide." In other words, as far as the World Court was concerned, Bosnia had already won this lawsuit for genocide against the rump Yugoslavia. The conclusion is inevitable, therefore, that in the opinion of the World Court all that Bosnia must now do is to continue through the merits phase of the proceedings in order to obtain a pre-ordained Judgment on the merits that the rump Yugoslavia has indeed committed acts of genocide against the People and the Republic of Bosnia and Herzegovina, both directly and indirectly by means of its surrogate Bosnian Serb military, paramilitary, and irregular armed forces.

This second Order of 13 September 1993 was purposefully designed by the World Court to be even more of an outright pre-judgment on the merits of the issue of genocide in favor of Bosnia than was the first Order of 8 April 1993. In other words, the World Court was telling the entire world, and especially the member states of the Security Council, that the Court had essentially found that genocide was currently being inflicted by the rump Yugoslavia against the People and the Republic of Bosnia and Herzegovina, both directly and indirectly by means of its Bosnian Serb surrogates. Therefore, the World Court was deliberately saying in this Second Order that all 100+ states parties to the Genocide Convention as well as the member states of the Security Council, and especially its Permanent Members, had an absolute obligation to terminate this ongoing genocide by means of the immediate and effective implementation of its first Order of 8 April 1993.

Paragraph 53 of the 13 September 1993 World Court Order makes even more findings of fact that are conclusive on the infliction of genocide by the rump Yugoslavia and its Bosnian Serb surrogates against the People and the Republic of Bosnia and Herzegovina:

> 53. Whereas, since the Order of 8 April 1993 was made, the grave risk which the Court then apprehended of action being taken which may aggravate or extend the existing dispute over the prevention and punishment of the crime of genocide, or render it more difficult of solution, has been deepened by the persistence of conflicts on the territory of Bosnia-Herzegovina and the commission of heinous acts in the course of those conflicts;

The "grave risk" language quoted above was taken from Paragraph 45 of the 8 April 1993 Order, which was mentioned by the World Court in Paragraph 49 of the second Order of 13 September 1993 as follows: "49. Whereas in paragraph 45 of its Order of 8 April 1993 the Court concluded that there was a grave risk of acts of genocide being committed..." I have already pointed out why Paragraph 45 of the 8 April 1993 Order was tantamount to a pre-judgement on the merits of the case that the rump Yugoslavia had indeed inflicted genocide against the People and the Republic of Bosnia and Herzegovina, as conceded by the late Judge Tarassov in his Declaration of 8 April 1993.

By means of Paragraph 53 of the second Order, the World Court expressly stated that since 8 April 1993 this "grave risk" of "...the crime of genocide... has been deepened..." Once again the World Court was telling the entire world and especially the Permanent Members of the Security Council that the rump Yugoslavia was currently inflicting even worse genocide against the People and the Republic of Bosnia and Herzegovina than the Serbs had been doing as of 8 April 1993. Also, the World Court's reference to "heinous acts" only strengthened the conclusion that in the opinion of the Court the rump Yugoslavia was indeed committing even worse acts of genocide against the People and the Republic of Bosnia and Herzegovina. Finally, this Paragraph 53 also indicates that in the opinion of the World Court, the rump Yugoslavia had violated the provisional measure set forth in Paragraph 52B of its 8 April 1993 Order, inter alia.

Paragraph 55 of the 13 September 1993 World Court Order provides conclusive proof of the fact that the Owen-Stoltenberg Plan would have destroyed Bosnia's Statehood and robbed the Republic of Bosnia and Herzegovina of its Membership in the United Nations Organization:

> 55. Whereas the Security Council of the United Nations in

resolution 859 (1993) of 24 August 1993 which, inter alia, affirmed the continuing membership of Bosnia-Herzegovina in the United Nations,...

At the very outset of the Owen-Stoltenberg negotiations in Geneva, on 29 July 1993 around 7:30 p.m. then Foreign Minister (later Prime Minister) Haris Silajdzic asked me to analyze the Owen-Stoltenberg Plan for President Izetbegovic. After working all night to prepare a formal Memorandum on the Plan for the President, and with a heavy heart, I informed Bosnia's Foreign Minister at breakfast around 8 a.m. Geneva time: "Briefly put, ...they will carve you up into three pieces, destroy your Statehood, and rob you of your U.N. Membership." At the end of our lengthy conversation, Foreign Minister Silajdzic instructed me: "You brief the press, I will tell the President!" Pursuant to his instructions, I immediately proceeded to explain to the world news media that the Owen-Stoltenberg Plan called for Bosnia to be carved up into three ethnically based mini-states, for Bosnia's Statehood to be destroyed, and for Bosnia to be robbed of its Membership in the United Nations Organization. I distributed my Memorandum dated 30 July 1993 to the world's news media in support of my conclusions.*

Several hours later, I received an urgent telephone call from Muhamed Sacirbey, Bosnia's Ambassador to the United Nations Headquarters in New York, asking me what he should do: "Convene an emergency meeting of the Security Council! Tell them they are stealing our U.N. Membership! Distribute my Memorandum! Try to stop it!" The net result of Ambassador Sacirbey's prodigious efforts in New York was Security Council Resolution 859 (1993) that guaranteed Bosnia's Membership in the United Nations despite the Machiavellian machinations of Owen and Stoltenberg in Geneva.

At the time everyone in Geneva knew full well that if Bosnia were to lose its U.N. Membership, then the Bosnian People would go the same way that the Jewish People did starting in 1939. Indeed, that was the entire purpose of the exercise in Geneva by Owen, Stoltenberg, and their lawyer Szasz: Implementing the "final solution" to the inconvenient "problem" presented by the gallant resistance to genocide mounted by the People and the Republic of Bosnia and Herzegovina since March of 1992. But in the late summer of 1993 the Bosnians refused to go the same way the Jews did in 1939!

During the course of this second round of provisional measures proceedings before the World Court in July and August of 1993, I had requested the World Court to rule against the legality of the Owen-Stoltenberg carve-up of the Republic of Bosnia and Herzegovina on the grounds that this partition

---

*See Francis A. Boyle, *The Bosnian People Charge Genocide* 233-45 (1996).

would subject 1.5 to 2 million more Bosnians to "ethnic cleansing," which I had already argued to the Court was a form of genocide. In response, the World Court did rule against the legality of the Owen-Stoltenberg Plan in Paragraph 42 of its Second Order by means of the following language:

> ...whereas, on the other hand, in so far as it is the Applicant's contention that such "partition and dismemberment," annexation or incorporation will result from genocide, the Court, in its Order of 8 April 1993 has already indicated that Yugoslavia should "take all measures within its power to prevent commission of the crime of genocide," whatever might be its consequences;...

In other words, by a vote of 13 to 2, the World Court effectively prohibited the Owen-Stoltenberg carve-up of Bosnia because it would result from acts of genocide, which were already prohibited by its 8 April 1993 Order. Nevertheless undeterred, thereafter Owen and Stoltenberg continued to plot their tripartite carve-up of Bosnia under the new rubric of the so-called "Contact Group Plan" with the full support of the United States, Britain, France, Russia, the United Nations, the European Union and its other member states.

In this second Order of 13 September 1993, the World Court then indicated that its first Order of 8 April 1993 was so sweepingly comprehensive that it did not need to be supplemented, but only "should be immediately and effectively implemented":

> 59. Whereas the present perilous situation demands, not an indication of provisional measures additional to those indicated by the Court's Order of 8 April 1993, set out in paragraph 37 above, but immediate and effective implementation of those measures;

Notice here the World Court's express finding of fact that the situation in the Republic of Bosnia and Herzegovina was "perilous." In other words, the rump Yugoslavia was currently perpetrating even worse acts of genocide against the People and the Republic of Bosnia and Herzegovina than the Serbs had been doing as of 8 April 1993. The very existence of the Republic of Bosnia and Herzegovina was in jeopardy.

Furthermore, it becomes crystal clear from reading through this second Order of 13 September 1993 that the World Court was indirectly criticizing the member states of the U.N. Security Council for having refused to fulfill their obligation "to prevent" the ongoing genocide in Bosnia. Pursuant to its own terms the World Court's first Order of 8 April 1993 was transmitted to the Security Council. The World Court noted in Paragraph 54 of the second Order of 13 September 1993 that the Security Council duly "took note of" its first Order in Resolution 819 (1993) of 16 April 1993. But the Serb acts of genocide against the Bosnians continued apace "...despite many resolutions of the Security Council of the United Nations..." to the great harm of the Bosnian People, as the World Court expressly found in Paragraph 52 of its second Order of 13 September 1993. In other words, in the opinion of the World Court, the Security Council had failed to adopt prompt and effective measures to terminate the ongoing genocide against the People and the Republic of Bosnia and Herzegovina, and especially despite its first Order of 8 April 1993.

In accordance with its own terms, this second World Court Order of 13 September 1993 was also transmitted to the U.N. Secretary General for transmission to the U.N. Security Council. It is obvious from reading through this second Order that the World Court was calling upon the member states of the U.N. Security Council to immediately and effectively implement its first Order of 8 April 1993 against the rump Yugoslavia in order to stop the ongoing genocide against the People and the Republic of Bosnia and Herzegovina. This the member states of the Security Council were required to do under the terms of both the Genocide Convention and the United Nations Charter. But despite this second, even stronger Order by the World Court on 13 September 1993, the Security Council and its Permanent Members refused to do anything to stop the Serb genocide and aggression against the People and the Republic of Bosnia and Herzegovina for the next two years until the Fall of 1995.

Article 31(3) of the Statute of the International Court of Justice provides: "If the Court includes upon the Bench no judge of the nationality of the parties, each of the parties may proceed to choose a judge as provided in paragraph 2 of this article." It was this author's decision to nominate Professor Elihu Lauterpacht of Cambridge University as Bosnia's Judge ad hoc in this case. Professor Lauterpacht is one of the leading Professors of Public International Law in the world today. He is also a man of great experience, integrity, and judgment. Finally, he is a distinguished member of the prominent Jewish community in Britain and thus, in my opinion, bore a special understanding for a race of people currently being victimized by genocide. Professor Lauterpacht had no prior connection with the Republic of Bosnia and Herzegovina.

By comparison, the Serb government nominated Milan Kréca to serve as their Judge ad hoc in this case. In accordance with his submitted resume, Mr. Kréca was a Serb lawyer who had worked for the Serb government. In other words, unlike Professor Lauterpacht, Mr. Kréca was not independent of the Serb government.

For this reason, at the time of Mr. Kréca's nomination by the Serb government to be their Judge ad hoc in this case, I repeatedly argued to the Deputy Registrar of the World Court that the President of the Court (then Judge Robert Jennings of Britain) should disqualify Mr. Kréca on the basis of his resume alone because he obviously was not independent of the Serb government. Eventually I was informed by the Deputy Registrar that the President of the World Court had taken the position that in the event I insisted upon my objection to Mr. Kréca's qualifications, there would have to be a formal hearing by the full Court on my objections and that this hearing would undoubtedly postpone the then scheduled World Court hearing on my Second Request for provisional measures of protection for Bosnia against the rump Yugoslavia that the Court had already ordered to take place on August 25 and 26, 1993.

Of course, under no circumstances could I risk jeopardizing that World Court hearing on my Second Request for provisional measures. It would be the only chance I had to stop the Owen-Stoltenberg carve-up of Bosnia into three pieces as well as to break the genocidal arms embargo against Bosnia. So I told the Deputy Registrar to inform the President of the Court that under these dire circumstances I had no choice but to accept Mr. Kréca as Serbia's Judge ad hoc, but that I protested his presence on the Court in the strongest terms possible.

It would serve no purpose here for me to analyze Judge ad hoc Lauterpacht's lengthy Separate Opinion attached to the World Court's Order of 13 September 1993. It speaks for itself, and--I might add--quite eloquently so. Nevertheless, within his erudite exposition, I wish to draw to the reader's attention the critical passage found in Paragraph 102 of Judge ad hoc Lauterpacht's Separate Opinion:

> 102. Now, it is not to be contemplated that the Security Council would ever deliberately adopt a resolution clearly and deliberately flouting a rule of *jus cogens* or requiring a violation of human rights. But the possibility that a Security Council resolution might inadvertently or in an unforeseen manner lead to such a situation cannot be excluded. And that, it appears, is what has happened here. On this basis, the inability of Bosnia-Herzegovina sufficiently strongly to fight back against the Serbs and effectively to prevent the implementation of the Serbian policy of ethnic cleansing is at least in part directly attributable to the fact that Bosnia-Herzegovina's access to weapons and equipment has been severely limited by the embargo. Viewed in this light, the Security Council resolution can be seen as having in effect called on members of the United Nations, albeit unknowingly and assuredly unwillingly, to become in some degree supporters of the genocidal activity of the Serbs and in this manner and to that extent to act contrary to a rule of *jus cogens*.

In other words, Judge ad hoc Lauterpacht had pointed out for the entire world to see that the Security Council's arms embargo against the Republic of Bosnia and Herzegovina had aided and abetted genocide against the Bosnian People! Furthermore, Judge ad hoc Lauterpacht knew full well that his Separate Opinion would be transmitted with the Second Order of 13 September 1993 to the United Nations Security Council. Thus, Judge ad hoc Lauterpacht had purposefully and officially placed on notice the member states of the Security Council that their arms embargo against Bosnia was aiding and abetting genocide against the People and the Republic of Bosnia and Herzegovina.

During the early morning hours of 14 September 1993, the author rose to fly to Geneva for further consultations with President Izetbegovic, Vice President Ejup Ganic, and then Foreign Minister Silajdzic. It was my advice to all three that the next step for Bosnia and Herzegovina at the World Court would be to sue the United Kingdom for aiding and abetting genocide against the Bosnian People in order to break the genocidal Security Council arms embargo of Bosnia and to stop the genocidal carve-up of the Republic pursuant to the proposed so-called Contact Group Plan. This recommendation was taken under advisement.

Pursuant to the authorization of President Izetbegovic, on November 10, 1993 the author was instructed by Ambassador Sacirbey to institute legal proceedings against the United Kingdom for violating the Genocide Convention and the Racial Discrimination Convention in accordance with my previous recommendation. On 15 November 1993, Ambassador Sacirbey convened a press conference at U.N. Headquarters in New York in which he stated Bosnia's solemn intention to institute legal proceedings against the United Kingdom. Later that day, the author filed with the World Court a Communication that I had drafted, which was entitled *Statement of Intention by the Republic of Bosnia and Herzegovina to Institute Legal Proceedings Against the United Kingdom Before the International Court of Justice.** Ambassador Sacirbey had also distributed this *Statement* at his press conference.

In this 15 November 1993 *Statement,* the Republic of Bosnia and Herzegovina formally stated its solemn intention to institute legal proceedings against the United Kingdom before the International Court of Justice for violating the terms of the 1948 Convention on the Prevention and Punishment of the Crime of Genocide; of the 1965 International Convention on the Elimination of All Forms of Racial Discrimination; and of the other sources of general international law set forth in Article 38 of the World Court's Statute. This 15 November 1993 *Statement* also indicated that the Republic of Bosnia and Herzegovina had issued instructions to the author to draft an Application and a Request for Provisional Measures of Protection against the United Kingdom, and to file these papers with the Court as soon as physically possible. Ambassador Sacirbey had this *Statement* circulated at United Nations Headquarters in New York as an official document of both the Security Council and the General Assembly.

On 30 November 1993, by telephone the author personally informed

---

*See Francis A. Boyle, *The Bosnian People Charge Genocide* 365-67 (1996).

Ambassador Sacirbey in Geneva that these documents were ready to be filed with the World Court at any time. But by then it was too late. In immediate reaction to Ambassador Sacirbey's public *Statement* of Bosnia's intention to institute legal proceedings against the United Kingdom on 15 November 1993, a Spokesman for the British Foreign Office said that this announcement "would make it difficult to sustain the morale and commitment of those [British troops and aid workers] in Bosnia in dangerous circumstances." This story continued: "Foreign Office sources said there were no plans to remove the Coldstream Guards, who have just begun a six-month deployment to Bosnia. But Whitehall would take account of whether the Bosnian threat of legal action was in fact taken to the International Court of Justice in The Hague."

In addition to the British government, several European states threatened the Republic of Bosnia and Herzegovina over the continuation of Bosnia's legal proceedings against the United Kingdom before the World Court in accordance with the 15 November 1993 *Statement*. The basic thrust of their collective threat was that all forms of international humanitarian relief supplies to the starving People of the Republic of Bosnia and Herzegovina would be cut-off if my Application and Request for Provisional Measures against the United Kingdom were to be actually filed with the World Court. For these reasons of severe duress and threats perpetrated by the United Kingdom, other European states, and David Owen, the Republic of Bosnia and Herzegovina was forced to withdraw from those proceedings against the United Kingdom by means of concluding with it a coerced "Joint Statement" of 20 December 1993.

Nevertheless, on the afternoon of Monday, 3 January 1994, the author called the Registrar of the International Court of Justice in order to make three basic Points to him for transmission to the Judges of the World Court:

1. The Bosnian decision to withdraw the lawsuit against the United Kingdom was made under duress, threats, and coercion perpetrated by the British government and the governments of several other European states upon the highest level officials of the Bosnian government in Geneva, London, and Sarajevo. Therefore the so-called agreement to withdraw the lawsuit against Britain was void *ab initio*. I reserved the right of the Republic of Bosnia and Herzegovina to denounce this agreement at any time and to institute legal proceedings against the United Kingdom in accordance with the *Statement* of 15 November 1993.

2. The British government demanded that the author be fired as the General Agent for the Republic of Bosnia and Herzegovina before the Court. The British government knew full well that the author was the one responsible for the Bosnian strategy at the World Court, and especially for the recommendation to sue Britain.

3. Toward the end of my conversation with the Registrar on 3 January 1994, the author made an oral Request that the World Court indicate provisional measures, *proprio motu* in order to protect the People and the

Republic of Bosnia and Herzegovina from extermination and annihilation by the rump Yugoslavia and the Republic of Croatia. I pointed out to the Registrar that this oral Request was in accordance with the terms of the written Request for provisional measures, *proprio motu* in advance that was already set forth in Bosnia's Second Request for Provisional Measures of 27 July 1993. The Registrar informed me that the Court was paying close attention to the situation in the Republic of Bosnia and Herzegovina.

Pursuant to Point 2, above, the author was relieved of his responsibilities as General Agent for the Republic of Bosnia and Herzegovina before the World Court on 12 January 1994.

On February 5, 1994, a mortar shell struck the marketplace in the center of Sarajevo, killing 69 people and wounding more than 200. The international outrage over this wanton atrocity inflicted upon innocent people by the Bosnian Serbs was so enormous that the Clinton administration was forced to seize the initiative for the so-called Bosnian peace negotiations from the United Nations and the European Union, and thus to take the matter directly into its own hands. The net result of this American effort was the Washington Agreements of March 1994.

The author analyzed the Washington Agreements in great detail in a *Memorandum of Law to the Parliament of the Republic of Bosnia and Herzegovina on the so-called Washington Agreements of 18 March 1994,* that I prepared and submitted to the Bosnian Parliament on March 24, 1994. This *Memorandum* is a public document that was considered by the Bosnian Parliament during the course of their deliberations over the Washington Agreements. It was originally published on the Bosnian Computer Newsgroup Bosnet (i.e., BIT.LISTSERV.BOSNET), and later elsewhere.

Instead of carving up Bosnia into three *de jure* independent states, the Washington Agreements prepared the way for carving up the Republic of Bosnia and Herzegovina into only two *de facto* independent states. One such *de facto* independent state—consisting of approximately 49 per cent of the Republic's territory—would be designated for the Bosnian Serbs, thus ratifying the results of their ethnic cleansing, genocide, mass rape, war crimes, and torture. The second such *de facto* independent state was actually created by the Washington Agreements and was called a "Federation" between the legitimate Bosnian government and the extreme nationalist Bosnian Croats working for separation at the behest of the ex-Communist apparatchik Croatian President Franjo Tudjman.

In theory, the so-called Federation was supposed to control 51 per cent of the territory of the Republic of Bosnia and Herzegovina. Nevertheless, it was clear from reading through the Washington Agreements that its American State Department drafters contemplated that ultimately this so-called Federation would be absorbed by the Republic of Croatia; and likewise, that the Bosnian Serb state would ultimately be absorbed by the Republic of Serbia. In other words, the Washington Agreements paved the way for the *de facto* partition of the Republic of Bosnia and Herzegovina between the Republic of Croatia and the Republic of Serbia. That had been the longstanding plan of Tudjman and Serb President Slobodan Milosevic to begin with, going all the way back to their secret agreement to partition Bosnia at Karadjordjevo in March of 1991.

The Washington Agreements of March 1994 became the basis for the drafting and the conclusion of the Dayton Agreement in December of 1995. Indeed, the Dayton Agreement can only be understood and interpreted by reference to the Washington Agreements. In other words, despite its public protestations to the contrary, throughout 1994 and 1995 the Clinton administration actively promoted and consistently pursued the *de facto* carve-up of a United Nations member state into two parts, and then Bosnia's *de facto* absorption by two other U.N. member states.

After imposing the Washington Agreements upon the Bosnian government, the Clinton administration then fruitlessly spent the next year and a half trying to convince Serbia and the Bosnian Serbs to go along with this *de facto* carve-up and absorption of 49 per cent of the Republic of Bosnia and Herzegovina. This would have required the Bosnian Serbs to voluntarily give up about 20 percent of the 70 percent of Bosnian territory that they had stolen and ethnically cleansed. That they proved unwilling to do until the use of military force against them by NATO in the Fall of 1995.

In the meantime, the siege and bombardment of Sarajevo and the other Bosnian cities persisted and the Bosnian Serbs continued to ethnically cleanse Bosnian towns of their Muslim and Croat citizens, with the active support and assistance of Serbia. The entire world watched and did nothing as the slaughter and carnage by the Bosnian Serb army continued relentlessly. This genocide culminated in the Serb massacres of thousands of Bosnian Muslims at the so-called U.N. "safe havens" of Zepa and Srebrenica during the Summer of 1995.

On September 8, 1995, the Clinton Administration imposed a so-called *Agreement on Basic Principles* upon the Bosnian government in Geneva as part of the run-up to Dayton. It was clear to the author that the Geneva Agreement constituted the next stage in the American plan to carve up the Republic of Bosnia and Herzegovina into two *de facto* independent states that had been initiated by the 1994 Washington Agreements. In order to warn the Bosnian Parliament of these machinations, I prepared a formal *Memorandum of Law to the Parliament of the Republic of Bosnia and Herzegovina Concerning the Agreement on Basic Principles in Geneva of September 8, 1995*, dated 11 September 1995. This *Memorandum* was submitted to the Bosnian Parliament and considered during the course of their deliberations. It was published on Bosnet on September 12, 1995.

At about the same time, it also appeared from published reports and from my own sources that the United States government was going to impose the partition of Sarajevo upon the Bosnian government as part of the so-called "final solution" for Bosnia. This is exactly what David Owen had planned to do in Geneva during the summer of 1993. In order to head off this partition plan, I prepared yet another *Memorandum of Law to the Parliament of the Republic of Bosnia and Herzegovina*, entitled *Saving Sarajevo*, dated September 13, 1995, and published on Bosnet, September 13, 1995. A Bosnian language translation of this *Memorandum* was published on Bosnet, September 24, 1995.

Briefly put, this *Memorandum* on Sarajevo resurrected the proposal that I had originally designed and drafted at the request of President Izetbegovic while serving as Bosnia's Lawyer at the Owen-Stoltenberg negotiations in Geneva during the summer of 1993: Turn Sarajevo into a Capital District like Washington, D.C., instead of partitioning the city. Although I was not at Dayton, as far as I can tell from the published sources, my proposal constituted the opening position for the disposition of Sarajevo that was presented by the Bosnian Government at the Dayton negotiations.

Fortunately, it proved unnecessary to implement my proposal at Dayton. For there the President of Serbia, Slobodan Milosevic, proved willing to concede a unified Sarajevo to the control of the so-called Federation on the grounds that President Izetbegovic "deserved it" for having courageously endured the three and a half year siege and bombardment of that capital city by Milosevic's surrogates. However, my proposal could still serve as a model for the organization of Sarajevo on a multi-ethnic basis as the capital of a reconstituted Republic of Bosnia and Herzegovina at some point in the not-too-distant future.

On 26 September the Clinton administration imposed yet another "Agreement" upon the Bosnian government in New York in order to pave the way for the carve-up of the Republic in Dayton. Once again, in order to alert the Bosnian Parliament to these machinations, I drafted a *Memorandum of Law to the Parliament of the Republic of Bosnia and Herzegovina Concerning the New York Agreement of 26 September 1995*, dated September 28, 1995. This *Memorandum* was submitted to the Bosnian Parliament for their consideration and then published on Bosnet, September 29, 1995.

Next, His Excellency President Alija Izetbegovic asked me to analyze the first draft of the so-called Dayton Peace Agreement that was submitted to him by Richard Holbrooke. For obvious reasons, this *Memorandum of Law* is and shall remain private and confidential. However, several of my basic criticisms were incorporated into the final text of the Dayton Agreement. For example, it is a matter of public record that the first draft of the Holbrooke Plan would have constituted a *de jure* carve-up of the Republic of Bosnia and Herzegovina. That never happened!

After the public initialling of the Dayton Agreement, I was asked by then Bosnian Foreign Minister Muhamed Sacirbey as well as by the Parliament of the Republic of Bosnia and Herzegovina to produce an analysis of the Dayton Agreement for the purpose of their formulating a package of reservations, declarations and understandings (RDUs) to the Agreement. This was done by means of a formal *Memorandum of Law* by me that was submitted to the Parliament of the Republic of Bosnia and

Herzegovina concerning the Dayton Agreement, dated November 30, 1995. This *Memorandum* is in the public domain and was published on Bosnet, December 1, 1995.

Pursuant to this self-styled Dayton Peace Agreement, on 14 December 1995 the Republic of Bosnia and Herzegovina was carved-up *de facto* in Paris by the United Nations, the European Union and its member states, the United States, Russia and the many other states in attendance, despite the United Nations Charter, the Nuremberg Principles, the Genocide Convention, the Four Geneva Conventions and their two Additional Protocols, the Racial Discrimination Convention, the Apartheid Convention, and the Universal Declaration of Human Rights, as well as two overwhelmingly favorable protective Orders issued by the International Court of Justice on behalf of Bosnia on 8 April 1993 and 13 September 1993. This second World Court Order effectively prohibited such a partition of Bosnia by the vote of 13 to 2. This U.N.-sanctioned execution of a U.N. member state violated every known principle of international law that had been formulated by the international community in the post World War II era.

Bosnia was sacrificed on the altar of Great Power politics to the Machiavellian god of expedience. In 1938 the Great Powers of Europe did the exact same thing to Czechoslovakia at Munich. The partition of that nation state did not bring peace to Europe then. Partition of the Republic of Bosnia and Herzegovina will not bring peace to Europe now.

On 11 July 1996—the first anniversary of the Srebrenica massacre of several thousand Bosnian Muslims by the Bosnian Serb army with the assistance of Serbia—the International Court of Justice issued a *Judgment* in which it overwhelmingly rejected all of the spurious jurisdictional and procedural objections made by the rump Yugoslavia against Bosnia's Application/complaint for genocide that the author had filed with the Court on 20 March 1993. The World Court had already rejected these same objections twice before in its Orders of 8 April 1993 and 13 September 1993. But under the Court's Rules of Procedure, the rump Yugoslavia was entitled to a separate hearing and decision on these preliminary issues alone. Nevertheless, despite the overwhelming merits of Bosnia's claims for genocide against the rump Yugoslavia, enormous pressure has been brought to bear upon the Bosnian government by the United States, the United Nations, the European Union and its member states, Carl Bildt, and Richard Holbrooke, *inter alia,* to drop this World Court lawsuit in order to placate Slobodan Milosevic. Why?

When I drafted all of the World Court papers for Bosnia and also when I orally argued the two sets of Provisional Measures before the Court in April and August of 1993, I was quite careful and diligent to file and plead as much material as I could that personally implicated Milosevic in ordering, supervising, approving and condoning genocide against both the People and the Republic of Bosnia and Herzegovina. I personally attacked and repeatedly accused him of primary responsibility for the genocide in Bosnia for the entire world to see and to hear. For this reason, it will prove to be impossible for the United States, the United Nations, and Europe to rehabilitate Milosevic once the World Court renders its final Judgment on the merits of the case in favor of Bosnia, which will inevitably occur unless prevented.

Bosnia has already won what is tantamount to two pre-judgments on the merits of the case in the World Court's Order of 8 April 1993 and the Court's Order of 13 September 1993, as conceded by the late Judge Tarassov in his Declaration attached to the first Order, and in his Dissenting Opinion attached to the second Order. In other words, under the leadership of Slobodan Milosevic, the rump Yugoslavia has indeed committed genocide against the People and the Republic of Bosnia and Herzegovina, both directly and indirectly by means of its surrogate army under the command of two individuals already indicted for international crimes in Bosnia: Radovan Karadzic and Ratko Mladic. Nevertheless, for almost four years the entire international community refused to discharge their solemn obligation under Article I of the Genocide Convention "to prevent" this ongoing genocide against the Bosnian People that was so blatantly taking place in the Republic of Bosnia and Herzegovina.

Hence, except for the Bosnians, everyone mentioned above wants this World Court lawsuit to disappear from the face of the earth. For they are all guilty of complicity in genocide. As this essay goes into print, it does not appear that Bosnia's lawsuit will survive much longer. If and when Bosnia is forced to drop its World Court lawsuit for genocide against the rump Yugoslavia, then the negation of the international legal order will be total and shameless. The so-called Western powers and the United Nations will have confirmed their complete moral bankruptcy and gross legal hypocrisy for the rest of the world to see everyday in the former Republic of Bosnia and Herzegovina.

But there is something that the People of Bosnia and Herzegovina can do about this situation: The Bosnian People must stand up as One and make it absolutely clear to the great powers of the world, and especially to the United States and to Europe, that under no circumstances will they withdraw their lawsuit against the rump Yugoslavia for genocide. This World Court lawsuit is the only justice that the Bosnian People will ever get from anyone in the entire world on this or any other issue!

If this lawsuit is withdrawn, then the rump Yugoslavia and its supporters around the world, together with the United States, the United Nations, the European Union and its member states, will be able to rewrite history by arguing that genocide never occurred against the People and the Republic of Bosnia and Herzegovina. All the great powers and these international institutions will then argue that the reason why Bosnia dropped its lawsuit for genocide against the rump Yugoslavia was because Bosnia was afraid of losing its World Court lawsuit. In this manner these great powers together with the United Nations and the European Union will be able to justify their refusal to prevent the ongoing genocide against the

People and the Republic of Bosnia and Herzegovina for almost four years despite the obvious requirements of the 1948 Genocide Convention, the 1945 United Nations Charter, and the two World Court Orders of 8 April 1993 and 13 September 1993.

As I have established in this paper, Bosnia has already won this World Court lawsuit. All that Bosnia must do now is to see this lawsuit through to its ultimate and successful conclusion. It is inevitable that the World Court will rule that the rump Yugoslavia and its surrogate Bosnian Serb armed forces have committed genocide against the People and the Republic of Bosnia and Herzegovina. At that time, the claims of the Bosnian People for genocide will be vindicated for the entire world to see and for all of history to know. After all that they have suffered, and endured, and accomplished, the Bosnian People owe it to themselves and to their children and to their children's children, as well as to all the other Peoples of the world and to their children and to their children's children, to prosecute this World Court lawsuit through to its successful conclusion.

MAY GOD ALWAYS BE WITH THE PEOPLE AND THE REPUBLIC OF BOSNIA AND HERZEGOVINA!

APPENDIX II

Common Article 3 of the Geneva Conventions

In the case of armed conflict not of an international character occurring in the territory of one of the High Contracting Parties, each Party to the conflict shall be bound to apply, as a minimum, the following provisions:

(1) Persons taking no active part in the hostilities, including members of armed forces who have laid down their arms and those placed 'hors de combat' by sickness, wounds, detention, or any other cause, shall in all circumstances be treated humanely, without any adverse distinction founded on race, colour, religion or faith, sex, birth or wealth, or any other similar criteria.

To this end, the following acts are and shall remain prohibited at any time and in any place whatsoever with respect to the above-mentioned persons:

(a) violence to life and person, in particular murder of all kinds, mutilation, cruel treatment and torture;

(b) taking of hostages;

(c) outrages upon personal dignity, in particular humiliating and degrading treatment;

(d) the passing of sentences and the carrying out of executions without previous judgment pronounced by a regularly constituted court affording all the judicial guarantees which are recognized as indispensable by civilized peoples.

(2) The wounded and sick shall be collected and cared for.

An impartial humanitarian body, such as the International Committee of the Red Cross, may offer its services to the Parties to the conflict.

The Parties to the conflict should further endeavour to bring into force, by means of special agreements, all or part of the other provisions of the present Convention.

The application of the preceding provisions shall not affect the legal status of the Parties to the conflict.

APPENDIX III

UN GENOCIDE CONVENTION

Convention on the Prevention and Punishment of the Crime of Genocide

Convention on the Prevention and Punishment of the Crime of Genocide. Adopted by Resolution 260 (III) A of the United Nations General Assembly on 9 December 1948.

Article 1:

The Contracting Parties confirm that genocide, whether committed in time of peace or in time of war, is a crime under international law which they undertake to prevent and to punish.

Article 2:

In the present Convention, genocide means any of the following acts committed with intent to destroy, in whole or in part, a national, ethnical, racial or religious group, as such:

> (a) Killing members of the group;
> (b) Causing serious bodily or mental harm to members of the group;
> (c) Deliberately inflicting on the group conditions of life calculated to bring about its physical destruction in whole or in part;
> (d) Imposing measures intended to prevent births within the group;
> (e) Forcibly transferring children of the group to another group.

Article 3

The following acts shall be punishable:

> (a) Genocide;
> (b) Conspiracy to commit genocide;
> (c) Direct and public incitement to commit genocide;
> (d) Attempt to commit genocide;
> (e) Complicity in genocide.

Article 4

Persons committing genocide or any of the other acts enumerated in Article

3 shall be punished, whether they are constitutionally responsible rulers, public officials or private individuals.

Article 5

The Contracting Parties undertake to enact, in accordance with their respective Constitutions, the necessary legislation to give effect to the provisions of the present Convention and, in particular, to provide effective penalties for persons guilty of genocide or any of the other acts enumerated in Article 3.

Article 6

Persons charged with genocide or any of the other acts enumerated in Article 3 shall be tried by a competent tribunal of the State in the territory of which the act was committed, or by such international penal tribunal as may have jurisdiction with respect to those Contracting Parties which shall have accepted its jurisdiction.

Article 7

Genocide and the other acts enumerated in Article 3 shall not be considered as political crimes for the purpose of extradition. The Contracting Parties pledge themselves in such cases to grant extradition in accordance with their laws and treaties in force.

Article 8

Any Contracting Party may call upon the competent organs of the United Nations to take such action under the Charter of the United Nations as they consider appropriate for the prevention and suppression of acts of genocide or any of the other acts enumerated in Article 3.

Article 9

Disputes between the Contracting Parties relating to the interpretation, application or fulfilment of the present Convention, including those relating to the responsibility of a State for genocide or any of the other acts enumerated in Article 3, shall be submitted to the International Court of Justice at the request of any of the parties to the dispute.

Article 10

The present Convention, of which the Chinese, English, French, Russian and Spanish texts are equally authentic, shall bear the date of 9 December 1948.

Article 11

The present Convention shall be open until 31 December 1949 for signature on behalf of any Member of the United Nations and of any non-member State to which an invitation to sign has been addressed by the General Assembly.

The present Convention shall be ratified, and the instruments of ratification shall be deposited with the Secretary-General of the United Nations.

After 1 January 1950, the present Convention may be acceded to on behalf of any Member of the United Nations and of any non-member State which has received an invitation as aforesaid. Instruments of accession shall be deposited with the Secretary-General of the United Nations.

Article 12

Any Contracting Party may at any time, by notification addressed to the Secretary-General of the United Nations, extend the application of the present Convention to all or any of the territories for the conduct of whose foreign relations that Contracting Party is responsible.

Article 13

On the day when the first twenty instruments of ratification or accession have been deposited, the Secretary-General shall draw up a proces-verbal and transmit a copy of it to each Member of the United Nations and to each of the non-member States contemplated in Article 11.

The present Convention shall come into force on the ninetieth day following the date of deposit of the twentieth instrument of ratification or accession. Any ratification or accession effected subsequent to the latter date shall become effective on the ninetieth day following the deposit of the instrument of ratification or accession.

Article 14

The present Convention shall remain in effect for a period of ten years as from the date of its coming into force.

It shall thereafter remain in force for successive periods of five years for such Contracting Parties as have not denounced it at least six months before the expiration of the current period.

Denunciation shall be effected by a written notification addressed to the Secretary-General of the United Nations.

Article 15

If, as a result of denunciations, the number of Parties to the present

Convention should become less than sixteen, the Convention shall cease to be in force as from the date on which the last of these denunciations shall become effective.

Article 16

A request for the revision of the present Convention may be made at any time by any Contracting Party by means of a notification in writing addressed to the Secretary-General.

The General Assembly shall decide upon the steps, if any, to be taken in respect of such request.

Article 17

The Secretary-General of the United Nations shall notify all Members of the United Nations and the non-member States contemplated in Article 11 of the following:

> (a) Signatures, ratifications and accessions received in accordance with Article 11;
> (b) Notifications received in accordance with Article 12;
> (c) The date upon which the present Convention comes into force in accordance with Article 13;
> (d) Denunciations received in accordance with Article 14;
> (e) The abrogation of the Convention in accordance with Article 15;
> (f) Notifications received in accordance with Article 16.

Article 18

The original of the present Convention shall be deposited in the archives of the United Nations

A certified copy of the Convention shall be transmitted to all Members of the United Nations and to the non-member States contemplated in Article 11.

Article 19

The present Convention shall be registered by the Secretary-General of the United Nations on the date of its coming into force.

APPENDIX IV

ROME STATUTE OF THE INTERNATIONAL CRIMINAL COURT

PART 2. JURISDICTION, ADMISSIBILITY AND APPLICABLE LAW

Article 5
Crimes within the jurisdiction of the Court

1.   The jurisdiction of the Court shall be limited to the most serious crimes of concern to the international community as a whole. The Court has jurisdiction in accordance with this Statute with respect to the following crimes:

(a)   The crime of genocide;

(b)   Crimes against humanity;

(c)   War crimes;

(d)   The crime of aggression.

2.   The Court shall exercise jurisdiction over the crime of aggression once a provision is adopted in accordance with articles 121 and 123 defining the crime and setting out the conditions under which the Court shall exercise jurisdiction with respect to this crime. Such a provision shall be consistent with the relevant provisions of the Charter of the United Nations.

Article 6
Genocide

For the purpose of this Statute, "genocide" means any of the following acts committed with intent to destroy, in whole or in part, a national, ethnical, racial or religious group, as such:

(a) Killing members of the group;

(b) Causing serious bodily or mental harm to members of the group;

(c) Deliberately inflicting on the group conditions of life calculated to bring about its physical destruction in whole or in part;

(d) Imposing measures intended to prevent births within the group;

(e) Forcibly transferring children of the group to another group.

Article 7
Crimes against humanity

1. For the purpose of this Statute, "crime against humanity" means any of the following acts when committed as part of a widespread or systematic attack directed against any civilian population, with knowledge of the attack:

    (a) Murder;

    (b) Extermination;

    (c) Enslavement;

    (d) Deportation or forcible transfer of population;

    (e) Imprisonment or other severe deprivation of physical liberty in violation of fundamental rules of international law;

    (f) Torture;

    (g) Rape, sexual slavery, enforced prostitution, forced pregnancy, enforced sterilization, or any other form of sexual violence of comparable gravity;

    (h) Persecution against any identifiable group or collectivity on political, racial, national, ethnic, cultural, religious, gender as defined in paragraph 3, or other grounds that are universally recognized as impermissible under international law, in connection with any act referred to in this paragraph or any crime within the jurisdiction of the Court;

    (i) Enforced disappearance of persons;

    (j) The crime of apartheid;

    (k) Other inhumane acts of a similar character intentionally causing great suffering, or serious injury to body or to mental or physical health.

2. For the purpose of paragraph 1:

    (a) "Attack directed against any civilian population" means a course of conduct involving the multiple commission of acts referred to in paragraph 1 against any civilian population, pursuant to or in furtherance of a State or organizational policy to commit such attack;

    (b) "Extermination" includes the intentional infliction of conditions of life, *inter alia* the deprivation of access to food and medicine, calculated to bring about the destruction of part of a population;

(c) "Enslavement" means the exercise of any or all of the powers attaching to the right of ownership over a person and includes the exercise of such power in the course of trafficking in persons, in particular women and children;

(d) "Deportation or forcible transfer of population" means forced displacement of the persons concerned by expulsion or other coercive acts from the area in which they are lawfully present, without grounds permitted under international law;

(e) "Torture" means the intentional infliction of severe pain or suffering, whether physical or mental, upon a person in the custody or under the control of the accused; except that torture shall not include pain or suffering arising only from, inherent in or incidental to, lawful sanctions;

(f) "Forced pregnancy" means the unlawful confinement of a woman forcibly made pregnant, with the intent of affecting the ethnic composition of any population or carrying out other grave violations of international law. This definition shall not in any way be interpreted as affecting national laws relating to pregnancy;

(g) "Persecution" means the intentional and severe deprivation of fundamental rights contrary to international law by reason of the identity of the group or collectivity;

(h) "The crime of apartheid" means inhumane acts of a character similar to those referred to in paragraph 1, committed in the context of an institutionalized regime of systematic oppression and domination by one racial group over any other racial group or groups and committed with the intention of maintaining that regime;

(i) "Enforced disappearance of persons" means the arrest, detention or abduction of persons by, or with the authorization, support or acquiescence of, a State or a political organization, followed by a refusal to acknowledge that deprivation of freedom or to give information on the fate or whereabouts of those persons, with the intention of removing them from the protection of the law for a prolonged period of time.

3.   For the purpose of this Statute, it is understood that the term "gender" refers to the two sexes, male and female, within the context of society. The term "gender" does not indicate any meaning different from the above.

Article 8
War crimes

1.   The Court shall have jurisdiction in respect of war crimes in particular when committed as part of a plan or policy or as part of a large-scale commission of such crimes.

2.   For the purpose of this Statute, "war crimes" means:

(a)   Grave breaches of the Geneva Conventions of 12 August 1949, namely, any of the following acts against persons or property protected under the provisions of the relevant Geneva Convention:

(i)   Wilful killing;

(ii)   Torture or inhuman treatment, including biological experiments;

(iii)   Wilfully causing great suffering, or serious injury to body or health;

(iv)   Extensive destruction and appropriation of property, not justified by military necessity and carried out unlawfully and wantonly;

(v)   Compelling a prisoner of war or other protected person to serve in the forces of a hostile Power;

(vi)   Wilfully depriving a prisoner of war or other protected person of the rights of fair and regular trial;

(vii)   Unlawful deportation or transfer or unlawful confinement;

(viii)   Taking of hostages.

(b)   Other serious violations of the laws and customs applicable in international armed conflict, within the established framework of international law, namely, any of the following acts:

(i)   Intentionally directing attacks against the civilian population as such or against individual civilians not taking direct part in hostilities;

(ii)   Intentionally directing attacks against civilian objects, that is, objects which are not military objectives;

(iii)   Intentionally directing attacks against personnel,

installations, material, units or vehicles involved in a humanitarian assistance or peacekeeping mission in accordance with the Charter of the United Nations, as long as they are entitled to the protection given to civilians or civilian objects under the international law of armed conflict;

(iv)   Intentionally launching an attack in the knowledge that such attack will cause incidental loss of life or injury to civilians or damage to civilian objects or widespread, long-term and severe damage to the natural environment which would be clearly excessive in relation to the concrete and direct overall military advantage anticipated;

(v)   Attacking or bombarding, by whatever means, towns, villages, dwellings or buildings which are undefended and which are not military objectives;

(vi)   Killing or wounding a combatant who, having laid down his arms or having no longer means of defence, has surrendered at discretion;

(vii)   Making improper use of a flag of truce, of the flag or of the military insignia and uniform of the enemy or of the United Nations, as well as of the distinctive emblems of the Geneva Conventions, resulting in death or serious personal injury;

(viii)   The transfer, directly or indirectly, by the Occupying Power of parts of its own civilian population into the territory it occupies, or the deportation or transfer of all or parts of the population of the occupied territory within or outside this territory;

(ix)   Intentionally directing attacks against buildings dedicated to religion, education, art, science or charitable purposes, historic monuments, hospitals and places where the sick and wounded are collected, provided they are not military objectives;

(x)   Subjecting persons who are in the power of an adverse party to physical mutilation or to medical or scientific experiments of any kind which are neither justified by the medical, dental or hospital treatment of the person concerned nor carried out in his or her interest, and which cause death to or seriously endanger the health of such person or persons;

(xi)   Killing or wounding treacherously individuals

belonging to the hostile nation or army;

(xii)   Declaring that no quarter will be given;

(xiii)   Destroying or seizing the enemy's property unless such destruction or seizure be imperatively demanded by the necessities of war;

(xiv)   Declaring abolished, suspended or inadmissible in a court of law the rights and actions of the nationals of the hostile party;

(xv)   Compelling the nationals of the hostile party to take part in the operations of war directed against their own country, even if they were in the belligerent's service before the commencement of the war;

(xvi)   Pillaging a town or place, even when taken by assault;

(xvii)   Employing poison or poisoned weapons;

(xviii)   Employing asphyxiating, poisonous or other gases, and all analogous liquids, materials or devices;

(xix)   Employing bullets which expand or flatten easily in the human body, such as bullets with a hard envelope which does not entirely cover the core or is pierced with incisions;

(xx)   Employing weapons, projectiles and material and methods of warfare which are of a nature to cause superfluous injury or unnecessary suffering or which are inherently indiscriminate in violation of the international law of armed conflict, provided that such weapons, projectiles and material and methods of warfare are the subject of a comprehensive prohibition and are included in an annex to this Statute, by an amendment in accordance with the relevant provisions set forth in articles 121 and 123;

(xxi)   Committing outrages upon personal dignity, in particular humiliating and degrading treatment;

(xxii)   Committing rape, sexual slavery, enforced prostitution, forced pregnancy, as defined in article 7, paragraph 2 (f), enforced sterilization, or any other form of sexual violence also constituting a grave breach of the Geneva Conventions;

(xxiii)   Utilizing the presence of a civilian or other protected person to render certain points, areas or military forces immune from military operations;

(xxiv) Intentionally directing attacks against buildings, material, medical units and transport, and personnel using the distinctive emblems of the Geneva Conventions in conformity with international law;

(xxv) Intentionally using starvation of civilians as a method of warfare by depriving them of objects indispensable to their survival, including wilfully impeding relief supplies as provided for under the Geneva Conventions;

(xxvi) Conscripting or enlisting children under the age of fifteen years into the national armed forces or using them to participate actively in hostilities.

(c) In the case of an armed conflict not of an international character, serious violations of article 3 common to the four Geneva Conventions of 12 August 1949, namely, any of the following acts committed against persons taking no active part in the hostilities, including members of armed forces who have laid down their arms and those placed *hors de combat* by sickness, wounds, detention or any other cause:

(i) Violence to life and person, in particular murder of all kinds, mutilation, cruel treatment and torture;

(ii) Committing outrages upon personal dignity, in particular humiliating and degrading treatment;

(iii) Taking of hostages;

(iv) The passing of sentences and the carrying out of executions without previous judgement pronounced by a regularly constituted court, affording all judicial guarantees which are generally recognized as indispensable.

(d) Paragraph 2 (c) applies to armed conflicts not of an international character and thus does not apply to situations of internal disturbances and tensions, such as riots, isolated and sporadic acts of violence or other acts of a similar nature.
(e) Other serious violations of the laws and customs applicable in armed conflicts not of an international character, within the established framework of international law, namely, any of the following acts:

(i) Intentionally directing attacks against the civilian population as such or against individual civilians not taking direct part in hostilities;

(ii)   Intentionally directing attacks against buildings, material, medical units and transport, and personnel using the distinctive emblems of the Geneva Conventions in conformity with international law;

(iii)   Intentionally directing attacks against personnel, installations, material, units or vehicles involved in a humanitarian assistance or peacekeeping mission in accordance with the Charter of the United Nations, as long as they are entitled to the protection given to civilians or civilian objects under the international law of armed conflict;

(iv)   Intentionally directing attacks against buildings dedicated to religion, education, art, science or charitable purposes, historic monuments, hospitals and places where the sick and wounded are collected, provided they are not military objectives;

(v)   Pillaging a town or place, even when taken by assault;

(vi)   Committing rape, sexual slavery, enforced prostitution, forced pregnancy, as defined in article 7, paragraph 2 (f), enforced sterilization, and any other form of sexual violence also constituting a serious violation of article 3 common to the four Geneva Conventions;

(vii)   Conscripting or enlisting children under the age of fifteen years into armed forces or groups or using them to participate actively in hostilities;

(viii)   Ordering the displacement of the civilian population for reasons related to the conflict, unless the security of the civilians involved or imperative military reasons so demand;

(ix)   Killing or wounding treacherously a combatant adversary;

(x)   Declaring that no quarter will be given;

(xi)   Subjecting persons who are in the power of another party to the conflict to physical mutilation or to medical or scientific experiments of any kind which are neither justified by the medical, dental or hospital treatment of the person concerned nor carried out in his or her interest, and which cause death to or seriously endanger the health of such person or persons;

(xii)   Destroying or seizing the property of an adversary unless such destruction or seizure be imperatively demanded by the necessities of the conflict;

(f) Paragraph 2 (e) applies to armed conflicts not of an international character and thus does not apply to situations of internal disturbances and tensions, such as riots, isolated and sporadic acts of violence or other acts of a similar nature. It applies to armed conflicts that take place in the territory of a State when there is protracted armed conflict between governmental authorities and organized armed groups or between such groups.

3.   Nothing in paragraph 2 (c) and (e) shall affect the responsibility of a Government to maintain or re-establish law and order in the State or to defend the unity and territorial integrity of the State, by all legitimate means.

APPENDIX V

Protocol Additional to the Geneva Conventions of 12 August 1949, and relating to the Protection of Victims of International Armed Conflicts (Protocol I), 8 June 1977

[Only sections related to general humanitarian protections are included]

PART I. GENERAL PROVISIONS

Art 1. General principles and scope of application

1. The High Contracting Parties undertake to respect and to ensure respect for this Protocol in all circumstances.

2. In cases not covered by this Protocol or by other international agreements, civilians and combatants remain under the protection and authority of the principles of international law derived from established custom, from the principles of humanity and from dictates of public conscience.

3. This Protocol, which supplements the Geneva Conventions of 12 August 1949 for the protection of war victims, shall apply in the situations referred to in Article 2 common to those Conventions.

4. The situations referred to in the preceding paragraph include armed conflicts in which peoples are fighting against colonial domination and alien occupation and against racist regimes in the exercise of their right of self-determination, as enshrined in the Charter of the United Nations and the Declaration on Principles of International Law concerning Friendly Relations and Co-operation among States in accordance with the Charter of the United Nations.

Art 2. Definitions

For the purposes of this Protocol

(a) "First Convention," "Second Convention," "Third Convention" and "Fourth Convention" mean, respectively, the Geneva Convention for the Amelioration of the Condition of the Wounded and Sick in Armed Forces in the Field of 12 August 1949; the Geneva Convention for the Amelioration of the Condition of Wounded, Sick and Ship-wrecked Members of Armed Forces at Sea of 12 August 1949; the Geneva Convention relative to the Treatment of Prisoners of War of 12 August 1949; the Geneva Convention relative to the Protection of Civilian Persons in Time of War of 12 August 1949; "the Conventions" means the four Geneva Conventions of 12 August 1949 for the protection of war victims;

(b) "Rules of international law applicable in armed conflict" means the rules applicable in armed conflict set forth in international agreements to which the Parties to the conflict are Parties and the generally recognized principles and rules of international law which are applicable to armed conflict;

(c) "Protecting Power" means a neutral or other State not a Party to the conflict which has been designated by a Party to the conflict and accepted by the adverse Party and has agreed to carry out the functions assigned to a Protecting Power under the Conventions and this Protocol;

(d) "Substitute" means an organization acting in place of a Protecting Power in accordance with Article 5.

Art 3. Beginning and end of application

Without prejudice to the provisions which are applicable at all times:

(a) the Conventions and this Protocol shall apply from the beginning of any situation referred to in Article 1 of this Protocol.

(b) the application of the Conventions and of this Protocol shall cease, in the territory of Parties to the conflict, on the general close of military operations and, in the case of occupied territories, on the termination of the occupation, except, in either circumstance, for those persons whose final release, repatriation or re-establishment takes place thereafter. These persons shall continue to benefit from the relevant provisions of the Conventions and of this Protocol until their final release repatriation or re-establishment.

Art 4. Legal status of the Parties to the conflict

The application of the Conventions and of this Protocol, as well as the conclusion of the agreements provided for therein, shall not affect the legal status of the Parties to the conflict. Neither the occupation of a territory nor the application of the Conventions and this Protocol shall affect the legal status of the territory in question.

Art 5. Appointment of Protecting Powers and of their substitute

1. It is the duty of the Parties to a conflict from the beginning of that conflict to secure the supervision and implementation of the Conventions and of this Protocol by the application of the system of Protecting Powers, including inter alia the designation and acceptance of those Powers, in accordance with the following paragraphs. Protecting Powers shall have the duty of safeguarding the interests of the Parties to the conflict.

2. From the beginning of a situation referred to in Article 1, each Party to the conflict shall without delay designate a Protecting Power for the purpose of applying the Conventions and this Protocol and shall, likewise without delay and for the same purpose, permit the activities of a Protecting Power which has been accepted by it as such after designation by the adverse Party.

3. If a Protecting Power has not been designated or accepted from the beginning of a situation referred to in Article 1, the International Committee of the Red Cross, without prejudice to the right of any other impartial humanitarian organization to do likewise, shall offer its good offices to the Parties to the conflict with a view to the designation without delay of a Protecting Power to which the Parties to the conflict consent. For that purpose it may inter alia ask each Party to provide it with a list of at least five States which that Party considers acceptable to act as Protecting Power on its behalf in relation to an adverse Party and ask each adverse Party to provide a list or at least five States which it would accept as the Protecting Power of the first Party; these lists shall be communicated to the Committee within two weeks after the receipt or the request; it shall compare them and seek the agreement of any proposed State named on both lists.

4. If, despite the foregoing, there is no Protecting Power, the Parties to the conflict shall accept without delay an offer which may be made by the International Committee of the Red Cross or by any other organization which offers all guarantees of impartiality and efficacy, after due consultations with the said Parties and taking into account the result of these consultations, to act as a substitute. The functioning of such a substitute is subject to the consent of the Parties to the conflict; every effort shall be made by the Parties to the conflict to facilitate the operations of the substitute in the performance of its tasks under the Conventions and this Protocol.

5. In accordance with Article 4, the designation and acceptance of Protecting Powers for the purpose of applying the Conventions and this Protocol shall not affect the legal status of the Parties to the conflict or of any territory, including occupied territory.

6. The maintenance of diplomatic relations between Parties to the conflict or the entrusting of the protection of a Party's interests and those of its nationals to a third State in accordance with the rules of international law relating to diplomatic relations is no obstacle to the designation of Protecting Powers for the purpose of applying the Conventions and this Protocol.

7. Any subsequent mention in this Protocol of a Protecting Power includes also a substitute.

Art 6. Qualified persons

1. The High Contracting Parties shall, also in peacetime, endeavour, with the assistance of the national Red Cross (Red Crescent, Red Lion and Sun) Societies, to train qualified personnel to facilitate the application of the Conventions and of this Protocol, and in particular the activities of the Protecting Powers.

2. The recruitment and training of such personnel are within domestic jurisdiction.

3. The International Committee of the Red Cross shall hold at the disposal of the High Contracting Parties the lists of persons so trained which the High Contracting Parties may have established and may have transmitted to it for that purpose.

4. The conditions governing the employment of such personnel outside the national territory shall, in each case, be the subject of special agreements between the Parties concerned.

Article 7. Meetings

The depositary of this Protocol shall convene a meeting of the High Contracting Parties, at the request of one or more of the said Parties and upon the approval of the majority of the said Parties, to consider general problems concerning the application of the Conventions and of the Protocol.

Part. II WOUNDED, SICK AND SHIPWRECKED

Section I : General Protection

Art 8. Terminology

For the purposes of this Protocol:

a) "Wounded" and "sick" mean persons, whether military or civilian, who, because of trauma, disease or other physical or mental disorder or disability, are in need of medical assistance or care and who refrain from any act of hostility. These terms also cover maternity cases, new-born babies and other persons who may be in need of immediate medical assistance or care, such as the infirm or expectant mothers, and who refrain from any act of hostility;

b) "Shipwrecked" means persons, whether military or civilian, who are in peril at sea or in other waters as a result of misfortune affecting them or the vessel or aircraft carrying them and who refrain from any act of hostility. These persons, provided that they continue to refrain from any act of hostility, shall continue to be considered shipwrecked during their rescue until they acquire another status under the Conventions or this Protocol;

c) "Medical personnel" means those persons assigned, by a Party to the conflict, exclusively to the medical purposes enumerated under sub-paragraph(e) or to the administration of medical units or to the operation or administration of medical transports. Such assignments may be either permanent or temporary. The term includes:

i) medical personnel of a Party to the conflict, whether military or civilian, including those described in the First and Second Conventions, and those assigned to civil defence organizations;

ii) medical personnel of national Red Cross (Red Crescent, Red Lion and Sun) Societies and other national voluntary aid societies duly recognized and authorized by a Party to the conflict;

iii) medical personnel or medical units or medical transports described in Article 9, paragraph 2.

d) "Religious personnel" means military or civilian persons, such as chaplains, who are exclusively engaged in the work of their ministry and attached:

i) to the armed forces of a Party to the conflict;

ii) to medical units or medical transports of a Party to the conflict;

iii) to medical units or medical transports described in Article 9, Paragraph 2; or

iv) to civil defence organizations of a Party to the conflict.

The attachment of religious personnel may be either permanent or temporary, and the relevant provisions mentioned under sub-paragraph (k) apply to them;

e) "Medical units" means establishments and other units, whether military or civilian, organized for medical purposes, namely the search for, collection, transportation, diagnosis or treatment—including first-aid treatment—of the wounded, sick and shipwrecked, or for the prevention of disease. The term includes for example, hospitals and other similar units, blood transfusion centres, preventive medicine centres and institutes, medical depots and the medical and pharmaceutical stores of such units. Medical units may be fixed or mobile, permanent or temporary;

f) "Medical transportation" means the conveyance by land, water or air of the wounded, sick, shipwrecked, medical personnel, religious personnel, medical equipment or medical supplies protected by the Conventions and by this Protocol;

g) "Medical transports" means any means of transportation, whether military or civilian, permanent or temporary, assigned exclusively to medical transportation and under the control of a competent authority of a Party to the conflict;

h) "Medical vehicles" means any medical transports by land;

i) "Medical ships and craft" means any medical transports by water;

j) "Medical aircraft" means any medical transports by air;

k) "Permanent medical personnel," "permanent medical units" and "permanent medical transports" mean those assigned exclusively to medical purposes for an indeterminate period. "Temporary medical personnel" "temporary medical-units" and "temporary medical transports" mean those devoted exclusively to medical purposes for limited periods during the whole of such periods. Unless otherwise specified, the terms "medical personnel," "medical units" and "medical transports" cover both permanent and temporary categories;

l) "Distinctive emblem" means the distinctive emblem of the red cross, red crescent or red lion and sun on a white ground when used for the protection of medical units and transports, or medical and religious personnel, equipment or supplies;

m) "Distinctive signal" means any signal or message specified for the identification exclusively of medical units or transports in Chapter III of Annex I to this Protocol.

Art 9. Field of application

1. This Part, the provisions of which are intended to ameliorate the condition of the wounded, sick and shipwrecked, shall apply to all those affected by a situation referred to in Article 1, without any adverse distinction founded on race, colour, sex, language, religion or belief, political or other opinion, national or social origin, wealth, birth or other status, or on any other similar criteria.

2. The relevant provisions of Articles 27 and 32 of the First Convention shall apply to permanent medical units and transports (other than hospital ships, to which Article 25 of the Second Convention applies) and their personnel made available to a Party to the conflict for humanitarian purposes:

(a) by a neutral or other State which is not a Party to that conflict;

(b) by a recognized and authorized aid society of such a State;

(c) by an impartial international humanitarian organization.

Art 10. Protection and care

1. All the wounded, sick and shipwrecked, to whichever Party they belong, shall be respected and protected.

2. In all circumstances they shall be treated humanely and shall receive, to the fullest extent practicable and with the least possible delay, the medical care and attention required by their condition. There shall be no distinction among them founded on any grounds other than medical ones.

Article 11. Protection of persons

1. The physical or mental health and integrity of persons who are in the power of the adverse Party or who are interned, detained or otherwise deprived of liberty as a result of a situation referred to in Article 1 shall not be endangered by any unjustified act or omission. Accordingly, it is prohibited to subject the persons described in this Article to any medical procedure which is not indicated by the state of health of the person concerned and which is not consistent with generally accepted medical standards which would be applied under similar medical circumstances to persons who are nationals of the Party conducting the procedure and who are in no way deprived of liberty.

2. It is, in particular, prohibited to carry out on such persons, even with their consent:

(a) physical mutilations;

(b) medical or scientific experiments;

(c) removal of tissue or organs for transplantation, except where these acts are justified in conformity with the conditions provided for in paragraph 1.

3. Exceptions to the prohibition in paragraph 2 (c) may be made only in the case of donations of blood for transfusion or of skin for grafting, provided that they are given voluntarily and without any coercion or inducement, and then only for therapeutic purposes, under conditions consistent with generally accepted medical standards and controls designed for the benefit of both the donor and the recipient.

4. Any wilful act or omission which seriously endangers the physical or mental health or integrity of any person who is in the power of a Party other than the one on which he depends and which either violates any of the prohibitions in paragraphs 1 and 2 or fails to comply with the requirements of paragraph 3 shall be a grave breach of this Protocol.

5. The persons described in paragraph 1 have the right to refuse any surgical operation. In case of refusal, medical personnel shall endeavour to obtain a written statement to that effect, signed or acknowledged by the patient.

6. Each Party to the conflict shall keep a medical record for every donation

of blood for transfusion or skin for grafting by persons referred to in paragraph 1, if that donation is made under the responsibility of that Party. In addition, each Party to the conflict shall endeavour to keep a record of all medical procedures undertaken with respect to any person who is interned, detained or otherwise deprived of liberty as a result of a situation referred to in Article 1. These records shall be available at all times for inspection by the Protecting Power.

Art 12. Protection of medical units

1. Medical units shall be respected and protected at all times and shall not be the object of attack.

2. Paragraph 1 shall apply to civilian medical units, provided that they:

(a) belong to one of the Parties to the conflict;

(b) are recognized and authorized by the competent authority of one of the Parties to the conflict; or

(c) are authorized in conformity with Article 9, paragraph 2, of this Protocol or Article 27 of the First Convention.

3. The Parties to the conflict are invited to notify each other of the location of their fixed medical units. The absence of such notification shall not exempt any of the Parties from the obligation to comply with the provisions of paragraph 1.

4. Under no circumstances shall medical units be used in an attempt to shield military objectives from attack. Whenever possible, the Parties to the conflict shall ensure that medical units are so sited that attacks against military objectives do not imperil their safety.

Art 15. Protection of civilian medical and religious personnel

1. Civilian medical personnel shall be respected and protected.

2. If needed, all available help shall be afforded to civilian medical personnel in an area where civilian medical services are disrupted by reason of combat activity.

3. The Occupying Power shall afford civilian medical personnel in occupied territories every assistance to enable them to perform, to the best of their ability, their humanitarian functions. The Occupying Power may not require that, in the performance of those functions, such personnel shall give priority to the treatment of any person except on medical grounds. They

shall not be compelled to carry out tasks which are not compatible with their humanitarian mission.

4. Civilian medical personnel shall have access to any place where their services are essential, subject to such supervisory and safety measures as the relevant Party to the conflict may deem necessary.

5. Civilian religious personnel shall be respected and protected. The provisions of the Conventions and of this Protocol concerning the protection and identification of medical personnel shall apply equally to such persons.

Art 20. Prohibition of reprisals

Reprisals against the persons and objects protected by this Part are prohibited.

SECTION II. MEDICAL TRANSPORTATION

Art 21. Medical vehicles

Medical vehicles shall be respected and protected in the same way as mobile medical units under the Conventions and this Protocol.

Section III Missing and Dead Persons

Art 32. General principle

In the implementation of this Section, the activities of the High Contracting Parties, of the Parties to the conflict and of the international humanitarian organizations mentioned in the Conventions and in this Protocol shall be prompted mainly by the right of families to know the fate of their relatives.

Art 33. Missing persons

1. As soon as circumstances permit, and at the latest from the end of active hostilities, each Party to the conflict shall search for the persons who have been reported missing by an adverse Party. Such adverse Party shall transmit all relevant information concerning such persons in order to facilitate such searches.

2. In order to facilitate the gathering of information pursuant to the preceding paragraph, each Party to the conflict shall, with respect to persons who would not receive more favourable consideration under the Conventions and this Protocol: (a) record the information specified in Article 138 of the Fourth Convention in respect of such persons who have been detained, imprisoned or otherwise held in captivity for more than two weeks as a result of

hostilities or occupation, or who have died during any period of detention; (b) to the fullest extent possible, facilitate and, if need be, carry out the search for and the recording of information concerning such persons if they have died in other circumstances as a result of hostilities or occupation. 3. Information concerning persons reported missing pursuant to paragraph 1 and requests for such information shall be transmitted either directly or through the Protecting Power or the Central Tracing Agency of the International Committee of the Red Cross or national Red Cross (Red Crescent, Red Lion and Sun) Societies. Where the information is not transmitted through the International Committee of the Red Cross and its Central Tracing Agency, each Party to the conflict shall ensure that such information is also supplied to the Central Tracing Agency.

4. The Parties to the conflict shall endeavour to agree on arrangements for teams to search for, identify and recover the dead from battlefield areas, including arrangements, if appropriate, for such teams to be accompanied by personnel of the adverse Party while carrying out these missions in areas controlled by the adverse Party. Personnel of such teams shall be respected and protected while exclusively carrying out these duties.

Art 34. Remains of deceased

1. The remains of persons who have died for reasons related to occupation or in detention resulting from occupation or hostilities and those or persons not nationals of the country in which they have died as a result of hostilities shall be respected, and the gravesites of all such persons shall be respected, maintained and marked as provided for in Article 130 of the Fourth Convention, where their remains or gravesites would not receive more favourable consideration under the Conventions and this Protocol.

2. As soon as circumstances and the relations between the adverse Parties permit, the High Contracting Parties in whose territories graves and, as the case may be, other locations of the remains of persons who have died as a result of hostilities or during occupation or in detention are situated, shall conclude agreements in order:

(a) to facilitate access to the gravesites by relatives of the deceased and by representatives of official graves registration services and to regulate the practical arrangements for such access;

(b) to protect and maintain such gravesites permanently;

(c) to facilitate the return of the remains of the deceased and of personal effects to the home country upon its request or, unless that country objects, upon the request of the next of kin.

3. In the absence of the agreements provided for in paragraph 2 (b) or (c) and if the home country or such deceased is not willing to arrange at its expense for the maintenance of such gravesites, the High Contracting Party in whose territory the gravesites are situated may offer to facilitate the return of the remains of the deceased to the home country. Where such an offer has not been accepted the High Contracting Party may, after the expiry of five years from the date of the offer and upon due notice to the home country, adopt the arrangements laid down in its own laws relating to cemeteries and graves.

4. A High Contracting Party in whose territory the grave sites referred to in this Article are situated shall be permitted to exhume the remains only:

(a) in accordance with paragraphs 2 (c) and 3, or

(b) where exhumation is a matter or overriding public necessity, including cases of medical and investigative necessity, in which case the High Contracting Party shall at all times respect the remains, and shall give notice to the home country or its intention to exhume the remains together with details of the intended place of reinterment.

Part III. Methods and Means of Warfare Combatant and Prisoners-Of-War

Section I. Methods and Means of Warfare

Art 35. Basic rules

1. In any armed conflict, the right of the Parties to the conflict to choose methods or means of warfare is not unlimited.

2. It is prohibited to employ weapons, projectiles and material and methods of warfare of a nature to cause superfluous injury or unnecessary suffering.

3. It is prohibited to employ methods or means of warfare which are intended, or may be expected, to cause widespread, long-term and severe damage to the natural environment.

Art 37. Prohibition of Perfidy

1. It is prohibited to kill, injure or capture an adversary by resort to perfidy. Acts inviting the confidence of an adversary to lead him to believe that he is entitled to, or is obliged to accord, protection under the rules of international law applicable in armed conflict, with intent to betray that confidence, shall constitute perfidy. The following acts are examples of perfidy:

(a) the feigning of an intent to negotiate under a flag of truce or of a surrender;

(b) the feigning of an incapacitation by wounds or sickness;

(c) the feigning of civilian, non-combatant status; and

(d) the feigning of protected status by the use of signs, emblems or uniforms of the United Nations or of neutral or other States not Parties to the conflict.

2. Ruses of war are not prohibited. Such ruses are acts which are intended to mislead an adversary or to induce him to act recklessly but which infringe no rule of international law applicable in armed conflict and which are not perfidious because they do not invite the confidence of an adversary with respect to protection under that law. The following are examples of such ruses: the use of camouflage, decoys, mock operations and misinformation.

Art 41. Safeguard of an enemy hors de combat

1. A person who is recognized or who, in the circumstances, should be recognized to be hors de combat shall not be made the object of attack.

2. A person is hors de combat if:

(a) he is in the power of an adverse Party;

(b) he clearly expresses an intention to surrender; or

(c) he has been rendered unconscious or is otherwise incapacitated by wounds or sickness, and therefore is incapable of defending himself;

provided that in any of these cases he abstains from any hostile act and does not attempt to escape.

3. When persons entitled to protection as prisoners of war have fallen into the power of an adverse Party under unusual conditions of combat which prevent their evacuation as provided for in Part III, Section I, of the Third Convention, they shall be released and all feasible precautions shall be taken to ensure their safety.

Section II. Combatants and Prisoners of War

Art 43. Armed forces

1. The armed forces of a Party to a conflict consist of all organized armed forces, groups and units which are under a command responsible to that Party for the conduct or its subordinates, even if that Party is represented by a government or an authority not recognized by an adverse Party. Such armed forces shall be subject to an internal disciplinary system which, inter

alia, shall enforce compliance with the rules of international law applicable in armed conflict.

2. Members of the armed forces of a Party to a conflict (other than medical personnel and chaplains covered by Article 33 of the Third Convention) are combatants, that is to say, they have the right to participate directly in hostilities.

3. Whenever a Party to a conflict incorporates a paramilitary or armed law enforcement agency into its armed forces it shall so notify the other Parties to the conflict.

Art 44. Combatants and prisoners of war

1. Any combatant, as defined in Article 43, who falls into the power of an adverse Party shall be a prisoner of war.

2. While all combatants are obliged to comply with the rules of international law applicable in armed conflict, violations of these rules shall not deprive a combatant of his right to be a combatant or, if he falls into the power of an adverse Party, of his right to be a prisoner of war, except as provided in paragraphs 3 and 4.

3. In order to promote the protection of the civilian population from the effects of hostilities, combatants are obliged to distinguish themselves from the civilian population while they are engaged in an attack or in a military operation preparatory to an attack. Recognizing, however, that there are situations in armed conflicts where, owing to the nature of the hostilities an armed combatant cannot so distinguish himself, he shall retain his status as a combatant, provided that, in such situations, he carries his arms openly:

(a) during each military engagement, and

(b) during such time as he is visible to the adversary while he is engaged in a military deployment preceding the launching of an attack in which he is to participate.

Acts which comply with the requirements of this paragraph shall not be considered as perfidious within the meaning of Article 37, paragraph 1 (c).

4. A combatant who falls into the power of an adverse Party while failing to meet the requirements set forth in the second sentence of paragraph 3 shall forfeit his right to be a prisoner of war, but he shall, nevertheless, be given protections equivalent in all respects to those accorded to prisoners of war by the Third Convention and by this Protocol. This protection includes

protections equivalent to those accorded to prisoners of war by the Third Convention in the case where such a person is tried and punished for any offences he has committed.

5. Any combatant who falls into the power of an adverse Party while not engaged in an attack or in a military operation preparatory to an attack shall not forfeit his rights to be a combatant and a prisoner of war by virtue of his prior activities .

6. This Article is without prejudice to the right of any person to be a prisoner of war pursuant to Article 4 of the Third Convention.

7. This Article is not intended to change the generally accepted practice of States with respect to the wearing of the uniform by combatants assigned to the regular, uniformed armed units of a Party to the conflict.

8. In addition to the categories of persons mentioned in Article 13 of the First and Second Conventions, all members of the armed forces of a Party to the conflict, as defined in Article 43 of this Protocol, shall be entitled to protection under those Conventions if they are wounded or sick or, in the case of the Second Convention, shipwrecked at sea or in other waters.

Art 45. Protection of persons who have taken part in hostilities

1. A person who takes part in hostilities and falls into the power of an adverse Party shall be presumed to be a prisoner of war, and therefore shall be protected by the Third Convention, if he claims the status of prisoner of war, or if he appears to be entitled to such status, or if the Party on which he depends claims such status on his behalf by notification to the detaining Power or to the Protecting Power. Should any doubt arise as to whether any such person is entitled to the status of prisoner of war, he shall continue to have such status and, therefore, to be protected by the Third Convention and this Protocol until such time as his status has been determined by a competent tribunal.

2. If a person who has fallen into the power of an adverse Party is not held as a prisoner of war and is to be tried by that Party for an offence arising out of the hostilities, he shall have the right to assert his entitlement to prisoner-of-war status before a judicial tribunal and to have that question adjudicated. Whenever possible under the applicable procedure, this adjudication shall occur before the trial for the offence. The representatives of the Protecting Power shall be entitled to attend the proceedings in which that question is adjudicated, unless, exceptionally, the proceedings are held in camera in the interest of State security. In such a case the detaining Power shall advise the Protecting Power accordingly.

3. Any person who has taken part in hostilities, who is not entitled to prisoner-of-war status and who does not benefit from more favourable treatment in accordance with the Fourth Convention shall have the right at all times to the protection of Article 75 of this Protocol. In occupied territory, any such person, unless he is held as a spy, shall also be entitled, notwithstanding Article 5 of the Fourth Convention, to his rights of communication under that Convention.

Part IV. Civilian Population

Section I. General Protection Against Effects of Hostilities

Chapter I. Basic rule and field of application

Art 48. Basic rule

In order to ensure respect for and protection of the civilian population and civilian objects, the Parties to the conflict shall at all times distinguish between the civilian population and combatants and between civilian objects and military objectives and accordingly shall direct their operations only against military objectives.

Art 49. Definition of attacks and scope of application

1. "Attacks" means acts of violence against the adversary, whether in offence or in defence.

2. The provisions of this Protocol with respect to attacks apply to all attacks in whatever territory conducted, including the national territory belonging to a Party to the conflict but under the control of an adverse Party.

3. The provisions of this section apply to any land, air or sea warfare which may affect the civilian population, individual civilians or civilian objects on land. They further apply to all attacks from the sea or from the air against objectives on land but do not otherwise affect the rules of international law applicable in armed conflict at sea or in the air.

4. The provisions of this section are additional to the rules concerning humanitarian protection contained in the Fourth Convention, particularly in part II thereof, and in other international agreements binding upon the High Contracting Parties, as well as to other rules of international law relating to the protection of civilians and civilian objects on land, at sea or in the air against the effects of hostilities.

Chapter II. Civilians and civilian population

Art 50. Definition of civilians and civilian population

1. A civilian is any person who does not belong to one of the categories of persons referred to in Article 4 (A) (1), (2), (3) and (6) of the Third Convention and in Article 43 of this Protocol. In case of doubt whether a person is a civilian, that person shall be considered to be a civilian.

2. The civilian population comprises all persons who are civilians.

3. The presence within the civilian population of individuals who do not come within the definition of civilians does not deprive the population of its civilian character.

Art 51. Protection of the civilian population

1. The civilian population and individual civilians shall enjoy general protection against dangers arising from military operations. To give effect to this protection, the following rules, which are additional to other applicable rules of international law, shall be observed in all circumstances.

2. The civilian population as such, as well as individual civilians, shall not be the object of attack. Acts or threats of violence the primary purpose of which is to spread terror among the civilian population are prohibited.

3. Civilians shall enjoy the protection afforded by this section, unless and for such time as they take a direct part in hostilities.

4. Indiscriminate attacks are prohibited. Indiscriminate attacks are:

(a) those which are not directed at a specific military objective;

(b) those which employ a method or means of combat which cannot be directed at a specific military objective; or

(c) those which employ a method or means of combat the effects of which cannot be limited as required by this Protocol;

and consequently, in each such case, are of a nature to strike military objectives and civilians or civilian objects without distinction.

5. Among others, the following types of attacks are to be considered as indiscriminate:

(a) an attack by bombardment by any methods or means which treats as a single military objective a number of clearly separated and distinct military objectives located in a city, town, village or other area containing a similar concentration of civilians or civilian objects; and

(b) an attack which may be expected to cause incidental loss of civilian life, injury to civilians, damage to civilian objects, or a combination thereof, which would be excessive in relation to the concrete and direct military advantage anticipated.

6. Attacks against the civilian population or civilians by way of reprisals are prohibited.

7. The presence or movements of the civilian population or individual civilians shall not be used to render certain points or areas immune from military operations, in particular in attempts to shield military objectives from attacks or to shield, favour or impede military operations. The Parties to the conflict shall not direct the movement of the civilian population or individual civilians in order to attempt to shield military objectives from attacks or to shield military operations.

8. Any violation of these prohibitions shall not release the Parties to the conflict from their legal obligations with respect to the civilian population and civilians, including the obligation to take the precautionary measures provided for in Article 57.

Chapter III. Civilian objects

Art 52. General Protection of civilian objects

1. Civilian objects shall not be the object of attack or of reprisals. Civilian objects are all objects which are not military objectives as defined in paragraph 2.

2. Attacks shall be limited strictly to military objectives. In so far as objects are concerned, military objectives are limited to those objects which by their nature, location, purpose or use make an effective contribution to military action and whose total or partial destruction, capture or neutralization, in the circumstances ruling at the time, offers a definite military advantage.

3. In case of doubt whether an object which is normally dedicated to civilian purposes, such as a place of worship, a house or other dwelling or a school, is being used to make an effective contribution to military action, it shall be presumed not to be so used.

Art 53. Protection of cultural objects and of places of worship

Without prejudice to the provisions of the Hague Convention for the Protection of Cultural Property in the Event of Armed Conflict of 14 May

1954, and of other relevant international instruments, it is prohibited:

(a) to commit any acts of hostility directed against the historic monuments, works of art or places of worship which constitute the cultural or spiritual heritage of peoples;

(b) to use such objects in support of the military effort;

(c) to make such objects the object of reprisals.

Art 54. Protection of objects indispensable to the survival of the civilian population

1. Starvation of civilians as a method of warfare is prohibited.

2. It is prohibited to attack, destroy, remove or render useless objects indispensable to the survival of the civilian population, such as food-stuffs, agricultural areas for the production of food-stuffs, crops, livestock, drinking water installations and supplies and irrigation works, for the specific purpose of denying them for their sustenance value to the civilian population or to the adverse Party, whatever the motive, whether in order to starve out civilians, to cause them to move away, or for any other motive.

3. The prohibitions in paragraph 2 shall not apply to such of the objects covered by it as are used by an adverse Party:

(a) as sustenance solely for the members of its armed forces; or

(b) if not as sustenance, then in direct support of military action, provided, however, that in no event shall actions against these objects be taken which may be expected to leave the civilian population with such inadequate food or water as to cause its starvation or force its movement.

4. These objects shall not be made the object of reprisals.

5. In recognition of the vital requirements of any Party to the conflict in the defence of its national territory against invasion, derogation from the prohibitions contained in paragraph 2 may be made by a Party to the conflict within such territory under its own control where required by imperative military necessity.

Chapter IV. Precautionary measures

Art 57. Precautions in attack

1. In the conduct of military operations, constant care shall be

taken to spare the civilian population, civilians and civilian objects.

2. With respect to attacks, the following precautions shall be taken:

(a) those who plan or decide upon an attack shall:

(i) do everything feasible to verify that the objectives to be attacked are neither civilians nor civilian objects and are not subject to special protection but are military objectives within the meaning of paragraph 2 of Article 52 and that it is not prohibited by the provisions of this Protocol to attack them;

(ii) take all feasible precautions in the choice of means and methods of attack with a view to avoiding, and in any event to minimizing, incidental loss or civilian life, injury to civilians and damage to civilian objects;

(iii) refrain from deciding to launch any attack which may be expected to cause incidental loss of civilian life, injury to civilians, damage to civilian objects, or a combination thereof, which would be excessive in relation to the concrete and direct military advantage anticipated;

(b) an attack shall be cancelled or suspended if it becomes apparent that the objective is not a military one or is subject to special protection or that the attack may be expected to cause incidental loss of civilian life, injury to civilians, damage to civilian objects, or a combination thereof, which would be excessive in relation to the concrete and direct military advantage anticipated;

(c) effective advance warning shall be given of attacks which may affect the civilian population, unless circumstances do not permit.

3. When a choice is possible between several military objectives for obtaining a similar military advantage, the objective to be selected shall be that the attack on which may be expected to cause the least danger to civilian lives and to civilian objects.

4. In the conduct of military operations at sea or in the air, each Party to the conflict shall, in conformity with its rights and duties under the rules of international law applicable in armed conflict, take all reasonable precautions to avoid losses of civilian lives and damage to civilian objects.

5. No provision of this article may be construed as authorizing any attacks against the civilian population, civilians or civilian objects.

Chapter V. Localities and zones under special protection

Art 59. Non-defended localities

1. It is prohibited for the Parties to the conflict to attack, by any means whatsoever, non-defended localities.

2. The appropriate authorities of a Party to the conflict may declare as a non-defended locality any inhabited place near or in a zone where armed forces are in contact which is open for occupation by an adverse Party. Such a locality shall fulfil the following conditions:

(a) all combatants, as well as mobile weapons and mobile military equipment must have been evacuated;

(b) no hostile use shall be made of fixed military installations or establishments;

(c) no acts of hostility shall be committed by the authorities or by the population; and

(d) no activities in support of military operations shall be undertaken.

3. The presence, in this locality, of persons specially protected under the Conventions and this Protocol, and of police forces retained for the sole purpose of maintaining law and order, is not contrary to the conditions laid down in paragraph 2.

4. The declaration made under paragraph 2 shall be addressed to the adverse Party and shall define and describe, as precisely as possible, the limits of the non-defended locality. The Party to the conflict to which the declaration is addressed shall acknowledge its receipt and shall treat the locality as a non-defended locality unless the conditions laid down in paragraph 2 are not in fact fulfilled, in which event it shall immediately so inform the Party making the declaration. Even if the conditions laid down in paragraph 2 are not fulfilled, the locality shall continue to enjoy the protection provided by the other provisions of this Protocol and the other rules of international law applicable in armed conflict.

5. The Parties to the conflict may agree on the establishment of non-defended localities even if such localities do not fulfil the conditions laid down in paragraph 2. The agreement should define and describe, as precisely as possible, the limits of the non-defended locality; if necessary, it may lay down the methods of supervision.

6. The Party which is in control of a locality governed by such an agreement shall mark it, so far as possible, by such signs as may be agreed upon with the other Party, which shall be displayed where they are clearly visible, especially on its perimeter and limits and on highways.

7. A locality loses its status as a non-defended locality when its ceases to fulfil the conditions laid down in paragraph 2 or in the agreement referred to in paragraph 5. In such an eventuality, the locality shall continue to enjoy the protection provided by the other provisions of this Protocol and the other rules of international law applicable in armed conflict.

Art 60. Demilitarized zones

1. It is prohibited for the Parties to the conflict to extend their military operations to zones on which they have conferred by agreement the status of demilitarized zone, if such extension is contrary to the terms of this agreement.

2. The agreement shall be an express agreement, may be concluded verbally or in writing, either directly or through a Protecting Power or any impartial humanitarian organization, and may consist of reciprocal and concordant declarations. The agreement may be concluded in peacetime, as well as after the outbreak of hostilities, and should define and describe, as precisely as possible, the limits of the demilitarized zone and, if necessary, lay down the methods of supervision.

3. The subject of such an agreement shall normally be any zone which fulfils the following conditions:

(a) all combatants, as well as mobile weapons and mobile military equipment, must have been evacuated;

(b) no hostile use shall be made of fixed military installations or establishments;

(c) no acts of hostility shall be committed by the authorities or by the population; and

(d) any activity linked to the military effort must have ceased.

The Parties to the conflict shall agree upon the interpretation to be given to the condition laid down in subparagraph (d) and upon persons to be admitted to the demilitarized zone other than those mentioned in paragraph 4.

4. The presence, in this zone, of persons specially protected under the Conventions and this Protocol, and of police forces retained for the sole purpose of maintaining law and order, is not contrary to the conditions laid down in paragraph 3.

5. The Party which is in control of such a zone shall mark it, so far as possible, by such signs as may be agreed upon with the other Party, which shall be displayed where they are clearly visible, especially on its perimeter

and limits and on highways.

6. If the fighting draws near to a demilitarized zone, and if the Parties to the conflict have so agreed, none of them may use the zone for purposes related to the conduct of military operations or unilaterally revoke its status.

7. If one of the Parties to the conflict commits a material breach of the provisions of paragraphs 3 or 6, the other Party shall be released from its obligations under the agreement conferring upon the zone the status of demilitarized zone. In such an eventuality, the zone loses its status but shall continue to enjoy the protection provided by the other provisions of this Protocol and the other rules of international law applicable in armed conflict.

Chapter VI. Civil defence

Art 61. Definitions and scope

For the purpose of this Protocol:

(1) "Civil defence" means the performance of some or all of the undermentioned humanitarian tasks intended to protect the civilian population against the dangers, and to help it to recover from the immediate effects, of hostilities or disasters and also to provide the conditions necessary for its survival. These tasks are:

(a) warning;

(b) evacuation;

(c) management of shelters;

(d) management of blackout measures;

(e) rescue;

(f) medical services, including first aid, and religious assistance;

(g) fire-fighting;

(h) detection and marking of danger areas;

(i) decontamination and similar protective measures;

(j) provision of emergency accommodation and supplies;

(k) emergency assistance in the restoration and maintenance of order in distressed areas;

(l) emergency repair of indispensable public utilities;

(m) emergency disposal of the dead;

(n) assistance in the preservation of objects essential for survival;

(o) complementary activities necessary to carry out any of the tasks mentioned above, including, but not limited to, planning and organization;

(2) "Civil defence organizations" means those establishments and other units which are organized or authorized by the competent authorities of a Party to the conflict to perform any of the tasks mentioned under (1), and which are assigned and devoted exclusively to such tasks;

(3) "Personnel" of civil defence organizations means those persons assigned by a Party to the conflict exclusively to the performance of the tasks mentioned under (1), including personnel assigned by the competent authority of that Party exclusively to the administration of these organizations;

(4) "Matériel" of civil defence organizations means equipment, supplies and transports used by these organizations for the performance of the tasks mentioned under (1).

Art 62. General protection

1. Civilian civil defence organizations and their personnel shall be respected and protected, subject to the provisions of this Protocol, particularly the provisions of this section. They shall be entitled to perform their civil defence tasks except in case of imperative military necessity.

2. The provisions of paragraph 1 shall also apply to civilians who, although not members of civilian civil defence organizations, respond to an appeal from the competent authorities and perform civil defence tasks under their control.

3. Buildings and matériel used for civil defence purposes and shelters provided for the civilian population are covered by Article 52. Objects used for civil defence purposes may not be destroyed or diverted from their proper use except by the Party to which they belong.

Section II. Relief in Favour of the Civilian Population

Art 70. Relief actions

1. If the civilian population of any territory under the control of a Party to the

conflict, other than occupied territory, is not adequately provided with the supplies mentioned in Article 69, relief actions which are humanitarian and impartial in character and conducted without any adverse distinction shall be undertaken, subject to the agreement of the Parties concerned in such relief actions. Offers of such relief shall not be regarded as interference in the armed conflict or as unfriendly acts. In the distribution of relief consignments, priority shall be given to those persons, such as children, expectant mothers, maternity cases and nursing mothers, who, under the Fourth Convention or under this Protocol, are to be accorded privileged treatment or special protection.

2. The Parties to the conflict and each High Contracting Party shall allow and facilitate rapid and unimpeded passage of all relief consignments, equipment and personnel provided in accordance with this Section, even if such assistance is destined for the civilian population of the adverse Party.

3. The Parties to the conflict and each High Contracting Party which allow the passage of relief consignments, equipment and personnel in accordance with paragraph 2:

(a) shall have the right to prescribe the technical arrangements, including search, under which such passage is permitted;

(b) may make such permission conditional on the distribution of this assistance being made under the local supervision of a Protecting Power;

(c) shall, in no way whatsoever, divert relief consignments from the purpose for which they are intended nor delay their forwarding, except in cases of urgent necessity in the interest of the civilian population concerned.

4. The Parties to the conflict shall protect relief consignments and facilitate their rapid distribution.

5. The Parties to the conflict and each High Contracting Party concerned shall encourage and facilitate effective international co-ordination of the relief actions referred to in paragraph 1.

Section III. Treatment of Persons in the Power of a Party to the Conflict

Chapter I. Field of application and protection of persons and objects

Art 72. Field of application

The provisions of this Section are additional to the rules concerning humanitarian protection of civilians and civilian objects in the power of a Party to the conflict contained in the Fourth Convention, particularly Parts I and III thereof, as well as to other applicable rules of international law relating to the protection of fundamental human rights during international armed conflict.

Art 73. Refugees and stateless persons

Persons who, before the beginning of hostilities, were considered as stateless persons or refugees under the relevant international instruments accepted by the Parties concerned or under the national legislation of the State of refuge or State of residence shall be protected persons within the meaning of Parts I and III of the Fourth Convention, in all circumstances and without any adverse distinction.

Art 74. Reunion of dispersed families

The High Contracting Parties and the Parties to the conflict shall facilitate in every possible way the reunion of families dispersed as a result of armed conflicts and shall encourage in particular the work of the humanitarian organizations engaged in this task in accordance with the provisions of the Conventions and of this Protocol and in conformity with their respective security regulations.

Art 75. Fundamental guarantees

1. In so far as they are affected by a situation referred to in Article 1 of this Protocol, persons who are in the power of a Party to the conflict and who do not benefit from more favourable treatment under the Conventions or under this Protocol shall be treated humanely in all circumstances and shall enjoy, as a minimum, the protection provided by this Article without any adverse distinction based upon race, colour, sex, language, religion or belief, political or other opinion, national or social origin, wealth, birth or other status, or on any other similar criteria. Each Party shall respect the person, honour, convictions and religious practices of all such persons.

2. The following acts are and shall remain prohibited at any time and in any place whatsoever, whether committed by civilian or by military agents:

(a) violence to the life, health, or physical or mental well-being of persons, in particular:

(i) murder;

(ii) torture of all kinds, whether physical or mental;

(iii) corporal punishment; and

(iv) mutilation;

(b) outrages upon personal dignity, in particular humiliating and degrading treatment, enforced prostitution and any form of indecent assault;

(c) the taking of hostages;

(d) collective punishments; and

(e) threats to commit any of the foregoing acts.

3. Any person arrested, detained or interned for actions related to the armed conflict shall be informed promptly, in a language he understands, of the reasons why these measures have been taken. Except in cases of arrest or detention for penal offences, such persons shall be released with the minimum delay possible and in any event as soon as the circumstances justifying the arrest, detention or internment have ceased to exist.

4. No sentence may be passed and no penalty may be executed on a person found guilty of a penal offence related to the armed conflict except pursuant to a conviction pronounced by an impartial and regularly constituted court respecting the generally recognized principles of regular judicial procedure, which include the following:

(a) the procedure shall provide for an accused to be informed without delay of the particulars of the offence alleged against him and shall afford the accused before and during his trial all necessary rights and means of defence;

(b) no one shall be convicted of an offence except on the basis of individual penal responsibility;

(c) no one shall be accused or convicted of a criminal offence on account or any act or omission which did not constitute a criminal offence under the national or international law to which he was subject at the time when it was committed; nor shall a heavier penalty be imposed than that which was applicable at the time when the criminal offence was committed; if, after the commission of the offence, provision is made by law for the imposition of a lighter penalty, the offender shall benefit thereby;

(d) anyone charged with an offence is presumed innocent until proved guilty according to law;

(e) anyone charged with an offence shall have the right to be tried in his presence;

(f) no one shall be compelled to testify against himself or to confess guilt;

(g) anyone charged with an offence shall have the right to examine, or have examined, the witnesses against him and to obtain the attendance and examination of witnesses on his behalf under the same conditions as witnesses against him;

(h) no one shall be prosecuted or punished by the same Party for an offence in respect of which a final judgement acquitting or convicting that person has been previously pronounced under the same law and judicial procedure;

(i) anyone prosecuted for an offence shall have the right to have the judgement pronounced publicly; and

(j) a convicted person shall be advised on conviction or his judicial and other remedies and of the time-limits within which they may be exercised.

5. Women whose liberty has been restricted for reasons related to the armed conflict shall be held in quarters separated from men's quarters. They shall be under the immediate supervision of women. Nevertheless, in cases where families are detained or interned, they shall, whenever possible, be held in the same place and accommodated as family units.

6. Persons who are arrested, detained or interned for reasons related to the armed conflict shall enjoy the protection provided by this Article until their final release, repatriation or re-establishment, even after the end of the armed conflict.

7. In order to avoid any doubt concerning the prosecution and trial of persons accused of war crimes or crimes against humanity, the following principles shall apply:

(a) persons who are accused of such crimes should be submitted for the purpose of prosecution and trial in accordance with the applicable rules of international law; and

(b) any such persons who do not benefit from more favourable treatment under the Conventions or this Protocol shall be accorded the treatment provided by this Article, whether or not the crimes of which they are accused constitute grave breaches of the Conventions or of this Protocol.

8. No provision of this Article may be construed as limiting or infringing any other more favourable provision granting greater protection, under any applicable rules of international law, to persons covered by paragraph 1

Chapter II. Measures in favour of women and children

Art 76. Protection of women

1. Women shall be the object of special respect and shall be protected in particular against rape, forced prostitution and any other form of indecent assault.

2. Pregnant women and mothers having dependent infants who are arrested, detained or interned for reasons related to the armed conflict, shall have their cases considered with the utmost priority.

3. To the maximum extent feasible, the Parties to the conflict shall endeavour to avoid the pronouncement of the death penalty on pregnant women or mothers having dependent infants, for an offence related to the armed conflict. The death penalty for such offences shall not be executed on such women.

Art 77. Protection of children

1. Children shall be the object of special respect and shall be protected against any form of indecent assault. The Parties to the conflict shall provide them with the care and aid they require, whether because of their age or for any other reason.

2. The Parties to the conflict shall take all feasible measures in order that children who have not attained the age of fifteen years do not take a direct part in hostilities and, in particular, they shall refrain from recruiting them into their armed forces. In recruiting among those persons who have attained the age of fifteen years but who have not attained the age of eighteen years the Parties to the conflict shall endeavour to give priority to those who are oldest.

3. If, in exceptional cases, despite the provisions of paragraph 2, children who have not attained the age of fifteen years take a direct part in hostilities and fall into the power of an adverse Party, they shall continue to benefit from the special protection accorded by this Article, whether or not they are prisoners of war.

4. If arrested, detained or interned for reasons related to the armed conflict, children shall be held in quarters separate from the quarters of adults, except where families are accommodated as family units as provided in Article 75, paragraph 5.

5. The death penalty for an offence related to the armed conflict shall not be executed on persons who had not attained the age of eighteen years at the time the offence was committed.

Art 78. Evacuation of children

1. No Party to the conflict shall arrange for the evacuation of children, other than its own nationals, to a foreign country except for a temporary evacuation where compelling reasons of the health or medical treatment of the children or, except in occupied territory, their safety, so require. Where the parents or legal guardians can be found, their written consent

to such evacuation is required. If these persons cannot be found, the written consent to such evacuation of the persons who by law or custom are primarily responsible for the care of the children is required. Any such evacuation shall be supervised by the Protecting Power in agreement with the Parties concerned, namely, the Party arranging for the evacuation, the Party receiving the children and any Parties whose nationals are being evacuated. In each case, all Parties to the conflict shall take all feasible precautions to avoid endangering the evacuation.

2. Whenever an evacuation occurs pursuant to paragraph 1, each child's education, including his religious and moral education as his parents desire, shall be provided while he is away with the greatest possible continuity.

3. With a view to facilitating the return to their families and country of children evacuated pursuant to this Article, the authorities of the Party arranging for the evacuation and, as appropriate, the authorities of the receiving country shall establish for each child a card with photographs, which they shall send to the Central Tracing Agency of the International Committee of the Red Cross. Each card shall bear, whenever possible, and whenever it involves no risk of harm to the child, the following information:

(a) surname(s) of the child;

(b) the child's first name(s);

(c) the child's sex;

(d) the place and date of birth (or, if that date is not known, the approximate age);

(e) the father's full name;

(f) the mother's full name and her maiden name;

(g) the child's next-of-kin;

(h) the child's nationality;

(i) the child's native language, and any other languages he speaks;

(j) the address of the child's family;

(k) any identification number for the child;

(l) the child's state of health;

(m) the child's blood group;

(n) any distinguishing features;

(o) the date on which and the place where the child was found;

(p) the date on which and the place from which the child left the country;

(q) the child's religion, if any;

(r) the child's present address in the receiving country;

(s) should the child die before his return, the date, place and circumstances of death and place of interment

Chapter III. Journalists

Art 79. Measures or protection for journalists

1. Journalists engaged in dangerous professional missions in areas of armed conflict shall be considered as civilians within the meaning of Article 50, paragraph 1.

2. They shall be protected as such under the Conventions and this Protocol, provided that they take no action adversely affecting their status as civilians, and without prejudice to the right of war correspondents accredited to the armed forces to the status provided for in Article 4 (A) (4) of the Third Convention.

3. They may obtain an identity card similar to the model in Annex II of this Protocol. This card, which shall be issued by the government of the State of which the Journalist is a national or in whose territory he resides or in which the news medium employing him is located, shall attest to his status as a journalist.

Made in the USA
Middletown, DE
22 May 2024

54689603R00159